THE MOTHER
OF ALL
DECISIONS

THE MOTHER OF ALL DECISIONS

A MEMOIR OF MOTHER LOSS, LEGACY, AND ADOPTING KIDS IN MIDLIFE

BETSY ARMSTRONG

SHE WRITES PRESS

Published 2025
Printed in the United States of America
Print ISBN: 978-1-64742-893-8
E-ISBN: 978-1-64742-894-5
Library of Congress Control Number: 2024927040

For information, address:
She Writes Press
1569 Solano Ave #546
Berkeley, CA 94707

Interior Design by Andrea Reider

She Writes Press is a division of SparkPoint Studio, LLC.

Names and identifying characteristics have been changed to protect the privacy of certain individuals.

For Doug, Andrei, and Svetlana

Thank you for being the family I never thought I'd have.

PART ONE

CHAPTER 1

THE SUBJECT IS CHILDREN

SUBJECT LINE: "ADOPT A COUPLE OF KIDS?"

This was the only part of the email I changed, hoping to be a tad provocative, before I forwarded the information about adoption to my husband, Doug. It was a challenge to him, a gauntlet on the topic of family: Did we want one that included more than the two of us? I wasn't sure either, but I was tired of talking about children in fits and starts; of moving forward, then backtracking; of conversations that circled into nothingness; and mostly, of how we avoided a firm conclusion, never deciding on the same idea at the same time.

I could not believe I was doing this, prying the lid off of the Pandora's box labeled "Family" that existed in my mind and spilling the contents into an email to Doug. I was about to be forty-seven years old, and Doug was forty-nine. How would he answer? He might ignore me (which, with the hundreds of daily emails he received at work, was a possibility) or pretend he hadn't received it, if he wanted to avoid the subject. If he gave a flat-out no, would I feel bereft? Or, if he agreed, would I freak out? Would an affirmative response be enough to satisfy my demons and let me hope?

That I was even playing this game was my friend Debbie's fault.

Four years earlier, she and her husband, Jacob, had embarked on an unusual path. Jacob was divorced with a teenage son from a prior marriage. Debbie was pushing fifty with only passing mentions of maternal desire, so I'd never had an inkling that they wanted kids. They did. So much so that they had opted for a situation scary to all but the bravest of prospective parents: Older kids. Plural. From far, far away. They had adopted two sisters, nine and eleven, from Russia.

Debbie had been smart about it, though. Having heard the horror stories about uncontrollable kids with emotional problems and tempers, she had uncovered a way to minimize every mind-boggling risk associated with this sort of thing. They had met the girls here in the United States, brought them from Russia, and let them live in their house . . . before being *certain* about adopting them.

On the surface, it sounded horrifying—an audition with very high stakes. I'd never heard of such a thing and thought it seemed unethical and potentially damaging to everyone, especially a child who got rejected. What if it didn't work?

The thing was, it had for them, and they claimed it did for "most"—whatever that meant. Although this wasn't a common practice in the adoption world, groups of older orphans traveled to America and stayed with families—families who decided to move forward with them. Jacob and Debbie now had two healthy, happy Russian-American daughters.

Ever since Debbie had brought her girls home three years earlier, she had made it her mission to find parents for the friends they had left behind at the orphanage. Debbie had aimed her considerable charm and desire to do good at me, along with several others. Some of them had followed her lead and added at least one adopted child to their family. I admired the generosity of spirit these people displayed in welcoming the kids into their hearts and homes, but admiration alone wasn't enough for me to act. I could never adopt for some gold medal of selflessness. I wasn't that good of a person, honestly.

So, while I was uneasy, I was also intrigued by the idea of older children I could get to know—a ready-made family, if siblings were chosen. No diapers or terrible twos. I was curious. But only a very small, teeny-tiny bit. At least that was what I told myself.

Throughout my forties, I avoided discussions about kids. For females in my demographic, married and childless, bringing up the topic of babies usually resulted in one of three conversations I didn't want to have:

1. An assumption that "Of course I want children" and a dialogue about how much they would absolutely, unquestionably, without a doubt give my life Meaning. But did I? Would they?
2. A quick but gentle probing into the state of my fertility and a lengthy soliloquy from the other person oversharing about the state of theirs. The underlying message here was: I must do whatever it takes. This might be fine for the women who felt the lack of a baby as a phantom limb, something that was supposed to be there, that they could see and feel, but all that entered my mind was, *Really? Why?*
3. An emphatic assurance that always took some form of "You will change your mind." I didn't think so. Kids were a conundrum I didn't know how to crack.

As I racked up more birthdays, a fourth conversation was being tossed into the mix when children were mentioned. It started with the question, "Have you ever thought about adoption?" I never admitted it out loud to anyone besides Doug, but I had. Only briefly. Very rarely.

The first time Doug and I had a conversation about kids, not even about adoption, I hadn't been thinking about children at all.

It was a gray Christmas Eve, right before I was about to turn forty, a Chicago winter day studded with steel icicles threatening to fall from black rooftops. Doug and I drove down the streets of our colorful Roscoe Village neighborhood, which—in spite of the holiday—seemed darkly monochromatic. We were on our way to Doug's parents' condo on Lake Shore Drive.

Christmas Eve had been leaden for me since age twenty-three, when my mom had died in the early morning hours before Christmas dawned. From then on, December was the month of sadness. At Christmas parties and family gatherings, I resigned myself to forced gaiety until I was alone and able to release my pent-up tears in a waterfall of grief. So on this particular Christmas Eve, like many before, I'd been thinking about my mom, not children.

That is until we approached the shaded swoosh of the S curve on Lake Shore Drive, and the little gazebo at Michigan Avenue appeared. I saw fairy lights wrapped around the columns, illuminating the ornate pouf of a roof. The lights twinkled like bright stars and emitted a warm glow, a balm to the dusky day.

Doug didn't see what I saw; he saw something else. His eyes were drawn to a bundled-up father. The father's blue hat was dusted with powder as he laughed and pulled a little boy with cherry-red cheeks on an equally red sled through the newly fallen snow.

I watched Doug watching—his eyes, his face, staring as if he were starving for something he couldn't have and that little boy was the antidote, the cure for his hunger.

I'd *never* seen a look like this cross over Doug's face, the depth of his wistful expression. I wanted to, but couldn't, ignore him. The force, the magnetic pull of his need, made me ask, "What is it, honey? Are you okay?"

Doug answered, "That looks like so much fun." His voice overflowed with the saddest yearning I'd ever heard.

That moment was when I thought about children, real children, for the first time in my life. It was also the first time I realized that *not* having kids might deprive Doug of the family he imagined having. Was I willing to allow my ambivalence to outweigh what he wanted? For years, the answer had been yes. But now, after seven years, it was December again. And here was my fourth missive from Debbie about the Bridge of Hope, the program through which she and Jacob had found their girls. Emails whose contents I interpreted as, "Adopt girls just like ours." Although Debbie's emails had never formally spelled those words out, I had watched the girls thrive and prosper. It seemed implied.

The Bridge of Hope event was an annual happening. Orphans would be arriving this summer, and here was my yearly reminder.

The first time I'd received one of her emails, it was too much. I was forty-four, and I opened it but didn't bother to finish the whole thing. I forwarded it to Doug with the note, "She's kidding, right?"

Doug didn't reply to me. I didn't reply to Debbie, either.

The next year, I managed to read through to the end. *Huh, interesting,* entered my mind unbidden, followed by, *Did Doug and I really want a kid with us for three or four weeks next summer?* Of course, the larger issue was, *What about after?* But I ignored that and focused on logistics. We both worked at jobs we loved, and bringing a child in for the summer would require taking off huge chunks of valuable time. And I had to face the fact: Doug and I had never even babysat. We had never even offered to help our many friends who had been blessed with babies. What would we *do* with a child? The way we usually spent our vacation time indicated that we'd take the kid out for cocktails by a pool somewhere tropical. So, no. I doubted Bridge of Hope would be a workable situation. Although scared of what his answer might be, I didn't ever ask Doug. I deleted Debbie's email.

The third year, Debbie's email contained something new: an attachment. I clicked on it, and the file opened wide. Pictures of children were waiting on the other side, like silent ghosts. I was unsettled, seeing how real they were.

I saw eight-year-old Elena's enormous blue eyes and fluffy hair bow. I took in seven-year-old Aleks's blond crew cut and red knit sweater, along with six-year-old Sasha's puffy skirt and prim smile. I read bits of the accompanying bios. Elena embroiders. Aleks is a leader. Sasha's favorite food is any kind of fruit.

I perused the nine pages and flipped back to the email. Then I saw my out. "The application deadline for the Bridge of Hope program is January 15." It was already late February.

But then I scrolled up to Debbie's note: "They are extending the deadline, but you'd have to move fast. Interested?"

Elena. Aleks. Sasha. A kid? I didn't mention their names to Doug, but that evening over dinner, we conducted our version of a conversation about kids.

"So, what do you think about this Bridge of Hope thing?" I began.

"It seemed to work for Jacob and Debbie. Do you want to look into it?" Doug asked.

"Well . . . I'm not sure. She sent me an email about it today. Maybe?"

"Well . . . What are we waiting for?"

I shrugged. "I don't know. I just . . . don't feel ready."

"Will you ever feel ready? This might be the kind of thing you just *do*," he said. "Let's go for it!"

His response made me feel panicky. "There's so much to consider. Do you really think it's a good idea?"

"Well, yeah, I do. But we don't have to do it if you don't want to. I'm fine with that," Doug gamely tried to conclude.

I restarted the debate. "But what if I'm *not* really fine with that?"

It was exhausting. It was also clear that Doug, in spite of the fact that he wanted children at least a little bit more than I did, would follow my lead wherever I led, which was obviously in circles. We finally blamed the deadline for stressing us out and therefore stalling us out. A decision of this magnitude shouldn't be hurried. The next day I wrote back to Debbie, "Thanks for sending this. We don't want to rush it. Maybe next year."

And now, it was the next year. Why had I told her maybe?

When the email from Debbie inevitably arrived, I'd been working from home, sitting at our dining room table while sunshine poured golden light through the December windows. All was serene until I saw Debbie's name pop up, and my stomach dropped. I knew exactly what the email was. A cursory glance confirmed that she was well ahead of schedule this time.

Scanning through the program info, I learned what I already knew: There were older kids available for adoption. The kids would come to visit in July for three to four weeks. The adoption agency was searching for families to "host" kids. After meeting and getting to know the child, parents could decide about adopting. It was sort of brilliant and kind of awful, like a last chance for these kids to find someone to call Mom and Dad.

Was it my last chance too?

I opened the attachment, looked at the pictures and bios. Elena, Aleks, and Sasha had been replaced with new kids: Oksana, Dmitry, and Raisa. And Maxim, Yuliya, and Petr. And others. The bright sun in the room seemed suddenly glaring. I pushed away from the computer and closed my eyes.

When I leaned back into my laptop to stare more closely at the photos, I found myself asking *what* I wanted instead of *whom* I wanted. Did I feel this? Did I want to be a mother? At all? Ever? The eyes stared back at me, but the pictures could not answer.

Even I couldn't answer. And in spite of the humor I displayed publicly and the roundabout conversations with Doug, I had been wrestling with the complicated knot of my ambivalence for years. Tangled in my mind were words like "Mom," "dead," and "cancer." The phrases "Only forty-six years old" and "What if it happens to me too?" were present also. My brain felt like a twisted tapestry, where pulling on a string and following a thread only ever managed to unravel me.

My forty-seventh birthday loomed. In just a few weeks, I'd be older than my mom had ever been.

Forty-seven was uncharted water for me. I would soon be Columbus, sailing the ocean without a map, unsure if there was an edge from which to fall. Actually, I was a motherless, child-less Columbus, searching for the shore of my maternal instinct to reveal itself. I might wash up on the sands of a couples-only Club Med or a family-friendly beach, where little ones in diapers would build sandcastles, but I didn't know my preference. I had never steered this boat. Should I take charge, or sit back and allow the currents to carry me toward my fate?

My decision had always been no decision. But now, something was different. I could finally look into the future and see myself, living my life, and going about my business as a forty-seven-year-old. Sitting with my laptop in the sunshine of my serene life, something inside of me wanted to set sail in a new direction and discover the answer. My curiosity trumped my doubt, and off went the email to Doug with the provocative subject line: "Adopt a couple of kids?"

Minutes later, my computer dinged. Doug's response—a calendar invite. I sat up a little straighter and read, "Bridge of Hope, Host Family Information Session, Saturday, January 15, 2011, 10:00 a.m.–noon."

Without any delay, without conscious thought, I watched as my hand moved. My fingers guided the cursor to hover right over the Accept button. And then . . . *click.*

It sounded like yes to me.

CHAPTER 2

LOSING MOM

I rushed to Fairview Southdale Hospital as soon as I got off work at the University of Minnesota. At the age of twenty-three, I was on the six-year plan—still plugging away at my undergraduate degree, working full-time and going to school part-time. The heat of the sticky July day clung to me as I hurried. Mom, who was one of those "never sick a day in her life" people, had undergone surgery to try to diagnose a series of mysterious symptoms she'd had during the first few months of summer. Starting two months earlier in May, she'd begun getting blood clots in her legs that were so bad, she had been rushed to the ER. The doctors discovered she was anemic and exhausted. Then she found blood in her stool, and an exploratory surgery was scheduled.

When I walked from the oppressive humid afternoon into the chill of the hospital lobby, I was surprised to find my stepdad, Herman, waiting for me. He was a giant of a man, six-four and over four hundred pounds. He had a hair-trigger temper that was even bigger than his size too, and in the years my mother had been married to him, I'd learned the hard way to be wary of him.

"How is she?" I asked.

"She's out of surgery. Come with me." He steered me toward the cafeteria.

"What's going on? Why aren't we going to her room?"

"We need to talk first. Sit down." We settled across from each other on hard gray chairs, the smell of bleach and old egg salad assaulting my nostrils. Herman was staring at the floor as he said, "There's no good way to say this. It's the big C, Betsy. It doesn't look good."

I slumped in my chair, shocked. "Cancer?" I asked. "No. No." My eyes filled; the room blurred.

He nodded. "Colon cancer."

Herman heaved himself out of his chair, clapped me on the back with his huge hand, and said, "She's upstairs. Just coming out of the anesthetic. She doesn't know yet, so pull yourself together before you come."

Up in her room, surrounded by family—my stepbrothers and my brother, and their wives—the doctor told us that the cancer had already metastasized to her liver and he couldn't get it all. In the awkward silence that followed, Herman asked, "How long does she have?"

I hated Herman for asking that question. It felt so mean, as if he were inviting sickness and death in to stay. Weren't we supposed to fight?

The doctor reflected my sentiments, answering, "I don't want to discuss timelines. Let's see what the chemo can do." And yet, by sidestepping the question, I also knew unequivocally that my mom was going to die. And she must have too, because I watched her face crumple and felt my heart lurch painfully in my chest.

All I remember from the rest of that night was holding my mom's hand, focusing on tenderly caressing it as our tears fell. I couldn't look at her. It hurt too much. I think I was hoping that by concentrating my loving attention on her hand, I could somehow rub away this terrible diagnosis. The wishful thinking had already kicked in.

Mom rallied in August and September, but in October we learned the chemo had had zero effect on the tumors. All it did was make Mom miserable, so she quit and we called hospice.

Mom wished to die at home and, at first, Herman and I became allies to fulfill this last request. I dropped out of school but kept my full-time job at the university, arranging my time to be with Mom when he wasn't. Thankfully, I lived on my own in an apartment near campus, just a thirty-minute drive away from their house. Part of her regimen was a daily injection of medicine, but Herman wouldn't administer it. The first time we had to give her a dose at home, he looked at me and said, "I can't handle causing her pain."

The hospice nurse taught me how to stab an orange with a needle and coached me on how to give the shot to Mom. Every day while she was sick, I went to her, even if only to give her the shot. Mom worried about the pain, fearing its iron grip, so as her condition worsened, I gave her morphine too sometimes, until she was woozy.

On one long weekend in early November, I stayed with Mom while Herman was away on a business trip. She'd started to want to give things away, and she pressed a two-carat emerald-cut diamond and platinum ring into the palm of my hand. The sharp edges hurt. I refused it, saying, "Mom, I can't take this. What are you doing?"

"It's from your father. My engagement and wedding ring. It should go to you."

I protested, but she insisted. Then she asked me to get her jewelry box, which she had hidden under the guest bathroom sink, and to bring it to her.

"Why wasn't this on your dresser?" I asked. I'd never seen it anywhere but there.

"Because of him," she told me. I knew she meant Herman. Her eyes and expression begged me to stop asking questions. "I want to tell you who should get what when I die."

"Please, please don't make me do this," I pleaded. It made her impending death too real. I wanted to lay my head down and bawl, to pretend this wasn't really happening. But I couldn't. I loved her too much to deny her. Big fat tears sprang to my eyes, falling onto the table next to the ring, another prism that caught light.

"I have to, Betsy. Before I can't remember what's what," she begged. "Please."

I finally consented, and she picked out the first jewel, a sapphire ring, and designated it should go to my brother's wife. We continued our mournful inventory until the last gem had a future keeper. Then she put them all back in the box, except her wedding ring, which she pushed me to wear home. It fit perfectly.

"Take them all, and give them out after I die," she said. "I need you to, Betsy. I don't trust him."

Neither did I, so I did as she told me, bringing the box with me when I left to go to my apartment.

The next day, I went to work as usual. My desk was in the rear corner of the admissions and records department at the U. Working full-time allowed me to take classes for free, a perk I couldn't get from any other job. But when Mom became ill, I put my education on hold to care for her on nights and weekends.

My phone jangled, and I picked up. I'd barely said hello before Herman bellowed a stream of expletives so loudly my office mates could hear. It startled and scared me, and I quickly hung up.

The phone rang again—Herman. "You stole the jewelry, you scheming little bitch! Bring it back!" This is how Herman spoke when he was angry.

"Mom gave it to me," I said as calmly as I could before crashing the receiver down. I didn't want to talk to him, especially at work. Arguing with Herman was impossible under normal circumstances, and it felt good to be able to shut him up so effectively.

He called back repeatedly. I didn't want to answer, except that I could hear Mom in the background pleading with him to leave me alone. The whole episode was unbelievable and so embarrassing. But it was classic Herman, acting like an obsessed lunatic. His temper, his rage, his hunger for a fight. I never knew what would set him off, or how unreasonable he would become—only that his attack was inevitable.

After thirty minutes of him calling and me hanging up, my supervisor picked up his call.

"Sir, you need to leave Betsy alone while she is at work. This is a place of business, after all."

I heard Herman yelling profanities at my boss.

"Sir . . . sir, please. Sir! Please stop yelling!" Now she was raising her voice too. He had that effect on people.

"Tell that little bitch that I'm on my way," I heard him say through the receiver. "I'm coming to get what she stole!"

I panicked at the thought of him showing up at my office. It was a public building, and I could picture the scene he'd make. A huge, obese, angry man screaming at me at full volume with crowds of students and all of my coworkers watching as he humiliated me. I knew Herman. He was relentless and would relish the opportunity to humiliate me. Worse than that, I was frightened that he would somehow bar me from seeing Mom. She was getting weaker and more dependent on him. What if he used this "theft" as an excuse to shut me out?

At his threat, I motioned to my boss to hand me the phone.

"Herman." I spoke over him. "Herman! I'll bring the jewelry back tonight after work. Do you hear me?" I didn't want to, but I didn't see what choice I had.

Herman grumbled his response, "You better! Thief!" And then he hung up on me.

I put the receiver back in the cradle and looked at my boss's face, her brow wrinkled with concern. Something about her sympathy cracked me open. No one outside our family had ever seen the way Herman treated me. I was so ashamed; I put my hands over my face and began to sob convulsively. I bent over and held my stomach, hoping the knot of grief and anger would ease. I finally went to the bathroom to pull myself together, but my hands, my entire body, wouldn't stop trembling for the rest of the day.

That evening, I relinquished the jewelry box, minus the engagement ring Mom had bestowed upon me. Even though Herman had what he wanted, he spent a full hour rampaging through the house, blaring insults and nonsense from the top of his lungs. He stomped away, returned to scream, stomped away, and returned. He repeated this pattern until Mom, who'd been in bed resting, crept into the room and said, "I'm dying! Can I please have some peace?"

Hearing her plea broke my heart. Why was he making her say that? Mom had to repeat herself three more times before Herman finally stopped. I hoped, silently and fervently, that he was ashamed of himself, but I doubted it.

When she finally fell asleep that night, I let myself out. I didn't care what Herman did; I only knew it was one of the saddest days of my life.

The following weekend, Herman called a family meeting, something our family had never done. Trepidatious, I sat in a small, hard living room chair. My older brother, Paul, was across the room as far away from Herman as he could get. When I was still in high school, their relationship had imploded during a horrible argument that ended with Herman kicking Paul out. That our mother had allowed Herman to make that ruling was something I never forgot when I lived under Herman's roof. Each of our two stepbrothers claimed opposite ends of the large, cushy couch. Herman and Mom sat on two matching chairs in front of the big window, the sun outside turning them into shadow-dark profiles against the brightness.

Herman prompted Mom, who was clearly woozy from pain-killers, to tell each of us what we would receive upon her death, forcing her to make a cruel inventory of the things she'd leave behind. I hated him for this, certain this sudden "transparency" was meant to warn me off removing anything else from the house, even if Mom tried to force it upon me. *The ring*, I thought. *At least I have the ring.*

I don't remember what she bequeathed to anyone else that day, but I do know she didn't mention any of her jewelry. That was Herman's way of communicating that the jewelry was *his* to distribute. Mom said I would be given her antique trunk along with my great-grandmother's wooden rocking chair. All the rest, we were told, would be divided up among us four kids after Herman passed.

Hearing that, I wished it was Herman, instead of my mom. Why did she have to be the one who left me?

Mom slipped into a coma a month later, just five days before Christmas. An ambulance took her to the hospital, where we waited through the long days and nights by her side. My brother and I were alone with her in the early hours of Christmas Eve morning, when her heart stopped beating its cadence of love and went completely silent. Our mom—my mom—was gone.

A week or so after Mom's funeral, I showed up at the house and crunched my way up the frozen January sidewalk. It was the kind of winter day where you felt your nostril hairs stick together, frozen, when you inhaled. I rubbed my hands together in a futile attempt to make heat.

I had asked Herman if I could come over to pick up the things Mom had left to me. In arranging this visit, he'd told me he needed to be there. We hadn't spoken since the funeral, and he wouldn't let me in the house alone. Although I didn't care to see him, I wanted what Mom had chosen for me, so I went anyway.

As I stepped through the front door, Herman had the trunk and rocking chair waiting for me in the entryway. The golden tones of the trunk glowed in the winter sunshine angling through the glass screen door. I stroked the old wood, feeling the large slats across the top and then the worn leather handles at the side, remembering the day when Mom had brought the trunk home after a day spent antiquing—one of her favorite hobbies. She'd been over the moon at her "find" and regaled me with the history that the store owner had passed on to her. "It's from the early 1900s!" she explained. "So long ago, but in great shape!" It was a beautiful piece, and it would always remind me of her.

The rocking chair sat next to the trunk, modest in size and plain in design. The rocker was precious because it had belonged to Mom's grandmother on her dad's side, who we always referred to as Great-Grandma Phoebe. I vaguely recalled Great-Grandma Phoebe as a benevolent presence who doled out generous portions of homemade gingersnap cookies from her kitchen and who sat, sewing everything from quilts to clothing, on this chair. Mom told me that her husband made the chair for her as a young bride, and it showed the spare designs reminiscent of their Scandinavian heritage, simple and painted in chalk paint without varnish.

The chair didn't shine like the trunk, but it was a solid piece of maternal history that was now mine.

I carried the empty trunk to my little Mazda hatchback and then took the rocking chair, fussing with it until I put it upside down on the passenger seat so the small car could accommodate both items. When I turned around, Herman was gone, and the door was closed.

I'd allowed myself to believe he'd let me poke around in the basement, combing through the memories stored there by my mom. She had a hope chest, a very old-fashioned cedar trunk filled with tablecloths, hand-embroidered napkins, and other treasures she'd brought to her marriage to my father. The hope chest had been emptied out over the years, then filled up again with things reminiscent of my "real" family. My parents' wedding picture book had been stored there. I used to adore caressing the pages in which Mom's snow-colored dress and Dad's white tuxedo stood out in a sea of dark suits and summer dresses.

The hope chest also contained all the baby paraphernalia my brother and I had accumulated. I knew there were long-ago baby pictures, tiny shoes, little knitted dresses, and a Baby's First Year book full of memories and a history of my infant double pneumonia.

The basement held so many treasures that reminded me of Mom. Besides my baby things, there was my Christmas stocking that Mom hand-beaded and embroidered, and the flotsam and jetsam of my youth: my drill team uniform, homecoming and prom pictures, art projects, and mementos from boys I'd dated. Mom had saved these memories, which were all things that meant nothing to Herman.

I approached the front door again and tried to open it. The knob was solid metal, a freezing block in my hand. It refused to turn in spite of my three attempts to shake it loose, each attempt becoming more violent.

My frozen hand could barely make a fist. I *rap-rap-rapped* painfully on the unforgiving surface of the door again and again, but Herman didn't answer. A cloud of breath drifted in the air between me and the door, clouding my vision, but Herman seemed deaf to my ever-louder knocks. Was he ignoring me? The doorbell didn't work.

Finally, I went to the car to retrieve the house key I'd rarely ever used, because we had always been people who didn't believe in locking doors. I fumbled through my purse for the pocket where I'd hidden it. Trudging back up to the door, the cold steel key burned my fingers as I tried to enter it into the grooves of the lock. It didn't fit. It took a minute for the reality to sink in. My fingers were icy claws by this time. I pounded on the door and yelled my stepdad's name. Pulling off my winter hat, I laid my warm ear on the frigid door and listened carefully, trying to slow down my steaming breath. The TV was on, and I strained to discern how loud it was and if there were any noises related to Herman. Nothing.

The porch stoop felt like a Siberian tundra with my icicle hands, cold ears, and the wind's fingers running up under my jacket. I huddled against the porch rail and mulled over the options, but nothing made sense. He ignored my knocking; my key didn't fit; he was inside and wouldn't let me in. I glanced down the sidewalk through my car's windows to see the graceful silhouette of the rocking chair's rockers forming two twin slopes from the headrest to the dashboard. My heart plummeted as if it had been punched.

The stark knowledge of what was unfolding hit me all at once. I had been shut out for good. There would be no retrieving these things that meant so much to me. Mom was gone, along with everything she'd owned, and all of the things that were *not* in my car. This wasn't home anymore. Herman wasn't my family anymore. I wasn't getting anything else. Ever.

I ran to the Mazda, buckled in, and took a last look at the last house my mother had lived in. Icy tears froze on my cheeks. Slowly, I turned the car and drove away. I would never speak to Herman or my stepbrothers again.

The last words Mom ever said to me were, "I'll never leave you."

All these years later, mulling over the possibility of children and family, I remembered those words. I thought about what I might pass on to a child—love, fear, anxiety, and rage—and I realized Mom was right. Who she was, what she did or didn't do, what I was left with when she died, and what I became . . . have never left me. These things are from her. And with me, always.

CHAPTER 3

ADOPTION INFORMATION SESSIONS

oug and I hadn't fully discussed having children before we got married, but Doug's intentions had been obvious from the moment I set foot in his apartment. Pictures of him holding or playing with his various nieces and nephews hung on his refrigerator, and their grade school photos were tucked into the corners of other frames displaying his younger self on camping trips. Doug talked about his family with such fondness and love that I knew he wished for kids. I thought that choosing a partner who wanted children might bridge the gap between maybe and yes that yawned before me whenever the question of children was spoken aloud. I couldn't seem to make myself leap across that distance, however. It was a chasm filled with fog, a cold mist of ambivalence that shape-shifted and changed but wouldn't clear.

I wished that babies stirred me into a gooey mess of adoration the way puppies and kittens did. Whenever I came across a baby animal, I couldn't stop my hand from reaching to feel the exquisite softness of their velvet fur while my entire body beckoned to cuddle them closely. Conversely, if the creature being held was a human baby, my reaction was the opposite. I was compelled to take a step back, to observe with clinical curiosity this little alien I didn't want to know and never felt the urge to touch. My response to babies made me feel mean and unnatural. It seemed there was something missing in me, that I had an icy, miserly hole in my heart where the warm longing for a child should live.

Because I felt obligated to, I brought up the subject of fertility at my annual pap smear during my first post-wedding visit to my ob-gyn when I was thirty-four. I asked the doctor about biological clocks and told him I didn't want to worry about having kids until I'd enjoyed marriage for a while, so he reassured me there was nothing magical about the age of thirty-five—one whole year away.

The doctor's words felt like a blessing. I threw myself into my marriage and a newly minted postgraduate-school career in non-profit marketing, which had sprung from my deep love of distance running combined with a desire to make a difference in the world. Although I'd always been somewhat athletic, after my mom died, running provided solace from my grief, as if sweating was just a different form of crying. The meditative motion of putting one foot in front of the other over and over and over again reminded me that I was still alive. Five miles became ten, then twenty, and more. For decades following her passing, I continued chasing that feeling and ran from the demons Mom's death had unleashed.

But then a few years into my marriage, that same ob-gyn began to lecture, "Don't come to me when you're forty and expect a baby." A current of disquiet arrived with his words. If my ambivalence were a boat floating on the river of my uncertainty, this comment made it rock. Should I, or shouldn't I? Should I, or shouldn't I? I couldn't decide if letting the boat tip would be a disaster that ruined my life, or a blessing that would teach me I had something to swim for, a shore where people who loved me waited, a real family.

Meanwhile, everywhere around us, friends had babies. Some of them had to really work for it too—through multiple miscarriages, fertility drugs, and IVF. Frozen eggs, frozen sperm, frozen embryos. The list of things one endured to get pregnant seemed way too long. My best friends educated me about Clomid and cervical mucus, and there were a few times, roaming the aisles of CVS, when I considered buying one of those thermometers for charting your cycles, but I never did.

Doug and I didn't *try* for babies in the same way our friends who ultimately had triplets did. Doug was bewildered by my "if it doesn't happen by itself, it's not meant to be" approach. He had expected a wave of maternal desire to swamp me and for me to sweep him along on a quest for our baby. I waited for that too, but deep down I hoped he would go first and discover an undeniable paternal urge that would force me into what I believed were the desperate, only-sometimes-fruitful actions that other females demanded of their reproductive organs. He never did.

By the time I was approaching forty, after we didn't make a baby the old-fashioned way, I did what the doctor recommended and submitted to the various tests for infertility, although I was blasé about their outcomes. The blood test showed that my ovaries were still releasing eggs. The hysterosalpingogram (HSP), the test to ensure my fallopian tubes weren't blocked, was awful, and I wept silently as I lay flat on the X-ray table while they shot the indigo dye through my ovaries. No one warned me it would hurt so much. I wanted nothing to be wrong, and that's what I got: a diagnosis of "unexplained infertility."

Afterward, I sat alone in the blue cubicle of the hospital changing room, the hard pinching inside of me subsided to a dull ache while I hugged the flowered cotton gown around myself and allowed my tears to flow. I missed my mom, already dead sixteen years, unable to be with me, to guide me to motherhood herself.

While I stewed in my funk of grief and relief, Doug submitted to a test too, one that required giving a sperm sample. He dragged his feet for months, his lack of action suggesting to me that I'd read him wrong. Maybe he didn't want children as badly as he claimed? Finally, he went to the clinic, but came home aghast and embarrassed. They had given him a cup and directed him to a bathroom stall. There were none of the expected accoutrements: no comfortable place to sit, no pictures or magazines to get his desire—*ahem*—flowing. "The nurses were right outside the door!" he told me. We both ended up laughing, verging on hysterics, at his comically awful experience, especially after he was cleared a few days later. His "boys" were swimmers, and there were plenty of them.

Not long after that, I searched the website of a well-known adoption agency in Chicago and signed Doug and I up to attend an adoption information session. As I filled out the online form, I told myself that we could always cancel, but when I informed Doug after the fact, he agreed to go. We were both trepidatious, telling ourselves we were going just to listen.

We walked into the agency office in Evanston, a diverse city just north of Chicago that is home to Northwestern University, not knowing what to expect. We were greeted by mismatched, out-of-date furniture, lots of little cubbies crammed with desks in improbable nooks, and pictures of children everywhere. The pea-green walls were papered with colorful flyers, some of their edges curled. "Pregnant? You have options," one of them announced. There were stairs up, stairs down, a theater's worth of folding chairs, and a table littered with handouts. The conference room was full. There must have been sixty to seventy people, everyone crammed close together. We took the papers and two seats toward the back.

I watched couples voraciously read the informational packet, searching the words for the lifeline it might provide. The air was loaded heavily with hope and desperation. The bobbed hair of the woman in front of me was so severely straight, the edge looked like it could cut glass, and her brittle posture suggested a readiness to shatter into a million pieces. The sense of competition among us was striking. I felt as if I'd entered into a famine-struck country and we'd landed in a bread line with too many hungry people and not enough bread.

The session began and proceeded. The facilitator read the packet aloud to us. It covered domestic adoption: White babies, Black babies, Hispanic babies, mixed-race babies. International adoption: Guatemala, China, Haiti, and Korea—where, if not babies, then toddlers would be the option. The costs of babies and trips. The requirements of courts and judges. Open adoptions and birth mothers choosing the next, other, mother for their babies. The options were dizzying. And every single one was a *baby*. Did I truly want a baby? I pushed aside my reservations and kept listening.

Toward the end of the session, a perfect adoptive family was offered up for display. A gray-haired earth mother sat hugging one Chinese daughter while her earnest husband held the other smaller one. They were still astonished at the blessings these girls had brought, at the love they felt for these children who had begun life with different mothers. With reverence, they talked of preserving their girls' culture by learning the language and eating Chinese food. These parents spoke of their "adoption journey." This was the first time I'd ever heard this peculiar phrase, "adoption journey." My reaction wasn't positive, and I didn't know why.

Maybe I sensed the emotional part underlying the trip on a plane to go retrieve your new child and wasn't ready for it. It would be an interior journey that might feel like being put on a spaceship to land in an alien place without a map, oxygen, or a way back home, looking for that one, unique moonstone answer that had always eluded me here on earth. Or perhaps it was that everyone in the audience, except Doug and I, seemed to lurch forward, eager and willing to embark upon this path. Even the people who worked here leaned toward the audience, coaxing us to take that first step. The whole thing smelled unfailingly, impossibly, of an optimism I did not feel.

For the one and a half hours we sat there, Doug's inclination toward privacy dampened both of our emotional reactions. I simply listened.

At the end of the meeting, we were asked to fill out a form. Even though it was multiple-choice, the last question stopped us.

What is your next step? Check one:

_____ Yes, we would like to schedule a personal visit with a social worker as soon as possible;

_____ Maybe, we are interested in proceeding sometime in the future;

_____ No, we are not interested at this time.

I held the blue piece of paper on my lap, on top of the packet of information we'd been given. Looking at Doug, I raised my eyebrows and used the pen to point to each of the options. Doug shook his head. We left without turning it in.

In the car on the way home, I asked him, "Why not at least get more information?"

"That was already more information than I expected," he said. "I never thought we'd have so many choices. I'm not ready."

"It was kind of overwhelming," I agreed, relieved that he was the one who said no first.

I ran a fifty-mile ultramarathon the next summer. I was forty-two, two years before we got the first email missive from Debbie.

Doug made the call to sign us up for the second adoption information session we attended. Earlier that year, for his forty-seventh birthday, I had taken him to a fundraiser where he could meet two of his heroes, the 2005 World Series–winning White Sox players Paul Konerko and Jim Thome. The fundraiser was for a child services agency on the west side of Chicago, and Doug had saved the information folder from the event.

The building looked institutional, and we walked into a big classroom with long tan tables and umber melamine chairs. Most of the unkempt offices we passed by on our way to the room had what looked like at least one abandoned Styrofoam cup of cold coffee left upon the cluttered desk.

The woman who led the session had spiky short hair, her no-nonsense shoes a sharp contrast to the glowing silver thumb rings that flashed as she talked with her hands. There was a male leader too, thin and pale, with long brown hair neatly tied back in a ponytail. He was the quiet one, meekly stooped while doling out pieces of paper.

They had packets, folders imprinted with a regal state stamp and filled with colored forms: the green one about foster care; the yellow one about the Department of Child and Family Services in Illinois; the pink one with lists of documents for parents, for kids, for courts. The leaders, again, read the forms aloud.

The people in this room were different than the sharp suburban crowd at the last session, less rigid and a little messier. These were city people with working-class clothes. They appeared more resigned about their adoption journeys. If they chose this path, they wouldn't be traveling in a plane; they would be driving within the borders of the state of Illinois. We talked about domestic adoption and kids from foster care.

When the time for questions arrived, three out of the thirty-plus families present were brave enough to raise their hands. One woman wanted only to overshare about her own adoption experiences and brag about how she had already adopted two children. She had the air of the neighborhood busybody who couldn't wait to spill her know-it-all gossip, who wished she could take charge of the rest of us and tell us what to do. The others had simple questions: Who are the kids? Why are they up for adoption? Where are they now? How long will this take? The facilitators dodged the questions, saying they couldn't be answered. Not yet, and maybe not at all—there were too many variables in each case.

These leaders were practical, and they chided us to be pragmatic too, because, after all, these were not fantasy children but real children. Older children, Black and Brown children, children whose families still hoped to keep the kids with *them*. The leaders told us about open adoptions and how the kids deserved to stay in touch with these parents and relatives, who had lost or failed their kids. They told us how complicated this could be. They were not encouraging.

Listening, I worried, a buzzing feeling filling my head. I considered how life with a child would be if the child were older and of another race, and how challenging it would feel when people around us blurted insensitive things. The leaders warned us about the judgments adoptive mixed-race families face, even if people never voiced their opinions out loud.

Guiding a child through such minefields would be even more difficult if the child's birth mother or family popped in and out of their lives, I thought, *arriving unexpectedly on a holiday, or not showing up on an important birthday.* Although the idea of older, somewhat autonomous children appealed to me, I knew the specter of a birth family nearby would haunt me.

This session made clear to Doug and me the unspoken hierarchy of adoption in the United States. Babies were best, ranked highest to lowest depending on their coloring, from White to Black; toddlers were second-best, their perceived value decreasing as the complexion of their skin grew darker, and problematic behaviors and delays in development increased; older children and teens were the bottom of the barrel, with the same preferential scale of skin tone and behaviors. It appalled me to learn the cold, hard, institutional fact that adoption agencies "charge less" for kids of color because there are so many more of them in the system. It broke my heart.

The female leader, assuming that everyone present preferred the palest, youngest child available, stated unprompted and unapologetically, "You will not get a perfect White baby here." The oversharing lady bristled at this news, all but snorted at the thought that *that* was what she was here for. But I noticed that the leader's disclosure seemed to have had the opposite effect on others, because some of the people sagged into their hard orange chairs.

At the end of the session, we were presented with another blue multiple-choice form. The same questions confronted us, and the last one stopped us, again.

What is your next step? Check one:

_____ Yes, we would like to schedule a personal visit with a
         social worker as soon as possible;
_____ Maybe, we are interested in proceeding sometime in
         the future;
_____ No, we are not interested at this time.

I turned toward Doug and pointed again at the options. This time, he nodded at me, took the pen, and checked the middle box, the "Maybe" box. My heart sped up a little, and I nodded back at him.

What I remember about the ride home most is the weather. It was cold, raining, and miserable. Our breath created little clouds of fog, cartoon bubbles of haze, when we talked.

"So, what about this 'Maybe'?" I asked.

"I like the idea of older kids," he answered, "and if we got brothers and sisters, we'd really be helping them."

Both Doug and I loved an underdog. It didn't surprise me that we agreed on that as I murmured my assent.

"It sounds like, if we do this, we'd prefer two kids, right? I think siblings are the way to go. They'd have each other too."

Doug nodded. He'd grown up with two sisters and a brother; I'd had my older brother and two stepbrothers.

"I don't know about the domestic adoption piece, though," I told him. "I know how pessimistic this sounds, but what if a relative shows up out of the blue, or the birth dad gets argumentative? Plus, if we adopt kids of color, we're going to get more attention. It would be as if we're proclaiming, 'These kids are adopted.'"

"Those are challenges we have to consider. If we're already getting older kids, the complexity of the adoption and bonding would definitely multiply. We'd have to be up for it, and I don't know that I am," he said.

"Yeah, I'm not sure I am, either. Does that make me a bad person?" I asked. I prided myself on being open-minded, and admitting I felt daunted didn't make me feel very good.

"This situation calls for 100 percent transparency," Doug said. "We have to be honest—it's real life, real kids. We don't want to mess it up."

In the weeks and months that followed, a caseworker called us several times. Both Doug and I ignored her calls. We got scared. We got busy. Whatever enthusiasm we had slowly fizzled.

I ran my twentieth and final marathon that October. I was forty-five.

Our third adoption information session happened on January 11, 2011. It was the one Debbie had prompted, the one I had furthered by forwarding to Doug with the provocative subject line, and the one to which he'd responded by inviting me to the Bridge of Hope information session.

Doug and I walked into a chalky gray building in a northern suburb of Chicago. The roof soared toward the sky like a church, but it wasn't a church. The room we were directed to had long windows, where the January sun was still high in the sky, reflecting light from the snow and dappling the white ceiling like so many spotlights.

There were only a handful of people, six or seven couples. They formed a semicircle on brown metal folding chairs. The couples looked like Doug and me. The men had the bearing of executives but wore their weekend uniforms of Gap jeans and polo shirts. The women sported designer denim skinnies, with tall black boots and long sweaters, foregoing their usual stay-at-home Lululemon yoga pants. The leader—there was only one—greeted us at the door. She was friendly, her draped, relaxed clothing matching her easy smile.

There were handouts and folders again. This time, the speech was not just reading from the material, but conversational. The talk was of Russia and Ukraine and possibly China. The adoption journey on offer was definitely across oceans and seas and lots and lots of land. Older children, living in foreign orphanages, would be coming to the United States in the summer for almost a month and needed host families to care for them.

We heard about requirements, ages, home visits, and the Illinois Department of Child and Family Services (DCFS)—what would be necessary if we wanted to meet these children, this summer, here at home instead of adoption-journeying all the way to where the kids were first. We were told what happens after the children are hosted. About flights and translators and money and court and costs. I was intrigued and curious in spite of myself. I liked that I would be able to suspend my decision, as if I were walking out onto a high dive, just to test it, but could still turn around and climb down without diving, without getting wet, without promising anything to anyone.

Before the session ended, before questions started, four new people entered the room and walked to the front. It was our friends Jacob and Debbie and their two Russian-born, adopted daughters, now twelve and sixteen. The girls were poised and smiling, Jacob and Debbie looking every bit the proud parents. Jacob had called Doug earlier that morning to warn us that the leader of the session had asked them to come that day. They were to be the ideal family put on display this time. Even though Doug and I knew their story, we sat next to each other on the metal chairs and listened. Doug's right leg was crossed over his left, and my left was crossed over my right. We were close enough that my boot touched his shoe in the middle.

At the end of this session, we knew what was coming. We were asked to fill out the same questionnaire. This time, the last question did not stop us.

What is your next step? Check one:

_____ Yes, we would like to schedule a personal visit with a social worker as soon as possible;

_____ Maybe, we are interested in proceeding sometime in the future;

_____ No, we are not interested at this time.

Just a month into my forty-seventh year, sitting at the Bridge of Hope information session, a shift occurred inside of me, not only in my ambivalent mind, but in my body too. I couldn't run anymore. My body had rebelled against the pounding and the miles, and I was irreparably injured. My brain, however, opened up to a new possibility, probably because I had survived past my mom. The stream of consciousness flowing through my head told me, *You're alive. You might live to see your children grow up. They won't be abandoned and put out. Maybe you should do this after all.*

This third time, Doug and I both looked at each other and nodded at the same time. We checked "Yes."

Instead of training for a race, I spent that summer preparing for a child.

CHAPTER 4

CROOKED

The reason I couldn't run was a fifty-degree curve in my spine.

Scoliosis. What an ugly word; it sounded like a combination of "scab" and "polio," and definitely like a disease. It meant curvature of the spine, and I had it. Not only was my spine crooked like an *S*, but it was twisted as well. My rib cage turned clockwise, my hips counterclockwise. The foundation of my body zigged and zagged in all the wrong directions.

I'd discovered my scoliosis when I was seventeen. Trying on outfits in front of my full-length mirror, I noticed how my new A-line jean skirt hung strangely from my hips, one side jutting out at an angle while the other fell in a straight line. I popped one hip out, then the other. The stiff garment held itself symmetrically only when my left hip was stuck out in an overly exaggerated way. I pulled the skirt off and put on a pair of pants. The right pant leg reached to my ankle, while the left pant leg hung closer to my heel. Off with the pants, on with some Levi's. Same discrepancy. As I stared at my body in the full-length mirror, I noticed my right side had an indentation at my waist, whereas my left side was straight. How had I never noticed this before? I called for my mom and allowed her slender fingers to swerve down the curves in my back. She dialed the pediatrician.

A few weeks later, the two of us sat in a pediatric spine specialist's office in a hospital in downtown Minneapolis. After being x-rayed, I waited on the exam table in a stiff paper gown while Mom sat next to me in a chair. It could have been any medical office but for the photographs on the walls. I examined pictures of children in ordinary postures of childhood—softball, gymnastics, the school play, Girl Scouts—all of them wearing back braces and body casts, wearing "look what I can do" expressions overflowing with the desire to prove how completely normal they were. I prayed, *Not me, not me, not me.* I sat up as straight as I possibly could.

When the doctor arrived, he set about examining me in a way I'd never been examined before. He asked me to bend and stretch, forward, backward, and side to side. He took out a measuring tape and used it like a seamstress making a dress, noting the size of my hips, rib cage, and the length of each leg. He pulled out a protractor, after slapping my X-rays up on the light box, drawing lines and assessing angles. He even weighed me in kilograms.

Upon completing his audit, he said, "Yes. Betsy has scoliosis. We measure scoliosis in terms of degrees. A mild case is less than twenty-five degrees, a moderate case is between twenty-five and forty, and anything over forty is considered severe. Betsy's degree of curvature is fifty." Hearing this, the air went out of me, and I slumped.

The doctor recommended that metal rods called Harrington rods be inserted into my back to straighten me. These would be two stainless steel surgical implants that hooked onto vertebrae at the top and bottom of the curve on each side of my spine, which would then be ratcheted during surgery until they pulled my spine straight. The rods would take eight hours to install; I'd be flat on my back in a hospital bed for six months, during which time I'd be flipped like a sandwich on a griddle every couple of hours. After that, I'd be in a body cast for a year while my vertebrae adjusted to their new position.

My mother, aghast, asked, "Will she be able to have children with those?" Her hands were tightly clasped together in her lap, her thumbs revealing her worry.

I looked up, embarrassed. After what the doctor had just described, I was incredulous that children were her first concern. *She knows I don't care* at all *about having kids.* That I didn't like dealing with babies and toddlers was a well-accepted fact in my family. I was the youngest, with only an older brother, so I never had to babysit anyone, had never changed a diaper, and when confronted with other people's little kids, I ignored them and stayed with the adults.

"She'll go on to live a normal life," the doctor said, "but she'll just have to be careful about what sports she plays." He went on, "Look at all these kids." He raised his pen, tapping on the picture nearest to him, as if it were proof of just how typical I could be. "They're amazing."

I looked away from them, staring at the floor with tears threatening to spill. All I could think was *Nooo!* What I couldn't express in front of the doctor was my complete unwillingness to commit social suicide by spending my junior year and part of my senior year in a hospital bed and a body cast. What about my friends and boyfriend? Or not dancing on drill team when I was about to be named the captain? And what about running? Running had become an important outlet for me to deal with the chaos of my homelife: a stepdad who didn't want me there, a father who lived across the country and couldn't intervene, and a mother who was helpless in the face of her husband's inexplicable rage.

Mom turned back to the doctor. "What happens if we don't have the surgery?"

"We monitor it. The main thing is, if we aren't going to correct it, we don't want it getting worse. She needs to come back every year, just so we can see what's happening."

"What are you looking for?" Mom asked.

"These cases can be dangerous if left unchecked," he explained. "People with untreated scoliosis can develop deformities like humpbacks, and in severe cases the curve constricts the lungs and other organs, causing breathing and functional problems. In that case, pregnancy becomes risky."

Mom told the doctor she would talk it over with my father before making a decision. Even though they were divorced, they were in touch with one another over matters pertaining to my brother and me. Her response brought relief. And hope.

My dad was my ace in the hole. He wouldn't go for such a surgery. He worked for an insurance company as a claims adjustor, which meant he visited with lots of people who had slipped on icy sidewalks and couldn't walk anymore, whose old football injuries meant surgery after surgery would never make their knees right again, and whose car accidents left them crippled with unending pain in spite of whatever treatments had been administered. It was my dad's job to help save the insurance company money by investigating what had happened and to recommend who should be paid for what. I'm sure he saved the insurance company lots of money.

When I was young, my dad believed that danger (or more likely financial ruin) lurked everywhere. After our family moved to a house with a pool, I invited my friends over to swim.

"Whoa, whoa, whoa!" said my dad. "Before anyone can swim, their parents have to sign a release."

"What?" I asked. "Why would we do that? These are my friends."

"You never know what might happen, Betsy. I refuse to be responsible if someone dives into the shallow end and breaks their neck."

"Now, Dell," Mom said, "I think that's going overboard. The kids are good kids. They'll obey the rules."

My dad finally relented but made a large plywood SAFETY sign listing various rules that should never be broken. No one ever got hurt, except my brother and me, when our parents got divorced when I was ten and they sold the house with the pool.

This time, though, my dad's leeriness of "quack doctors who only made things worse" worked in my favor. My parents' discussion ended in a veto for surgery. No surgery, just the yearly visits.

The most memorable step in this annual exam was not the bending and stretching, the protractor, or the kilograms, but the pictures. Actual images were taken, always by a male medical photographer, to document what my naked body looked like and if it appeared to curve or bulge or deform. Each time the man photographed me, the macabre thought crept up on me that these pictures were being accumulated for a book of medical anomalies. That *I* would be showcased as some kind of freak. It was horrifying.

The room where these pictures were taken was tucked away in the hospital basement, as if ashamed of itself. I felt certain the morgue was next door. I stood against a wall, shivering, in the whitest pair of cotton bikini underwear I owned, unable to use my hands to cover my breasts because I had to keep them at my sides. The doctor refused even to let me wear a bra in case my little AA cups grew lopsided. I always had the urge to cry after it was over, but I never did.

Six years after that first appointment, my mom died, and I made the decision to stop going to the annual examination. I was twenty-three. My mom was dead. And I had work, school, friends, boys, and *running* as necessary distractions. My back might be crooked, but it was fine. It didn't hurt. I believed that thinking it would make it so. After all, I was my mother's daughter.

CHAPTER 5

RUNNING AWAY

I didn't start out as a long-distance runner. I began running as a sophomore at Thomas Jefferson High School in Bloomington, Minnesota, when—during my second-year tryout for the drill team—the coach told me I was getting fat. That I wasn't didn't matter. His comment lodged in the part of my brain where my myriad insecurities lived, right next to the mean names Herman called me; the thought that my scoliosis made me defective; and the cultural ideal of thinness that was not only in my head but everywhere, impossible for teenage girls to ignore in America.

Joan Benoit had just become famous by winning the first Olympic women's marathon—26.2 miles. I had marveled watching her on television lope around the stadium track on her victory lap, the American flag she held rippling red, white, and blue above her. She was a one-woman parade, announcing to the world that women were just as strong as men. I filed her image in the back of my mind. I looked at her body, her legs, and internalized another message: "If I run, I'll look like that." *That* meant skinny.

At first, I ran because I didn't want to be fat—and it worked. The first street I ran up and down was 0.6 miles, with a big hill at the end rising up to the finish line of our driveway. I would awaken before dawn to shield my thighs, which now embarrassed me, from the eyes of our neighbors, one of whom was my unrequited crush. Sometimes, I'd imagine him seeing me and being amazed at how fit I was. Running soon became more than a body-shaper; it became a respite from my busy mind, keeping all those "I'm not good enough" thoughts at bay.

I graduated from that street to other blocks in the neighborhood, building my endurance. I could now run past familiar roads and schoolmates' houses, through the black-paved bicycle paths of the Hyland Park Nature Preserve, and all the way to Bush Lake. Every summer at the lake, a gaggle of us girls competed in the ritual of trying to transform our pale Scandinavian skin into burnished bronze, holding our arms next to each other, always comparing tans to see who was darker, while we combed Sun In into our already-blonde hair.

Those summer mornings when I ran, Bush Lake was all mine, a quiet refuge with nothing and no one to interrupt me. I would climb the lifeguard tower, feel the sweat drip down my legs onto the rough white wood platform, and breathe in the lake, matching my thoughts to the tranquil water until it was time to retrace my steps home. Winding my way back, feeling lighter with each footfall, my run both grounded and lifted me. The physical movement seemed to settle my unsettled heart while my mind expanded with dopamine's euphoria—I wondered sometimes if I kept going, might I take off and fly?

I also ran to be away from my homelife—from being a stepchild and living under my stepfather's roof. Ours was not a peaceful family, and I'd learned to tiptoe carefully through the minefield. In spite of the perfection I chased with my running and drill team and straight A's and watchful behavior, I still managed to rile Herman's temper. Everyone did. It was impossible not to.

When Mom divorced Dad, she replaced him with Herman, an inexplicably angry man who loved her but barely tolerated her children. My stepfather was like a policeman constantly scanning the horizon for evidence of our wrongdoing, calling attention to any, in his eyes, transgression we committed. He did so with a blind rage that came on like a tsunami, sweeping my mom, my brother, and I into an angry sea. There a screaming, cussing monster hurtled insults at us until his anger was spent and the tide turned calm again. He rarely directed his wrath at his own kids—he saved it for us. His fury could be triggered by something as random as the Vikings losing a football game or a newspaper inadvertently thrown away too soon, yet he always managed to make it someone's fault, and worse, his berating made us *believe* it was our fault.

When my mom got sick, I ran through her cancer.

On bleak, gray fall Saturdays, I would escape as she dozed comfortably in a drugged haze, and I would go for very long runs. Each footfall would echo in my head: *Kill. Cancer. Kill. Cancer. Kill. Cancer.*

Running made me a fierce warrior. I wanted to murder those cancer cells living inside her, my fury shielding me from the deep, dark, malignant fear of losing her that kept spreading inside of me.

One day in early November, after Mom had quit chemo, I crumpled onto the gritty, cold sand at Bush Lake, my tan long gone and a horrible chill enveloping me. I couldn't outrun my fear, and she couldn't outlast her cancer. She died just five months after her diagnosis. She was forty-six years old.

Her death, and the aftermath, changed me forever. I doubted I would ever want even a husband, let alone a family of my own.

CHAPTER 6

JUDGMENT DAY

The doorbell rang, and our dogs, Lulu and Roscoe, went nuts, rushing the front door and prancing in anticipation of a new person in our house. "Shush! Be quiet," I whisper-shouted at them. "Sit!" Then I called upstairs to Doug, "She's here!"

Doug jogged down to join me at the front door, asking quietly, "Ready for this?"

"Let's do it," I answered, holding on to a dog collar attached to a squirming ninety-pound dog with each hand. "Calm down!" I said to the dogs. I may as well have been saying it to myself, because my nerves were already frazzled.

The first, and biggest, hurdle in our adoption waited on the other side of the door: the social worker who was going to conduct our home study. The home study was described to us as a written record of our life that included our personal background, family history, educational background, and health and financial information, along with our views on parenting. For anyone hoping to adopt (or foster) children, passing the home study was the first and foremost step. Failing the home study meant no adoption. At all. My anxiety soared when I considered the high stakes of this meeting, and in these moments before we opened our door, the jitters in my body amplified until I was literally shaking.

With his hand on the doorknob, Doug looked me straight in the eyes and quietly said, "It's all going to be okay. Right?"

"Right," I answered.

Doug swung the door open, and together we chorused, "Hello! Welcome! C'mon in!"

Sandra, our social worker, had arrived. Her appearance on our doorstep was the result of checking "Yes" on the blue form at our last adoption information session. The x in that box set in motion phone calls and emails from multiple sources: the Bridge of Hope people based in Washington, DC; St. Mary's, the Illinois adoption agency that coordinated the process in state; and Sandra, a social worker from St. Mary's charged with figuring out our intentions and fitness for parenting.

All of the initial communication, no matter whether from Bridge of Hope, St. Mary's, or Sandra, pointed at one thing— paperwork. Paperwork was the precursor to any conversation about, or action toward, adoption, and Doug and I had been given a daunting catalog of items to gather in order to prepare for Sandra's visit. It had taken us four long months of trudging through the Chicago winter to assemble everything Sandra needed.

Fingerprints topped the list, so that four months of prep began with us rolling our fingertips across a series of glass plates in an overcrowded, slightly seedy place that reminded me of the DMV. Too many customers trying to hurry and too few workers, all of whom acted as if they had all the time in the world. The twenty finely lined electronic images Doug and I generated there were sent to the Illinois State Police to discover any criminal records we had.

The state records, while unsurprisingly clean, were insufficient. We also needed to send fingerprints to the FBI. The Bureau only accepted ink fingerprints, the kind taken in old TV police dramas. In our increasingly digitized world, we had to find the lone place in all of Chicago that still did it the old-fashioned way, where the sole worker there followed the protocol I'd only seen on television or the movies, rolling each finger on an ink pad and then across a canary-yellow index card printed with ten spaces on it, one for each digit's imprint.

The stamped papers were then mailed to the FBI in an effort to determine that we were both, in fact, who we said we were and had committed no federal crimes. Additionally, we filled out forms ominously named Child Abuse and Neglect Tracking System, or CANTS.

My nerves often got the best of me during those months. I worried I was a fraud—a mean, selfish person who knew nothing about kids but who masqueraded as a sweet, caring someone hoping to bring children into her life. And that feeling was surfacing again now as Sandra stood in our home. After all my years of yo-yoing uncertainty, I was sure some residue of ambivalence clung to me. What if I didn't have a satisfactory answer for why I was pursuing children *now* when I'd never yearned for any during the previous forty-seven years of my life?

Sandra was a small woman with a toothy smile, white against her olive skin and glossy dark hair. We greeted her in the foyer of our spick-and-span, zealously overcleaned house.

When she saw Lulu and Roscoe, she let us know in her melodious South American–accented voice, "I'm sorry, but I'm not a dog person. Is there a place we can go sit where the dogs won't disturb us?"

"Of course!" I said, inwardly kicking myself, sorry that my grand plan to avoid the red couch in the basement was foiled. Our basement was finished and actually very nice, but our house was unusual in that the open configuration and wide staircase didn't allow for a door to the basement; we could only lock our dogs in the upstairs living room, behind a baby gate. Unfortunately, our cat, Oliver, had peed on the basement couch months earlier, and though the stains were covered with a throw blanket, I didn't believe Sandra would look kindly upon a house with cat urine on the furniture. Downstairs we went, where Doug and I sat on the offending stains and Sandra, from the clean side of the couch, unknowingly complimented my immaculate housekeeping.

As we settled in, I fussed with the myriad files I'd organized, channeling my nervous energy into appearing competent and prepared. Besides our fingerprint and criminal record clearances, Doug and I completed applications and financial synopses; copied our licenses, passports, birth certificates, and marriage license; and also assembled pay stubs, the terms of our mortgage, car titles, and investment account balances. The stack of papers for Sandra was about three inches thick.

This cut-and-dried, factual information paled in comparison to the big project Doug and I undertook for this interview: a personal autobiography, which Sandra received via email in advance of our meeting and was going to use as the basis for her questions.

The first time I read through our draft, the Autobiography sections went on and on. It started easily with Identifying Information, followed by Educational Information, which was pretty straightforward, although I'd needed to search the internet for my high school's address. Health Information was the section where I began to wonder exactly how much I should share and whether the people reading this ever dove deeply.

One of the things I worried about was my scoliosis. The Bridge of Hope people told Doug and I we would need to bring chest X-rays to court—the unwieldy, large, plastic kind—to prove we didn't have tuberculosis. I pictured a slide slapped up on a light box in a courtroom, the curving, sloping of my spine on display for everyone to see. If I didn't confess such an obvious deformity in the home study, the judge might deny us after catching me in a lie. As I followed this line of reasoning, I decided to add the diagnosis to my health history, especially because I believed scoliosis to be a harmless condition that had no bearing on my capacity for parenting.

Completing the last two sections, Extended Family and Personal Information, of the Autobiography intimidated me more than anything else.

The final section alone had sixteen questions, including queries about our marriage, our parents' marriages, and our favorite childhood memories. People-pleasing, oversharing me answered each question with multiple paragraphs, while Doug, always more private, had mostly made bullet point lists. I asked him to change those to complete sentences with the argument that the social worker probably expected adjectives, nouns, *and* verbs in his self-descriptors.

After turning over the bulky file of our paperwork to Sandra, the three of us sat together for an hour. Doug sat between Sandra and me, and I held his hand while she questioned us.

We answered questions about our experience with children and what our upbringing had taught us. For Doug, his good memories centered on the things like his mom and dad piling all four kids into the station wagon to drive cross-country to visit their East Coast relatives every summer. I had gotten stuck when thinking about my favorite memories. My childhood remained in my mind as a series of frightening events interrupted by some happy ones, mostly out of my control, but I didn't want to disclose my messy memories. How could I explain to Sandra that the blended family which had formed me was largely responsible for my years of ambivalence about motherhood? Ultimately, I wrote about how my parents taught me the value of hard work and doing for myself, qualities that served me well after Mom died and I'd felt so abandoned.

Sandra asked, "How will you be like or unlike your own parents?" Afraid of being judged, I simply remarked that I wouldn't use corporal punishment, as my parents had. Doug mentioned hoping he would be as great as his parents had been.

Sandra couldn't leave without dropping the Big Question: "Why do you want to adopt?" She leaned forward and cocked her head sideways, staring directly into my eyes.

I didn't talk about ambivalence, or how I'd never babysat and was scared of babies. How I'd not once in my life changed a diaper and didn't want to break my streak. I didn't share the worry that haunted me, that I'd die young as my mom had and abandon my pretend children to fend for themselves, as I'd been forced to do. I didn't mention how the family dynamic I remembered stood out as one of the primary reasons taking care of children terrified me. What if I resented them, as Stepdad had resented me? What if the kids divided Doug and me, instead of bringing us together? Would I feel tied down and trapped? Triggered into running away? I couldn't admit any of this to Sandra.

What I relayed to Sandra instead was that during the dozen years Doug and I had been together, we had built a really wonderful life. Staying in that life, not rocking our safe little boat, would be fine, but something was missing. I laid out the "I've finally come to my senses" argument, which in the stew of my uncertainty about motherhood I only half-believed. Sandra jotted down notes and nodded at me, smiling.

But inside, past the joking about the diaper changes that would never be, I felt forlorn. I'd never ever met anyone like me, who didn't care when my reproductive organs grew a few too many years past ripe to be useful, when I blessed the childless life I enjoyed on the no-kids-allowed trips we took to islands with coconut drinks and lots of sun, when it seemed like nothing was missing. Truly, sitting in front of Sandra, I was still uncertain about leaving all that behind. For kids? I didn't, wouldn't, or couldn't share my trepidation with Sandra.

And yet, I was here because the idea of adoption refused to abandon me. Where my default propensity to turn away lived, a new path appeared in front of me, an opening that spilled over with generosity. Doug and I had a lot to give, to share, we reasoned, so why not? This last question was the single argument I fully embraced. We were ridiculously blessed. So, really, why *not* adopt children?

As we led Sandra on a tour through the living room, dining room, bedrooms, and bathrooms, the gravity and the weirdness settled upon me. It was very odd to open my house and my heart, to show my very handprints, to a total stranger whose job was to judge. To sit and account for my choices to her. To have her study my tax forms and copy down numbers. To have given her, someone who was not buying my home, permission to look in every nook, cranny, closet, and door so she could measure bedrooms to calculate square footage.

At the end of the interview, we stood in our kitchen, Doug and I leaning on our granite countertop across from Sandra. "You two have a lovely home," she said. "It's obvious that you have the room and resources to raise beautiful children here."

"Thank you, Sandra. What are the next steps from here?" Doug asked.

"I'll take all the information that you've provided and write up a report." She looked at me. "I'll be in touch with you if there are any details I need to complete it. You'll have a chance to edit it before it becomes final."

Is that really all we have to do? I wondered. "Anything else we can expect?"

Sandra looked around the kitchen as she packed her papers into her bag. "You might want to put away that wine bottle over there." She pointed her chin toward the half-empty pinot noir resting on the counter. "And you also need to lock up the medicine sitting on the bathroom counter."

Why didn't I think of that? flashed through my head just as I saw Sandra give me a big grin.

"That should be it," she said. "After we get the home study done, Bridge of Hope can begin referring children to you for consideration."

She turned around, and we all walked toward the front door. Thanks circled among the three of us, along with Sandra's promise to have a preliminary draft ready in a week or so. Finally, Doug swung the door shut and turned around to look at me. I let out a huge sigh of relief, ready to almost melt into the floor.

"That went well," Doug said. "Don't you think?"

"I guess so?" The ambivalent part of me refused to believe that one conversation was enough to undo decades of indecision.

In the end, all of it not only rang true to Sandra but was true. After two sets of fingerprints, three meetings, ten hours of instruction (required by DCFS), endless copies, and an extraordinary amount of back-and-forth editing, Sandra produced an official home study. Twelve pages long, the last sentence read, "Douglas and Elizabeth have met all of the requirements for adoption in the State of Illinois."

The words startled me as their import sunk in. Someone impartial thought I was fit to be a mother? If that were true, why did I doubt them so? The feeling that I could, maybe, get what I thought I wanted unsettled me. I didn't know if what I thought I wanted was really what I wanted. Yet inside of this rolling feeling lifting me up and then putting me down, as I rode the sea of doubt and fear, anticipation bubbled up from the depths. There was a chance Doug and I would become parents. We were a big step closer to the prospect of "our" children.

"Our" children? I might be someone's mom? I didn't dare say it out loud.

CHAPTER 7

HER NAME WAS JUDY

Her name was Judy. She was my mom, and she was everything to me, from the very beginning. I was born with double pneumonia and lived in an oxygen tent for the first three months of my life. The story was told that, during those months, she visited the hospital multiple times every day to hold and nurse me.

She was twenty-three years old at the time and looked like Audrey Hepburn, with short dark hair, shining caramel eyes, and a smile that carried the same glint of mischief in it, as if she and Audrey knew a secret they couldn't wait to tell you. Mom was into the power of positive thinking before it had a name, and she had a knack for getting what she wanted simply by believing it would happen. She believed with all her heart that I would make it. My dad was more practical, coming to terms with the idea that I might not survive. From the start, I was, have always been, my mother's daughter.

My dad used to tell us that he loved Mom from the moment he laid eyes on her. She had applied for a secretarial job at the office where he worked, and he'd passed a note to the boss that said, "This one is pretty. Let's keep her." That was June of 1959, right after she graduated from high school. They married in September. Their union lasted fifteen years and produced two kids.

Twenty-one years after the divorce, a few years after Mom died, my dad died too. Lung cancer from his lifelong habit of smoking one Pall Mall cigarette after another in succession, four packs a day, every day. When he was sick and I visited him, I went for long runs too, just like I did when Mom was ill.

"How in the world did I get a health nut for a kid?" Dad would wonder aloud, punctuating his sentence with a wet thwacking cough that only made me want to escape his tobacco-soaked house and run farther away.

He and I weren't very close, our relationship a casualty of the cross-country move to California, demanded by his employer, after the divorce. He and my brother developed an impenetrable father-son bond (which excluded me) formed by their mutual hatred of Herman. Neither of them understood that I hated Herman too, but I had no choice about where I lived. Dad's death wasn't as sudden or surprising as Mom's had been, but once he was gone, he was gone just the same. I felt, acutely, orphaned.

Packing up his house after he passed, I found my parents' wedding photo hidden underneath the brown and black socks. My dad looked so proud of himself and his young bride. She held her bouquet demurely against the big pouf of her white dress and looked down, not meeting the gaze of his adoring eyes.

I wouldn't find out until I was much older that my mom divorced my dad to marry Herman, an acquaintance of our family. Herman and both of my parents had worked at the same company before Dad married Mom, so we saw Herman occasionally over the years. As a child, I thought it was an innocent coincidence that he happened to call our house to talk to my mom, practically the day after Dad had moved out. But the older I got, the less I believed in the serendipity of that phone call.

My brother told me Mom had been having an affair with Herman, and Dad had been trying desperately to hang on to his one true love, while Stepdad did everything in his power to woo her and take her away from Dad.

After Dad lost that battle, his hatred of Herman burst into flames and burned steadily throughout the rest of my father's life. It singed the edges of our relationship too. When I graduated from high school, Mom threw a party for me and all of our friends and family in the home where we lived with Herman. Dad refused to enter the house, so I had to leave my celebration to ride around the block in his rental car, the hot leather seats searing the backs of my legs like a spanking, as if I had been the one who had done something wrong.

But after my parents' separation and before the divorce, there was an in-between time when my mom was suspended, torn, between her two men; it was then, while the wooing was happening and without the glue of my dad in the house, the chips in our family became cracks.

Mom had always worked full-time, selling furniture on commission, but those days she had taken to reminding my brother and I before she left each morning, "If I don't sell, I won't get paid." She told us this because we needed her paycheck, but also because left alone together, my brother and I did what siblings do: pick fights and then tattle on each other when things went too far. Being the runt of our two-person litter, I was the picked-on one who ended up the loser more often than not. Our arguments prompted tell-all phone calls that constantly interrupted Mom's work and cost her sales she would have made if it weren't for our unending quarreling.

Each morning, we swore we'd be nice to each other, and I sent her off with a hopeful, "Make it a thousand-dollar day!" Somehow, I knew that was the dollar amount that would keep our household above water, preventing us from slipping under and failing.

All this pressure, from men and money and children, made Mom lose her appetite. She got so skinny, her clothes began to hang off her frame alarmingly. There was a day when I asked Mom for ten dollars to buy a new pair of shorts: powder-blue, cuffed short-shorts that were all the rage and would have been the showpiece of my summer 1973 wardrobe. But Mom refused me with tears in her eyes, apologizing. That was how I knew she couldn't afford new clothes for herself, either. I began to pitch in a lot more, cleaning the house and cooking so I could greet her at the door after work with the Swanson's frozen chicken potpie I'd made, begging, "C'mon, Mom. Eat."

Most afternoons, while Mom was trying to sell couches and end tables, my brother and his friends would gather at our parent-less house to drink beer and smoke pot. I have no idea how or where they got it. A few years my senior, my brother had a better grasp of the triangular situation our parents and soon-to-be step-dad were in. He punished our mom for her sins. At thirteen, he was already six feet tall and close to two hundred pounds, and she couldn't control him.

I felt impotent anger when the drugs brought on the munch-ies and the boys swarmed the kitchen, gulping Pepsi and shoving chips in their mouths until only drops and crumbs remained. One time I pulled my brother aside to whisper furiously, "Make them stop. We don't have enough money to feed them."

When Mom arrived home, there would be yelling, but no words could pierce through the hazy veil of my brother's high. I never called Mom about the drugs or the booze; instead, I absorbed the stress around me and worried and worried.

When Herman formally entered the picture, it felt at first like rescue was imminent. I was reassured by his over-the-top court-ing, his generous gift-giving to both Mom and me. She received the big heart box of chocolates; I got the small one. She got dozens of red roses in crystal containers too big for the dishwasher, while I was gifted a trio of yellow roses in bud vases. There was even a trip to Disneyland. He charmed us as if he meant it.

Mom always told me she loved him, right through to the end, but I suspect some part of her acceptance came from being saved from the chaos that filled the space of her between-marriages life. I've always clung to the hope that going in, Mom was as naive as I was. I've chosen to believe she had zero knowledge of how very black the dark side of Herman was. But thirteen years after marrying him, when she died, there was no denying what kind of man he was.

And I was left, bereft, a newly blind person trying to decipher the braille bumps of Mom's reason for staying, trying to understand why, after all we had endured together, she never rescued us—why she didn't, wouldn't, and ultimately couldn't save us by running away.

CHAPTER 8

HERMAN BECOMES
STEPDAD

U pon Herman marrying my mom, our family had the awkward conversation about what to call our new parental figure. Intuitively, Herman knew that my brother and I wouldn't call him Dad, or Uncle, so he asked to be referred to by his last name. During the years he and my mom were married, I honored this request, but in the aftermath of her death, uttering his name was like poison in my mouth. I chose to banish him, his title, and the idea of him to a black shadow figure labeled "Stepdad"—a cardboard cutout, caricature of a man whose blood, thankfully, never ran through my veins.

From the beginning, life with Stepdad confused me. He was a man of extremes. He was unpredictable, a dangerous combination of highs and lows, passion and hatred, kindness and ambivalence. Before Stepdad and Mom got married, we had only been exposed to his positive side, but as soon as the rings were exchanged and our separate families became one, his nether side revealed itself.

On one of the first Mother's Days we spent as a blended family, when I was eleven, Mom decided to take the day off work.

After we'd had breakfast and she'd opened her gifts, everyone scattered. I don't know where the boys went, but Mom drove to the nursery to buy flowers to plant and Stepdad went to his Sunday golf game. Coming home with a car full of colorful greenery, Mom went out to our backyard to plant flowers and trim the lilac bushes that bordered our entire fence. I went along to help her.

It was one of those unusual spring days in Minnesota where the warmth of the sun permeated through the back of my T-shirt, while the cool grass I knelt on chilled my knees through my jeans. Immersed in lavender, green, and gold, we quietly cut lilacs and planted, our fingers in the dirt. After a couple of hours, a shadow fell over me.

"Judy! What are you doing out there? Come inside!" It was Stepdad, home from his golf game, and he sounded crabby. My heart squeezed.

"We're planting flowers. I want to get the yard in order while the weather is good," Mom said.

"I want you inside. I'm home and want to go out to eat," Stepdad said. His tone was less husbandly and more like a hungry six-year-old home from day camp, tired and cranky.

"We have about an hour until we finish, then I'll come inside."

Stepdad turned to walk away and harrumphed as he went through the back door.

"He must have had a bad golf game," Mom said to me.

We continued our work, but after only thirty minutes, Stepdad yelled through the back door again. "Judith! What's taking so long?"

"We're almost done. Can you wait another thirty minutes?"

I wished he was the kind of man who could just say, "No. I'm hungry," but he wasn't. Instead, he became an angry lion, roaring and ready to spring.

"I told you I want to go get something to eat. Now! I'm hungry! Can't you hurry up?"

Mom had gone still. She whispered, "Betsy, why don't you go inside and clean up?"

"I'll stay to help you," I whispered back.

She shook her head.

He heard us. "You two are thick as thieves! What are you saying about me?" He walked over to where we were crouched and stood right above us. At six-four and four hundred pounds, he was intimidating even when he wasn't upset.

"We're just finishing. Betsy, why don't you go inside and clean up?" She wasn't asking this time.

I reluctantly walked inside while he started yelling. When I got to the threshold of the house, I turned to look out the window, to watch helplessly. Stepdad was following Mom around the backyard, haranguing, screaming. "You stupid bitch, how selfish are you? How dare you make me wait. Don't you give a shit that I'm hungry?"

As Mom went back and forth from the flowers to the garage, putting away the planting tools, and from the hose to the flowers to water them, he trailed her and he raged, saying demeaning things, calling her humiliating names. It was all out there, in our backyard for the neighbors to hear. She tried to fight back, but the angry force field around him deflected her words into the dust.

A hot, burning shame choked me as Mom walked up the back porch stairs with Stepdad right on her tail, hulking over her with his loud, never-ending diatribe. Mom came over to the sink where I was washing my hands and began to scrub hers. She gave me a look that meant "clear out," so I vacated the sink and slinked up to my bedroom.

Stepdad began the whole argument again inside the house. His tirade continued from the kitchen sink, upstairs to the bedroom where Mom changed; he bellowed from the bedroom back down to the kitchen, where Mom tried to make him something to calm him and his hunger down. His anger screeched from the kitchen to the TV room. No matter where she went, she couldn't escape him. From upstairs, I could follow the progress of their fight from the footfalls and scuffles and shouting.

Whenever these fights occurred, my ears buzzed like static on a radio. I couldn't always hear the words, but the sounds were excruciating just the same. In an effort to shut them up and shut it out, I curled around myself on my bed, hugging my knees and making myself small. My eyes squeezed shut and then *zzzzz*, the fuzzy sound, consumed me.

I heard steps on the stairs, and Mom came into my room, Stepdad right behind her. I rolled off the bed into a standing position, ready.

"Come on, Betsy. We're leaving," Mom said.

Stepdad said, "Of course you're going to take her! Where do you think you're going?"

"We're going to my mother's. You're being completely unreasonable." Mom grabbed my hand and pulled me.

Stepdad barely stepped aside, and as we maneuvered past him, I felt the heat of his anger radiating from him. Mom and I rushed down the stairs, her hand my lifeline, where she grabbed her purse from the banister rail. The two of us ran out to the car. As Mom backed up, I watched Stepdad watching us from behind the front door. I felt his scowling gaze like a laser beam, burning into my body. I couldn't wait to get away. "Hurry up, Mom. I'm scared," I told her.

Mom drove through our neighborhood, past the grocery stores and businesses, until we turned onto the ramp that took us east on Interstate 494, toward where my grandparents lived. We passed France Avenue, Penn Avenue, I35W, Lyndale, Nicollet, and Portland and were about to pass the airport exit when Mom decided to turn off onto a little-used exit with a sign saying POST

ROAD. We got to the top, which seemed to feature . . . nothing. It was more of a half-grass, half-pavement parking lot, a bit ruined, with a few cars dotted here and there. Mom pulled up to a spot by one end and stopped the car.

"What's this? Why are we stopping here?" I questioned, not alarmed but confused.

"This is Post Road, Betsy. There's a post office for the airport way over there"—Mom indicated with her hand—"and this is just an old parking lot. Look what you can see." She pointed out the front windshield, where a view of the airport runways spread before us.

"Wow! I can see all the planes down there, driving around. That's cool," I exclaimed. "How did you know about this place?"

"I come here to think sometimes. Clear my head." Mom was staring out at the sky as if it held the answer to her dilemma. In the distance, further east out over the Minnesota River, I made out the dots of lights that indicated planes were coming in to land. The lights formed a line that moved across the sky in unison, toward the runways.

Sssswwwwwooooossshhhh! A plane was rising toward us, taking off. It was so close I could see the landing gear folding inward, tucking the wheels into place right above the car as it rose through the early evening sky.

"That was so *cool!*" I swiveled my head to try to follow its flight path, watching until it disappeared from view. "Where do you think they're going, Mom?"

"I don't know. Somewhere." She paused, lost in her thoughts. Then she turned toward me. "Where do you think they're going?"

"Maybe Arizona? Or Las Vegas?" I asked, naming the only two places I'd flown to in my eleven-year-old life.

"Yes!" Mom was enthusiastic. "Or what if they're going some-place we've never been? Like Hawaii? Or Paris?"

"And they're dancing hula on the beach! Or eating chocolate croissants!" I added.

I watched plane after plane rise, heard the incredible *woosh* noise and imagined going off to a peaceful island with my mom, someplace without Stepdad, where his terrible temper couldn't follow us.

"Look there, Betsy, over the river." Now Mom pointed at the string of plane lights moving across the deepening sky. "Those are the ones coming back home." Her voice was wistful, full of both sadness and hope.

We were quiet for a while, lulled by the graceful dance in front of us, rising and falling, flying away and returning home. The planes were a steady metronome, a beat that made time seem like it passed and stood still in the same moment.

"Mom, aren't we going to Grandma's?"

Mom sighed, still looking at the planes landing. "No, I guess we're not." Her gaze shifted to me. She smiled a wan smile and moved her hand to cup my cheek.

"Why can't we go to Grandma's? Please?"

"I know it's hard to understand, Betsy. Your grandmother wouldn't be in favor of me leaving another man. She would just tell me to go back anyway."

I didn't understand.

"I love him, Betsy. I'll do whatever I can to make things better." Her voice had more muster in it now, and she formed a smile that felt more real as she started the car and turned it toward home.

This was the first time Mom took me out to Post Road, but it wasn't the last. Each time we left the house and drove there, it seemed our focuses were different. I was fixated on the planes that took off and tried to discover a way to grow my own wings and fly away. But she was more interested in the planes that returned home, the ones that landed gracefully like a floating bird and carried their vacation happiness back to a tranquil home where feathers weren't ruffled.

That was Mom. She deluded herself, over and over, believing her love could quiet Stepdad's fury and calm him down—that if she just tried harder, we would be a happy family. That was her dream: to have a happy family. Even if that meant that we were always going to go back to Stepdad.

CHAPTER 9

THE FIRST PHONE CALL

I t had been almost a month since our social worker, Sandra, had given Doug and I a passing grade on our home study and, with all the paperwork done, we were doing what we didn't yet know would comprise a lot of our time for the next year— waiting. I was at work, typing, sun at my back, when my ringtone blasted and the caller ID popped up: Bridge of Hope. Our adoption agency. I answered as I pushed away from my desk, rolling across the old uneven floor to my messenger bag for the notebook where I kept all my adoption-related notes.

Patrice, our caseworker, sang out, "Betsy, I've got great news! We've found you a match!"

My stomach jumped with anxiety. I was still struggling with doubts about my ability to be a mother and remained stunned that DCFS had approved Doug and me to adopt *any* children, much less the real ones I was to hear about in the next few seconds. "Go ahead, tell me about them. Please!" I said, pulling myself back over to the desk and fumbling to open my binder and take notes.

"You are going to love these little blond cuties!" Patrice said.

"Blond. Cute," I scribbled, as if that really mattered.

Patrice went on. "They are a brother and sister, one-and-a-half and two-and-a-half years old. Total darlings!"

"Boy. Girl," I wrote. As I began writing "one-and-a-half," I dropped my pen. "What?" I said, registering their ages. Before I could stop myself, I said, "Patrice, I don't want babies."

"But *everyone* wants babies! I was so excited to present these toddlers to you, since everyone wants the youngest children they can get. These two are perfect!"

"I know," I said, my voice heavy with guilt. I bent over, resting the weight of my forehead on my desk.

Inside, I heard the voices of "everyone" screaming, *"She doesn't want a baby? What kind of monster rejects a baby?"*

Well, me. I was the abomination who did *not* want a baby. I didn't know how to reveal the dread, the sheer fear, that gripped me when the word "baby" was mentioned. I'd been avoiding babies for all of my forty-seven years, and I didn't have an explanation for why the concept of being responsible for toddlers flipped the switch of the panic button in my brain. I wasn't a baby-hater, just a baby not-wanter. But I knew this antipathy made me unnatural, unholy, and horrendous. Shame draped itself over me like a cloak.

"Can I just tell you about them?" Patrice's voice held hope. "Or email you the information and pictures? You can let me know after you look things over."

My guilt forced me to say, "Sure, Patrice. Send it."

"It's on the way. Talk to you soon!" she said.

My email pinged. I opened it and clicked on the attachments, two pieces of paper and one picture. Before I examined anything, I called Doug and, when he didn't pick up, left a message summarizing Patrice's call. Then I forwarded the email.

Each page Patrice had sent was jammed with statistics: birth weight and head circumference described in centimeters, which I converted to inches using Google. It didn't matter. I had no idea what was "normal." The paper listed current info about health and a paragraph describing each child's disposition. The words, translated from Russian, had the awkward phrasing provided by direct decoding. One child had an "elegant appetite." What could that possibly mean? With literal translations piled upon medical jargon, this information was not only overwhelming, it seemed like a horoscope. I understood how a prospective parent, desperate for a child, could read whatever they wanted into these descriptions. Again, I felt different, freakish, for not yearning for motherhood.

I picked my phone up again and dialed the pediatrician we'd been referred to. With five Chinese adopted daughters, he was an expert in international adoption. The agency had connected us for just this situation. We briefly discussed the toddlers' medical history, and he seized on the fact of their head circumferences. "When they were born, their heads were so small that neither of them were even on the charts," the doctor told me.

"What does that tell you?" I asked.

"It can indicate a lack of brain development. Or it might not," he said. "They are both still very small for their ages."

"So what would that mean for the adoptive parents?" I asked.

"It means that you won't know how smart they are until they go to kindergarten," he said, not unkindly.

"There aren't tests for that?"

"Nothing that spells it out clearly. It's why we look at the numbers we're looking at. The best predictors are where they started and how far they've come. To be honest, this information is not encouraging."

"I'm worried . . ." I wasn't sure I should tell him this, but I pressed on. "I'm scared that if we say no to these two, they won't give us another referral. In your experience, does that happen?"

"Oh . . . no. I understand how you might think that, but trust me, it doesn't work that way. There are too many children out there who need parents. An endless supply, unfortunately. The agency's job is to match you with the right children because they want you and the kids to succeed. Mismatching is a disaster waiting to happen." His final words stayed with me. "Don't give up until you find the children who were meant to be with you."

Uncertain such children existed, I simply said, "Thank you."

That evening, I relayed my conversation with both Patrice and the doctor to Doug, and we looked at the information, and the picture, together. We both agreed these little ones were cute, but the doc's comments on brain development stuck in my head.

"The younger the kids, the less we know about their potential, even though they'd be with us from the beginning," I said. "It's like, on one hand, we'd be able to shape them from a younger age, but we don't have a good idea of who or what we're working with."

"If we try for older kids, we'll know more about their capabilities," Doug said, "but the older they are, the more time they've had with the families who couldn't take care of them or the longer they've been in the orphanage."

It was a real conundrum. How young was too young? How old was too old? What exactly were we trying to measure? No formula existed.

I told Doug, "I've known from the get-go that babies or toddlers aren't my thing. And yes, that makes me a terrible person . . ."

Doug shook his head.

"But given what the doctor said, I'd rather tell Patrice we are passing these two kids up and wait to see who else they refer to us. Is that okay?" I felt sheepish, inadequate, my lack of maternal desire for babies pressing down on me.

"Honey," Doug said, "stop it. We both need to feel good about this. We'll say no now and see what happens."

I nodded, absolved, but questioned myself. *Why am I so relieved to say no?*

CHAPTER 10

LIFE WITH STEPDAD

Our family spent my teen years yo-yoing between happy and sad, calm and calamity, pleasure and pain. Never knowing what to expect from Stepdad kept me hyperaware of the sound of footfalls and the timbre of voices. I became a little meteorologist who could tell you the temperature of any room in the house at any given time, my antennae tuned in to the threat of storms.

The most confusing thing was that sometimes Stepdad could be his better self—the self he'd been when he was courting Mom. After dinner, on hot summer nights in our un-air-conditioned house, Stepdad would announce, "We're going for a drive. We'll get ice cream." All six of us would pile into the 1975 wood-paneled station wagon so harmoniously it was like a choreographed dance. Mom and Stepdad got the front. The three oversized boys, each over six feet tall and two hundred pounds, crowded into the back seat while I, the lone girl and the youngest, got to roll around in the square back space, the place of honor, all by myself.

Both Mom and Stepdad loved to people watch. They thought it was fun, or a curiosity, to bring us kids into the seedier parts of Minneapolis on Hennepin Avenue and Lake Street to check out the hippies or watch the pimps and sex workers parade up and down. It felt exotic and strange to me—but also fun. It was something my straitlaced father would never have thought to do, much less permitted.

We'd often drive to a newsstand-bookstore in Minneapolis where Stepdad liked to buy newspapers and the rest of us browsed through the books. Circling back toward home, we'd stop at Bridgeman's Ice Cream Parlor for cones that I'd have to eat fast, fast, fast, trying to finish all those sweet, chocolate drips before the hot wind whipping through the car melted it away. Those nights, it felt as if I had a family—a *real* family—and I always hoped it would last, but it never did.

I was fifteen and had just gotten my driving permit when spring break dawned on the horizon. Seemingly out of the blue, my mom proposed that she and I take a spring vacation to practice my driving. A trip like this, only Mom and me, was unprecedented. No Stepdad! I relished the chance to spend time with her as we wended our way down to Florida, seeing Disney World and heading to the beach. The fact that we took a brand-new 1979 Camaro Z28, provided by Stepdad's employment at a local car dealership, was a blessing (cool car!) and a curse (Stepdad would never let us forget his generosity). Nonetheless, Mom and I took off, leaving Stepdad and my brother, Paul, behind.

I was relieved it was only Mom and me, because Mom and Stepdad argued a lot over Paul, especially after Stepdad's two sons, who were older, left for college. Once it was just the four of us—Mom, Stepdad, Paul, and me—living in the house on Normandale Highlands Drive, Paul struggled to escape living under Stepdad's oppressive roof by working a full-time job while he was in high school. Paul did whatever he could to make his own money, buy his own car, and remain independent. Unfortunately, he did the minimum in high school and spent his spare time partying, hanging out with his girlfriend, and staying out late.

Paul's behavior gave Stepdad the ammunition he needed to turn our mom against Paul. Stepdad constantly complained to Mom about how ungrateful we were, how we didn't respect him, and what a burden caring for us had put on him. Taking a vacation with Mom removed us both from the pressure cooker of daily life with Stepdad and Paul.

We drove for two and a half days, alternating listening to Billy Joel's *The Stranger* and Olivia Newton-John's *I Honestly Love You* albums on 8-track tape. We loved to sing, albeit off-key, and Mom made her fingers dance on the top of the steering wheel in time to the music.

We made it to Florida on a Saturday afternoon, and we checked into a hotel (nothing fancy) somewhere outside of Orlando. Mom called home to check in.

I had just stretched out on one of the beds in the hotel room, the scratchy, sanitized comforter sticking to the back of my sweaty legs as Mom dialed. My thoughts turned to the ocean, to the moment I could lay a towel across the sand, flop down on it, and bask in the sun's glorious rays. I hoped Mom's call would be quick so we could at least go to the pool.

"Hello!" Mom said, smiling into the receiver. "We're here in Florida! Going to go to Disney World tomorrow." She was chipper and upbeat.

I couldn't make out Stepdad's response, but it was loud, causing Mom to move the phone away from her ear.

"Wait. What happened?" she said.

From the bed, I heard Stepdad's bellow and watched Mom's posture change from relaxed to rigidly upright in seconds.

"What do you mean, 'you had a fight'? Where's Paul now?" Mom sat with one hand strangling the phone and the other twisting the cord. "Let me talk to him!" All I could hear on the other end was more intense screaming.

"Paul? Are you all right? What happened?" she said.

The next words were Paul's, and I could make them out loud and clear. "Your gorilla hit me, Mom! He hit me. I'm leaving!"

Mom was on high alert now, pacing across the drab hotel carpet like a diplomat unsure of how to broker peace from afar. "He's not a gorilla," she said gently, trying to placate him. "Don't say that. Tell me what happened."

Between Paul's yelling and Mom's anxious interjections, I intuited that my brother and some of his friends had wanted to go somewhere warm for their senior spring break. Paul didn't think Stepdad should stop him, and the situation had devolved into a physical fight. I was horrified. And scared for Paul. Even though Paul had always been a big kid, he was David to Stepdad's Goliath, and no one could ever win against Stepdad.

"He shouldn't have hit you, but at least wait until Betsy and I get home."

At those words, any thought of my toes in the sand by the ocean evaporated. Everything was ruined.

"Paul . . ." she said, but he'd hung up on her.

I didn't doubt that Stepdad was capable of laying hands on my brother. He'd just never done it before. He abused us with his words; he punched his fist through walls and slammed doors until they broke. Now the progression of his anger had reached the next logical step.

"Do we really have to go home? We just got here." I was terrified of what he would do to us.

"I don't know what to do, Betsy." Mom's voice vibrated with so much anxiety I could feel my own throat, chest, and stomach tighten. She looked out the window with unseeing eyes, blind to the Florida landscape, formulating her plan. "I'm going to call Grandma and see if she can find Paul and have him stay there until we get back."

I wanted to help my mom, but cutting the trip short seemed so unfair. Why did I have to suffer because Paul and Stepdad had a fight? My hands were bunching and wringing the comforter on the bed. I wanted to throw a tantrum, but that would only upset Mom more. She sat across from me on the other bed. She looked small and defeated.

"Why don't you go out by the pool while I deal with this?" she asked.

I could see that she didn't want me there to hear all the details, so I quickly changed into my swimsuit, grabbed a book, and left. I slumped downstairs and around the corner to the pool. Finding a place in the sun, I unfolded myself slowly, vertebra by vertebra, until I was flat. A tear from each eye fell sideways down and into each ear, tickling me. I could feel this trip and Mom all slipping away. Disappointment overwhelmed me, and I turned onto my stomach, buried my face in the towel, and cried silent, bitter tears.

That evening, after Mom had spent the afternoon burning up the phone lines between Minnesota and Florida, between her and her mother, and her mother and Stepdad, and Stepdad and Mom, they came up with a response. Paul was gone. Mom and I were going home.

Although I was unhappy, I wasn't surprised. A trip with Mom and me had been too good to be true. It was inevitable that Stepdad would find a way to ruin it. I hated him for always pick, pick, picking away at us. And though I loved my mom, I hated that she couldn't, she wouldn't, stay away from Stepdad. Mom would get away, then come back, get away, then come back, and all I could think of as I lay in bed that night was, *I will* never *stay with a man like him.*

The moon hadn't yet given up its grasp of the sky when Mom and I pulled away from the hotel parking lot. Even our peppy little sports car seemed defeated as we steered north, back to the scene of the crime. We drove straight through, taking more than twenty-four hours, alternating turns at the wheel. The sunny morning gave way to a cloudy afternoon as we moved into purple evening and through velvet-black midnight. As the sun rose again, we crossed the bridge between Wisconsin and Minnesota.

The mood in the car was one of pressure, of worry, of speed, along with dread, uncertainty, and resignation. We didn't listen to Billy Joel or Olivia Newton-John. No happy fingers tapped the steering wheel on the way home.

I didn't understand why my brother couldn't just follow the rules. Instead of *telling* Stepdad about his spring break plans, he should have simply asked. Or called our mom to get her okay. I hated our living situation too, but rebelling against it, as he did, only made it worse. I'd taken the other tack: I sat down, shut up, and acted perfectly. Unfortunately, no matter what either of us did, Stepdad's resentment—and Mom's giving in to him—never went away.

It was early morning when we approached our street and pulled into the driveway, which was pitched at about a thirty-degree angle so sometimes, sitting in the car, it felt like you were in a rocket before takeoff. We were both exhausted from our round-the-clock drive. I wished we could hit "go" again and blast out of there. Mom sat next to me, frozen with her hands on the wheel, staring straight ahead. "Well," she whispered, "let's go face the music."

Before she could even get out of the car, Stepdad barreled out of the house. He'd been waiting.

"Judith! Come here now! I want to talk to you about your son." His voice, full of contempt, boomed over the quiet morning.

"Let's go inside," Mom said. "We don't need to wake the neighbors."

I began grabbing stuff out of the car, glowering at Stepdad.

"Don't you give me that look! Do you think this is your business?" he yelled at me. "*It's not!* Look what happens when you take your mom away, you selfish little ingrate! Go to your room!"

I scrambled to comply, but felt scared for Mom. What if he began hitting her too? Would he come for me next? And where was Paul?

Up in my room, I curled up again into my familiar fetal position, holding my breath, while Mom and Stepdad argued. I heard bits and pieces. It was all about Paul. Uncontrollable. Disrespectful. Dumb. Ungrateful. From my upstairs vantage point, I tracked where they were and hoped the argument wouldn't make its way up the stairs.

Mom's protests couldn't keep up with Stepdad's deluge. She was exhausted, worried, and anxious. Stepdad didn't know or care where Paul was. The two of them circled around each other; Stepdad was wearing her down. Finally, I fell asleep.

For the remaining days of spring break, Stepdad started in every morning, "He can't come back." Every night before he turned in for the night, it was the same. "He can't stay here."

Mom asked where Paul was supposed to go, but I never heard Stepdad respond to that. Witnessing them argue about whether my brother could live *in our home* was unbearable. Mom's love for Paul couldn't overcome the strength of Stepdad's resolve, or break away from Stepdad's magnetic pull on her heart. I agonized, alone in my bedroom, scared to make a peep lest Stepdad begin fighting to get rid of me too.

Paul finally walked through the door on Saturday night at the end of the long week off. When I heard him, I came downstairs. He held a small bag and had a bad sunburn. So he had gone somewhere warm. His curly brown hair was brassy and reeked of Sun In. And his eye—his left eye was completely bloodshot, the skin around it swollen and blooming with the dark red, deeply bruised color of a rose way past its prime.

"Does it hurt?" I whispered.

Paul shook his head. "Is he here?"

I shook my head.

"Mom?"

"Upstairs."

Paul trudged up the stairs as if he were walking to his death. I remained on the bottom step, anxious to hear what I could from my perch.

Mom's voice was high-pitched and angry; Paul's was low-pitched and frustrated. He was upset, asking for our dad. Mom said, "You can't be here when he gets home."

Paul said, "You're kicking me out? Because of *him*?" He made a strangled noise. "*Fuck you!*"

Before I knew it, Paul flew past me down the stairs, slamming the front door and then his car door. He revved the engine, the tires squealed, and the car roared away. My brother was gone.

CHAPTER 11

A GIRL NAMED MIYA

After deciding against the very young pair of "blond cuties," Doug and I were on hold with the adoption process, bolstered by the words of the pediatrician. He had told me to wait until we felt right about the match, and I took his advice seriously. Three weeks after our first referral, the phone rang again.

This time, there was a girl and boy from Ukraine, seven and five years old. On the line with Patrice, the social worker from Bridge of Hope, I felt a surge in my heart. Was it hope?

Patrice emailed the pictures and the page of medical information, one for each child. I talked with the same pediatrician. He pronounced, "I have no concerns." Doug and I talked about them, about Ukraine, that night. The next day, I called Patrice back.

"Yes," I said. "Doug and I agree. These two are a yes."

Two months later, Doug and I were at a Hampton Inn just outside of New York City, waiting in the lower-level cafeteria area where the free breakfast was served. The yellow walls cast a buttery glow while the juice and milk machines hummed. Earlier that day, we'd flown in from Chicago. We were anticipating the moment we would, at last, lay eyes on the little girl, flying across the world from Ukraine, who was taking her first steps toward a forever family where she might become our daughter. My whole body thrummed with hope and tension.

Her name was Miya. Her little brother, Viktor, was too young to travel with the group of orphans, so the orphanage sent Miya without him. One of the pictures we'd received, which I'd carried around in my purse, had made me fall in love with the idea of them. In it, her light brown hair was in pigtails, and her brown eyes stared delightedly at her handsome little brother. Viktor was painting, and Miya was focused completely on helping him. They were both smiling. Miya was looking at Viktor with love. I imagined her looking at me the same way.

Doug's cell phone rang. It was Linda, the director of Bridge of Hope. She and the group of children and caregivers were on their way from the airport. All of the kids except Miya were staying for three weeks with host families in the New York/Washington, DC area. As the only host family from Chicago, we would be flying Miya back with us the next day. On the phone, Linda sounded frazzled as she explained that she'd been lost, was nervously navigating the huge rental van, and that the children hadn't eaten yet. Doug offered to have pizza delivered to the hotel and called the nearby restaurant where we had just had dinner and a couple of drinks for courage. We waited. I took a deep breath and stretched, trying to roll the tension out of my neck.

All at once, we heard a hustle-bustle in the lobby and the sound of Russian and Ukrainian voices. The group had arrived. I felt jolted by nervous energy, an inside shakiness suddenly flooding my body. Linda's thick New York accent directed everyone to the cafeteria.

Seconds later, children shuffled down the stairs. They clutched plastic bags filled with melty chocolate, broken crayons, and single coloring book pages. Tousled and wrinkled after traveling by train, then plane, and finally in a van to this hotel in

America, each child wore a lanyard with their picture on one side and a picture of their host family on the other. An image entered my mind of very tired miniature conventioneers after a night of partying, weaving, bobbing, and settling themselves into chairs so they could eat something before they went to sleep.

The children were guided by four caregivers, three women and one man. The man strutted, a peacock aware of his handsomeness. Two of the women were young and quite beautiful, wearing sexy clothes and high heels that didn't look comfortable for travel. The third woman, Olga, was older and more sensibly attired. She bossed the others around, getting them to settle the kids at tables. In stark contrast to the little bags the children had, the Ukrainian adults all wrestled with enormous suitcases, which I found out later were for the American electronics, clothing, and makeup they planned to take back home with them. Amid all of the hubbub, I searched for Miya, attempting to match the picture in my mind with the face of one of the children before me.

Olga emerged from the crowd with her arm around a little girl, steering her toward us and speaking to her in Russian. My throat tightened, and tears shimmered in my eyes. I heard Olga mutter the words "mama" and "papa" and watched Miya shake her head with surprising vehemence. I knelt down, intending to hug her, but when her face told me not to try, I didn't. Instead, I presented the soft, sweet teddy bear I'd picked out as a welcome gift. With downcast eyes, she shoved a small handmade toy, braided from yellow yarn into the shape of an octopus, into my hand. I said, "*Spasibo*." She said nothing.

Olga firmly seated Miya at our table and plopped a piece of pizza in front of her. Miya dropped the teddy bear on the floor and rolled the pizza up like a tortilla, eating it burrito-style and eyeing us suspiciously. She silently sobbed between bites, choking down tears with tomato sauce and cheese. Olga and the other caregivers sat at a nearby table, chiding Miya to behave. I didn't understand Russian, but I understood that she didn't like us and they wished she would act as if she did. I wished she would act like it too.

The other children stared curiously and smiled at Doug and me, immune to the drama playing out before them. Miya took her lanyard off and threw it against the wall, where it slid down to the floor near my feet. I bent down and put it around my own neck, trying to smile.

Dinner went fast, and suddenly, it was time to go to our rooms. My stomach churned and I looked at Doug, silently wondering what we were supposed to do. We weren't leaving for Chicago until the next day, and although we'd thought Miya would sleep in our room, that plan didn't seem right anymore. He shrugged his shoulders.

Across the room, Linda and Olga were speaking urgently through a translator and looking over at us. Linda finally called out, "We think it's best if Miya sleeps with the group tonight." I let out the breath I didn't realize I'd been holding and felt a wave of relief flow over the tide of my anxiety. Miya raced over to join her caregiver and two other girls without a backward glance.

With heavy hearts, we left for our room. Our eyes met in the elevator, where Doug turned to me and said the obvious. "Well, that didn't go as we planned, huh?"

Suddenly, we were laughing, slightly hysterical, at how awful it was. "She hates us," I agreed, "but if I were her, I'd be rocking myself in the corner and banging my head on the wall."

And I would. My child self probably wouldn't have done any better than Miya, but my adult self was now dreading the next three weeks with her. I'd been told to let go of any Hallmark card expectations, but somehow I thought there'd at least be some receptivity on the part of the child too. I hadn't prepared myself for this kind of standoff. All the doubts I had about being a mom, and there were so many, started to throb in my head and hurt in my stomach. Oh Jesus, what had I done?

That night was just a foretelling of the next morning. Same cafeteria, only breakfast was laid out. Caregivers unwrapped yogurt and tried to get the kids to eat American cereal and cold milk. Olga made Miya sit with us. Miya wore yellow sunglasses on her head, pink capris, and a raggedy fuchsia sweater. She refused to look at us. Olga called out, saying Miya wished for a yellow swimsuit and a Hello Kitty purse, as if this might bribe her into liking us. I found myself hoping it would.

But the time came to leave, and it was as horrible as we imagined. Miya pitched a terrible fit, screaming in Russian, stamping her feet. I stood helplessly. Doug, terrified to touch her, was as helpless as I was. The only solace I had was the fact that we'd hired a translator to meet us at home in Chicago. Olga nodded at me. Linda said, "Please pick her up and just go. We find it's best."

So I wrapped Miya's squirming body in a bear hug and lifted her, my back twinging from the effort. She screamed louder. I began walking away with her, and she struggled. I held more tightly, straining the muscles in my back further, the pain drawing lightning bolts down my spine. Doug punched the elevator button, and the door closed.

We were alone, the three of us, together for the first time.

Flying home with Miya was not as difficult as I'd thought it would be. She refused to sit next to Doug, so I put myself between them with her perched next to me in the aisle seat, her entire small being on high alert but blessedly silent.

Midway through the flight, she tugged on my arm and pointed at her lap, saying, "Toy-lee-ette," which I understood to mean "bathroom." The two of us crammed into the tiny space together as I helped her navigate the buttons to flush and wash. She stared me down the entire time, glaring at me, suspicious. Once we settled back in our seats, it seemed I'd passed some test. She even snuggled into me and laughed at the Tinkerbell DVD I played for her. I nudged Doug and pointed out this turn of events. Maybe it wouldn't be so bad after all.

But then we landed. As Miya ascended the jetway, her eyes frantically searched the crowd, and her face began to cloud over. She became increasingly stormy with each step. Doug wanted to document our arrival with a happy photo, and I knelt down next to her, attempting to appear pleased. Miya would not smile. I felt the cold of the tile floor on my knee, and it seemed as if it were seeping into me, all the way into my heart. We kept going and alternately coaxed and struggled with Miya to follow us to our car. What was Miya thinking? Was she terrified of us? It would make sense. She was all alone in a strange place and didn't understand a word we said.

Getting her inside the car presented a new challenge. Again, the vehement shaking of the head. The stamping of her white-sandaled feet. She fought me as I strapped her into the car seat, my back screaming for mercy. I decided to sit next to her in the back seat, in case she decided to unleash herself midway.

While Doug navigated, our eyes constantly, nervously met in the rearview mirror, as I attempted to console the inconsolable Miya. She was sad. And pissed. She began a diatribe, yelling at me in Russian, with increasing emotion and volume. Lamely, I tried to comfort her, but she resisted my petting, batting at my hands. Finally, I just fell silent and let her rail away. The forty-minute ride from O'Hare had never felt so long.

We pulled into the alley leading to our garage. To our immense relief, we saw Tatiana, the interpreter we had hired to translate during Miya's visit, waiting outside in the July sunshine. Young and beautiful, with shining brown hair and big blue eyes, she had dressed modestly in a long skirt and blouse for her introduction to Miya. Tatiana possessed an air of old-fashionedness, as if she embodied old-country values. Her family had emigrated from the Ukraine when she was in high school, and she spoke fluent English, Ukrainian, and Russian, along with a little French and Spanish. I had been impressed when we interviewed her.

As Tatiana began to speak to Miya in Russian, Miya's suspicious expression lessened. When Tatiana knelt down to take Miya's hand, it was as if Tatiana were offering a lifeline to the little girl. Their hands clutched, and they started a fast-moving conversation.

Circling around them as Tatiana led Miya into our house, I hoped to get this situation back on track. I had imagined how this day would unfold, and it wasn't going according to plan. I wished it was my hand Miya grabbed for comfort, but why would she? We were strangers who had torn her away from everyone she knew. Unlike Tatiana, we didn't speak her language.

Tatiana finally noticed Doug and me and guided Miya over to sit on the couch by us. Miya chose to sit by Tatiana and leaned against her as we began to orient Miya to our house, our life, our family. We had assembled a picture book that we had been told would help Miya communicate. There were a series of photos: Doug, me, our pets, our house, the car, the car seat, Miya's bedroom, the bathroom, Doug eating, me sleeping, Doug taking a drink, me sitting in the bathtub fully clothed but pretending to wash my hair. The laughing expression I had in the picture was a contrast to the nerves that made my hand shake as I turned each page. These pictures were underlined with the Russian words that described what was happening so that Miya could show us the photo if she needed or wanted something but wasn't able to tell us. Miya pointed at a picture of me and told Tatiana she liked my haircut, which felt like progress.

We persevered, moving on to the calendar I had prepared for the three-week visit with a daily schedule on a big white poster board, so that Miya would know her activities each day. As we showed her, Tatiana and Miya spoke back and forth, with Miya becoming more animated with each exchange. Outside of their circle, I kept hoping, trying to tamp down the twinge of jealousy. My anxiousness was getting worse by the minute. Sitting next to me, I could feel Doug begin to relax.

Our plan was to walk to the nearby doggie day care where our pups, Lulu and Roscoe, were boarded, and to introduce Miya to them. Lulu was a sweet, energetic, eighty-pound chocolate Lab who frequently did not realize her strength. Roscoe was a striking mix of Siberian husky and Bernese mountain dog. We had rescued him after our first dog, Muddy, died. He was less subtle than Lulu but even bigger. Neither dog would ever intentionally hurt Miya (or anyone), but we didn't want Miya's first experience with our beloved pets to frighten her. I worried that our dogs would scare Miya or that she would start sneezing around Oliver, our geriatric cat. But when Miya met Oliver, she bravely picked him up, and my stomach settled a little bit more.

Tatiana, Miya, and I walked down our block together. Gorgeous summer sunshine poured down, and green trees arched over the street, framing the flowers blooming in our neighbors' yards. The colors seemed supersaturated in the bright light, and the July heat tilted toward oppressiveness. I felt a line of sweat dripping down my back.

We meandered. Miya and Tatiana talked. I listened without understanding, attempting to gauge the emotional temperature of their conversation and wondering if they were speaking about me. I recognized only three words of Russian: *spasibo, dah,* and *nyet.* Thank you, yes, and no.

I heard Tatiana say, "Mama Betsy—" and Miya instantly interrupted with a loud, "Nyet!" Doug and I had been told that in the orphanages, the kids called each caretaker "Mama," followed by the caretaker's first name, and that we could expect to be called "Mama Betsy" and "Papa Doug." Hearing Miya so blatantly refuse stung me, pouring gas on the fire of my nerves. What did Tatiana think? What was Miya saying?

Finally, unable to wait, I asked Tatiana to explain what they'd been talking about. In what felt like a single breath, Tatiana spilled all the information she'd been gleaning. She told me Miya was scared. Miya liked Oliver. Miya loved our piano. Miya worried that she would have no one to talk to here. Miya liked Tatiana. Miya had only gotten on the plane with us because one of the Ukrainian caregivers had promised to be in Chicago with Miya, but she wasn't there. Miya was not happy that she had been lied to. Miya was hot. Miya was tired. Miya was excited about meeting the dogs. A caregiver back in Ukraine, prepping Miya for the trip, had apparently told Miya that she would be kidnapped once she got here, that Doug and I would chop her up in little pieces and throw her away. The poor child! No wonder she had fought us! Now I felt even more atrocious for the way I'd picked her up and carried her away.

Last, Miya told Tatiana that she already had a mama. The agency hadn't shared her backstory with us, but clearly she believed she had a family waiting back in Ukraine, and she didn't need, or want, another one. Tatiana relayed that Miya would not call me Mama.

I tried to ignore the heaviness in my heart. I realized I hadn't fully anticipated the dynamics of a seven-year-old who spoke no English with a host family who spoke no Russian, nor that Miya might prefer our translator over me. I also wasn't certain of Tatiana's opinion of those adopting kids from her country and whether she would feel uneasy about her role as our advocate. I'd assumed that a translator's role was to translate verbatim, not have private conversations. That day, I recognized how stupid I'd been, which didn't help my heart, accelerating in my chest, or the panicked feeling flooding through my body.

We picked up the dogs. We walked home. I held the dogs' leashes and tried not to be jealous when Miya held Tatiana's hand instead of mine.

The rest of our day passed like a movie on fast-forward. We fed Miya. We bathed Miya. We put her to bed. Miya warmed a little to me, but not to Doug. Maybe Miya was so worn out at this point she had no energy left to resist me, but I hoped she was coming around.

Given how this first twenty-four hours unfolded, the mere thought of tomorrow and the next twenty-one days exhausted me. After Tatiana left for the night, I bowed my head into my quivering hands, trying to steady myself. What had I done? How was I going to get through this? All I wanted to do was run away. *How ironic*, I thought. *I bet Miya wishes she could run away too.*

CHAPTER 12

FLYING AWAY

My senior year in high school, I attended a college fair with a boy I'd been dating. We entered the huge room full of hope and expectation, eager to visit the booths staffed by college reps and to learn about what each school had to offer. As we browsed the tables emblazoned with mascots and school colors, I realized I didn't feel an affinity for any one institution, or major, or place. College was the post–high school destination I'd been groomed for, but to do what, exactly? I hadn't a clue. My mom had always told me, "You can do anything, Betsy!" And my father's advice only highlighted the practicality—and paycheck— of whatever job my education would lead toward. My parents had only graduated from high school; neither of them really knew how college worked, so walking around that room, I decided I'd have to figure it out on my own. The only thing I knew for sure was that I was going to go away to school. I wouldn't, couldn't, live at home anymore; the tension between Mom, Stepdad, and me was becoming untenable.

After Paul got kicked out, he moved in with his girlfriend's family, which meant all of the boys were out of the house. With Mom's retail schedule and Stepdad's traveling for work, I was often home alone until well after dark. During peaceful times after school, I'd make something to eat and bring it up to my bedroom.

Mom and I had painted the walls peach to match a quilt she had made for me, the very first handsewn quilt she'd ever made. When the afternoon sun hit the western window, the room was flooded with a warm, ember-colored glow. In the winter, I'd lay on my bed reading and soak up the sun, as if the light itself would fortify me for the night ahead. I always needed it.

The boy I went to the college fair with wanted to go to Pepperdine University, and as we approached the booth, I hung back a bit. I liked the way Pepperdine sounded, with its sharp *P* sounds and definitive *d*, but I saw the pamphlet with the picture of Malibu and college buildings spread out on the hills overlooking the Pacific Ocean, and it felt too far away. I needed to be close to Mom, so I kept my sights on Midwestern cities and towns: Madison, Wisconsin, and Drake University in Iowa.

The table for the University of North Dakota drew me in with its pictures of planes and its claim to be one of the best flight schools in the country. A clean-cut young man standing in the booth piqued my interest by telling me that he was a "student pilot" who had gotten his private pilot license in the first semester.

"What's it like to fly?" I asked him.

"It is . . . the coolest thing I've ever done." His smile gleamed, and his eyes looked off to a horizon that only he could see. He asked me, "How are your math grades?"

"All A's," I replied. My dual proficiencies at math and science, and reading and writing, were both a gift and a curse. The good grades I earned came from my deep fear of making a mistake rather than for a passion for any one subject.

The student looked me right in my eyes. "If you're good at math and you're willing to have an adventure, I think you'd like flying."

The confidence with which he appeared and spoke—*that* was how I wanted to feel. Piloting a plane, being a captain of my own destiny, appealed to me. When I began announcing I wanted to study aviation, other people's responses kindled my enthusiasm. That student pilot had no idea, but his remarks returned me to the times I sat in a car with my mom up above the airport runways, longing to be on one of the planes taking off. This was how I could leave home and fly away.

Six months later, on a late February evening, I came home to a thick envelope from the University of North Dakota informing me that I had been accepted into their Aviation Administration program and that I had been given a modest academic scholarship. I was going to learn to fly! Those papers were the ticket to the next phase of my life, what I'd been waiting for, but my anticipation was layered with worry. Could I really leave Mom behind with Stepdad? If I were gone, would he be better? Or worse?

A week or two later, Mom and I huddled at our dining room table, surrounded by financial aid forms, scholarship papers, pay stubs, and college information, trying to tabulate a budget for my freshman year. One number that stuck out was sixty-five dollars, the amount it cost to fly a Cessna 152, a little two-seat single-engine plane, per hour. In order to become a true commercial pilot, I'd need hundreds, if not thousands, of hours of flight time. And that was in addition to tuition, room and board, and all the other costs of a university education.

Mom's approach to this, like most things, was optimistic. The numbers for tuition and room and board were tight, but she had a way—probably the same way she convinced customers to dedicate money for furniture—of rounding up on income, of rounding down on expenses, of calculating the best possible outcome, and of making me feel as if anything were possible. Part of Mom's charm was that she avoided mention of calamity and disaster, believing instead that when the time came, she'd somehow bend the numbers to fit the budget. She taught me this too: how to pretend around a problem as if it didn't exist. But implicit in her positivity was Mom's promise to be there, to help me if I needed it.

When Stepdad came home and saw the two of us elbow deep in papers with the adding machine whirring as Mom typed in numbers and wrote notes on a yellow legal pad, he came over to the table and surveyed the scene. "Are you two figuring out the financial aid?" he asked.

Mom nodded.

"Would you like me to look it over?" he asked.

"Oh, I don't think that's necessary, honey," Mom said. "I think we've got it all under control."

"Really?" he asked, one of his eyebrows raised.

Stepdad was a financial manager and car buyer at a used car lot. His work was murky to me. I didn't know what he did, why he traveled, or what kind of money he earned, but inherent in every argument they had about money was the fact that he didn't think there was enough and he believed Mom spent too much. I suspected that Mom actually outearned Stepdad, maybe because her employer was the source of our entire family's health insurance, which he must have resented. Nevertheless, he was the person in the house who "did the bills" and ostensibly had the most say over the purse strings.

He didn't seem like he was mad or in a bad mood that evening, but my stomach jittered. Money, especially money related to my expenses, always triggered arguments. As my senior year had unfolded, it became very clear to me that I represented the final hurdle for Stepdad to overcome so that he could, finally, have all of Mom's time and attention. Not only was I the last kid in the house, I was *her* kid, and he deeply resented sharing her, sharing *anything,* with me. I'd had a part-time job since I was fifteen and tried to pay for all of my expenses but felt guilty for wanting, or needing, even a morsel of Mom's attention.

I sat very still at the table, holding my breath, and stared at the piece of paper in front of me.

Mom stood up and smiled at him. "Yes! We really are in good shape. Betsy got a scholarship, and she's been saving. You don't need to worry."

Stepdad's eyebrow returned to its usual position and his brow unfurrowed. "Okay, then." He smiled back at my mom. "What's for dinner?"

"I'll set the table," I said and began to gather up all the papers. *Crisis averted,* I thought, letting out a breath.

I hated the position Stepdad put my mom in, continually asking her to choose between us. And worse, if she gave me attention, he raged at her. I was left in a slurry of anger and sadness, fear and pain, knowing my very presence caused Mom's heartache. I would have made myself disappear if I could have, so my mother could live in peace without Stepdad's tormenting jealousy.

Later that night, after dinner and television, we followed our usual evening routine. I was upstairs reading in my bedroom. Mom and Stepdad were down the hall in theirs, watching the news. I could hear the murmur of the newscasters and the timbre of their conversation, but I was absorbed in my book.

Gradually, the murmurs got louder. The argument I'd anticipated had arrived, just later than expected. Their voices became angrier, and the volume increased, until I finally put my book down. I pulled my knees up to my chest and burrowed my head under the quilt, trying very hard to block them out.

"She's going to bankrupt us!" Stepdad yelled.

"Honey, she is not. She'll work . . . and she has scholarship money," Mom retorted ."Will you please leave it alone?"

Her asking him to stop only fueled his rage. I heard the sound of something being thrown on the floor, the creak of bedsprings as he stood up, and his bellow. "Is she *ever* going to leave? I'm tired of taking care of her! She's a spoiled, ungrateful brat, and you just keep on giving and giving. I'm sick of it."

Something about his blunt honesty triggered me. How much did he really hate me? What had I ever done but tried to be perfect? Why did he always try to make her choose between us?

A tornado of blackness descended on me, and I swirled with rage. This haze in my head—anger, sadness, hate, and fear—clouded my vision until I felt like a wild animal that had reached its breaking point, ready to strike out and bite the hand that both fed and punished it.

All this noise, all the loudness, all of the poisonous unspoken words I wasn't allowed to say leaked into and congealed in my brain. I crashed down the hall from my bedroom to theirs. I felt possessed when I staggered through their bedroom door.

It was as if I'd run with a gun onto a stage in the middle of a performance, interrupting a scene where the actors froze, mouths agape, startled into stillness. My mom, lying in bed in her nightgown, long legs stretched out, with her counted cross-stitch covering her lap; Stepdad, in his pajama bottoms, turning from where he stood next to his side of the bed, staring at the intruder; me, wild, in the doorway of their bedroom. Our bodies were statues, but our eyes scanned the room looking for the next line in this suddenly improvisational drama. I'd never—*never*—talked back.

"Stop. This. I hate this. Stop screaming at each other!" I spat. I heaved and I spewed. "I can't stand this anymore!"

No one moved. No one spoke.

And there was silence, blessed silence. For just a second . . . until Stepdad bellowed, "Who in the hell do you think you are?"

He took one menacing step toward me, and I screamed back, "No one! I'm no one!" I turned to go and said, "Just leave me alone," and I slumped back to my room.

That was all I wanted in that moment, to be invisible, to be away, to be no one. Not to need, never to have to ask, to stop being a problem. If Mom didn't have me, then she wouldn't have to fight for me anymore. As frightened as I was for her with him, I desperately wanted to stop being a burden and disappear. There was no place for me anymore. As I cried myself to sleep alone that night, I wished Mom would come to comfort me, but I knew she couldn't.

For months after that, the three of us tiptoed around each other. Both of them were absorbed in their work while I was finishing up my senior year, secure in the knowledge that North Dakota was waiting for me. There wasn't much conversation, but there wasn't as much fighting, either. The silence wasn't as loaded as it had been, but it was still foreboding. I'd been trained to wait for the next explosion, and I couldn't shake the feeling that whatever peace we'd gained could be shattered in an instant.

In May, I walked through the door after school and found Stepdad, planted in his big chair by the TV, waiting for me. He seemed uneasy, and my antenna for trouble rose up immediately. Without any preamble, he told me, "Elizabeth, your mother and I are breaking up."

"What?" I was stunned at his words. How had this come about?

"Your mother and I are getting divorced," he said again.

Although a breakup was the answer to a long-held dream, I didn't want to show my happiness. Partly because I didn't trust him, but more because for once, I wanted to be the one that hurt him with my nonchalance, to act as if he didn't matter at all. "When?" I asked.

"Once you've graduated."

"Okay," I said with a definitive nod and walked away, up the stairs to my bedroom.

I threw myself on my bed and commenced a series of silent postures, all demonstrating how exhilarated I was. My arms went up over my head in a victory position. I pumped my fists like a prizefighter; I kicked both feet in the air, mimicking Snoopy's happy dance. And then, the emotions overran me, and tears seeped out of my eyes as I cried with the feeling of finally releasing pent-up anger and sadness. My energy ran out, and I was exhausted with relief. The sun hadn't set yet, but I fell into an untroubled sleep that lasted until dawn the next day.

The next morning, Mom confirmed the news and answered all my questions about how this would go down. Stepdad would find an apartment, but Mom and I would stay in the house until I left for college, after which she would sell the house and buy a condo. She said to me, "A lot of people plan June weddings, but I'm planning a June divorce."

I was cautiously hopeful, while at the same time, somewhere deep inside of me, I thought of Post Road and the planes. Would she be able to resist her urge to return? I didn't know.

After I graduated, they put the house on the market and Stepdad got the promised apartment. The heavy, foreboding atmosphere in the house lifted when it was just Mom and me living there. Sometimes the relief I felt was so intense, it felt as if I were actually floating from room to room, or up the stairs. Unfortunately, both Mom and I worked so much—her at the furniture store, and me at a clothing store in the mall—that our crazy retail schedules didn't allow us much time together. The summer flew by, and suddenly it was the night before I left for Grand Forks, North Dakota.

That evening, after putting my final load into my car, I lay back on the hood, breathing in the late summer air. The wind was ferocious and carried the raggedy edges of clouds across the sky while the stars peeked through, shining and winking at me. I thought about flying, how it would feel to be one with the wind, riding on the clouds, and soaring through the heavens. A wave of hope surged within me. I wished the wind would sweep me up and send me forward into the night and toward the sun. I stayed there for an hour, letting my dreams out into the universe, praying that they'd all come through. Tomorrow I would leave home and start my new life, breathing easy that Stepdad and Mom were safely apart.

I returned home the Wednesday before Thanksgiving, having earned my pilot's license and logged thirty-seven hours of flight time. I was disoriented when I walked into the new town house Mom had bought and moved into while I was at school. She had decorated with mostly new furniture, a perk of her job being the discount she received on furnishings, and the unfamiliar decor and layout felt foreign. Mom seemed jumpy and anxious, fluttering about the kitchen and chattering nonstop as she laid out the plan to celebrate the holiday at my grandmother's house the next day.

"Herman and the boys, along with their wives, will be there," she told me. Her eyes darted around the room, avoiding eye contact with me.

Her words felt like a punch in my gut. I leaned against the counter for support. "What happened, Mom? Why are they coming to Thanksgiving?"

"Betsy, where will they celebrate?" she said. "I can't stand the thought of them having Thanksgiving at his apartment."

"But what about the divorce? Aren't you two divorced now?" I asked her.

She shook her head and looked down. "We haven't finalized anything. In fact"—she swallowed and took a deep breath—"we've been seeing each other. The threat of divorce has really changed him, Betsy."

I sighed and hung my head. "Mom! Why? How can you get back with him again?" The taste of disappointment was bitter in my mouth.

"I miss our family. I don't want to live alone!"

"Are you kidding me? Our *family*? What family?" I was aghast. "Do you remember all the arguing? The screaming and stomping and raging?" *How could she do this?*

"He's really changed. Just give him a chance, Betsy." She was pleading with me.

"Mom, just please, please promise me that if he ever—*ever*—hurts you, you'll leave?" I couldn't believe she was putting her trust in him again.

"He's not going to hurt me," she said. She sounded so certain.

That night, as I lay in my unfamiliar bedroom mulling over our conversation, I thought about Mom, living in this place alone, and I conceded that it probably *was* lonely for her. I was gone in North Dakota; Paul and his wife had bought a house of their own and lived on the other side of town. We were moving on with our lives. Was it fair of me to expect her to start all over? I punched my pillow and turned it over, restless even though I was exhausted and scared for her.

I remembered how charming I'd once believed Stepdad to be, and I was sure he was turning it on, wooing her once again, curbing his terrible temper until he had her back. I didn't understand how my mother could be such a moth to his flame. Didn't she remember what it felt like to be burned?

I finally fell into an uneasy sleep. I dreamed I was back at school, flying a Cessna 152. Improbably, I was trying to land at the Minneapolis airport, but the control tower wouldn't give me permission. In the dream, I saw Mom standing on the runway, waving to me. I felt desperate to get to her, but it was impossible. From the air, I watched her and worried as I circled and circled, never being able to set the plane down. I couldn't determine if she was signaling that she needed me to rescue her, or if she was simply waving goodbye, wishing me well on my journey. My confusion felt all too real.

CHAPTER 13

THE BEGINNING OF LEGACY

A t the beginning of the summer after my mom died, a few
months after Stepdad locked me out, I found myself at the
start line of a road race, the Grand Old Days 5 Miler. The
Minnesota May morning held a bit of chill, which soon burned
off with sunshine and sweat. I chose to run this particular event
because my tiny apartment was only a block away from the start,
and the route looped through the streets of Saint Paul and finished
on Summit Avenue, a beautiful neighborhood of stately homes that
included the Minnesota governor's mansion. I lived on the funky,
slightly bohemian street that ran parallel to Summit—Grand Avenue, the street that gave the event its name. After the race, I walked
away from the crowd of runners and reveled in early spring's yellow light, feeling the limitless blue sky and the peaceful energy
running gave me.

The rest of the afternoon, I hung out on the barely there bal-
cony of my vintage apartment. I had just enough room to set up
a lounge chair to watch the parade that followed the race. As the
pageantry marched by, I relaxed in the sun, my bare feet propped
on the porch rail, sipping a vodka tonic and savoring potato chips
that tasted like summertime to me.

In spite of my easy mood and the festivities around me, memories of my mom visited. May was her birth month. May had

Mother's Day in it. This was the first time we wouldn't celebrate these holidays together, but not the first time I had mulled over what she would have done with her life if she were still alive.

When Mom became sick, I had been called upon to do all of the things daughters do for their ailing mothers. Stepdad was often gone for business on weekends, putting me in charge of her care for forty-eight hours at a time. I slept over so I could help her up and out of bed, in and out of chairs; help her to the bathroom; and coax her to eat so the morphine wouldn't make her nauseous.

There were times when her medicine hit its sweet spot—strong enough to kill the pain and dull her inner censor, but weak enough to allow her lucidity—when she opened her heart to me. The idea of unfinished business, of regret, settled heavily upon her. It hurt to listen, but I couldn't bring myself to turn away. I understood how sacred these moments with my mom were, filled with precious information she felt compelled to confess to me.

The breath of the grim reaper down her neck stunned her. She simply couldn't believe that her life was destined to be so short, so suddenly. Mom, like most people, assumed she would have all the time in the world to live, that there would be a future "someday" when all of the things she'd put off for later would finally come to pass.

"What did you want to do, Mom?" I asked her one Sunday afternoon when these dark thoughts descended, making her cry.

The question opened up a seemingly unending list. She wanted to go antiquing and uncover treasures. She wanted to travel—to Paris, to Hawaii, to somewhere—but had never been anywhere but the lower forty-eight states her entire life. She thought she'd be there to watch me become an adult and do adult things, like giving her grandkids to play with and spoil, like taking mother-daughter trips together. She thought she would have time for more dinners with her best friend. She wished she could mend all the damage done during her marriage to Stepdad. Did she mean to fix what he'd done to her, or to my brother and me, or to all of us? I couldn't guess, and I refused to ask. It hurt too much. She wanted to read books, eat ice cream, maybe even go back to school. She wanted to do something besides selling furniture for a living.

I asked her, "What career would you have preferred, Mom?"

"Something creative. I wish I'd been more talented at crafting and been able to make a living that way. I won't"—her breath caught as she began to tear up—"I won't even have time to sew you a proper quilt, honey. I got to sew one for each of the boys, but not you."

"But you did! You made your very first one for me. I love it," I told her, but I knew what she meant. The peach quilt she made for me fit my twin-size mattress; it wasn't a quilt that I would ever share with a lover or life partner. My stepbrothers and brother, along with their wives, had each been gifted a handmade, king-size quilt as wedding gifts.

"And I won't be at your wedding." She hung her head at this thought, and tears dripped down her sallow cheeks onto the collar of her nightgown.

The mention of a wedding made me weep with her and project out into my own empty future, bereft for both of us. All the things she would miss, the things I would have to do alone, without her.

I told her what I'd been telling myself since she'd been diagnosed. "Mom, you'll be there. Somehow. I'll know you're there. I will always—*always*—carry you in my heart." I paused. "Plus, who says I'll ever get married?" I tried to chuckle to lighten our mood, but the sound that came out was strangled.

"Oh, honey, you have to get married. It's so important to have someone who loves you."

This topic wasn't new. Mom had been pushing marriage on me since the end of my junior year of high school, when I broke up with my older, bound-for-college boyfriend of two years. She adored the thought of us together and carried a picture of us all dressed up in our coordinated prom finery in her purse. She even had the nerve to stay in touch with him after he left for school, writing him letters and phoning him behind my back, encouraging him to "just stop by" whenever he was in town. This went on for two years and only stopped after she ran into him at the mall. After taking in his stylish ensemble of 1980s androgynous clothing, an earring, and eyeliner, she had broken the news to me that she suspected he was gay.

"Mom, getting married isn't the be-all and end-all," I sighed, not wanting to argue with her but truly confused. Her early marriage to my father had ended in divorce, and life with Stepdad? I couldn't imagine anything worse.

"Yes, Betsy, it is! Marriage brings us family! I want you to be happy. Please promise me that you'll keep our family together after I'm gone. I can't die in peace if our family falls apart. I know you don't like him and that he's difficult sometimes, but please, keep together, stay together." She was talking about Stepdad. I was gobsmacked at her request. How was I supposed to maintain a relationship with a pseudo-parent who didn't really want me? And with his kids, who never bothered to speak to me outside of our parents' presence? My brother and Stepdad barely acknowledged each other at this point. I couldn't see a way to bring all of these opposing forces together. Mom was asking for the impossible.

My mother's plea for our "family" angered me too. Cancer robbed her of her free will—there would be no divorce or standing up to his rage—and the sicker she became, the more she clung to him. He had all the power, and I was terrified that he would use it to cut me out of her life before she died. I agreed to her request only to ease her mind, saying, "Of course, Mom. Don't you worry about us."

But once she was dead, and after Stepdad did what he did, our "family" was over. Any sense of home I'd had was destroyed and the bridge back thoroughly burned. I was left alone with the charred ashes of her legacy, feeling as if I'd failed her, even if the promise she'd asked me to make had always been well beyond the bounds of possibility.

What stuck with me the most about those sad conversations, the unfulfilled dreams my mom had expressed, was the terrible medicine she had been forced to swallow, the bitter taste of regret at the end.

Her regrets haunted me.

Back on my stamp-sized porch, thoughts of my mom and her regrets swirled around me like dust, infiltrating any small crack in my heart they could find, and settling there to wait until I summoned the energy to blow them away.

As the sun met the evening horizon, I decided a second run would shake off my melancholy. I had never done this before— run twice in one day. But that day, I needed to escape my grief. I ran another six miles, up and down Summit Avenue.

The route I ran mirrored the last six miles of the Twin Cities Marathon, something that crossed my mind around mile five. I floated back to my little apartment feeling on the verge of . . . something I couldn't name. I had been so sad but felt almost euphoric after running so far. I yearned for more. As I turned the brass lock in the worn wooden door to my place, the idea clicked like a key in my mind: I was going to do the undoable. For my mom. I was going to run a marathon.

CHAPTER 14

EXPIRATION DATE

Running became my constant. I carried it with me, wherever I went, no matter who I liked or loved, no matter where I worked or spent my free time. Running provided a spirit connection to my mom, a place where the rustling of the leaves contained her murmur and the pounding of my feet echoed her heartbeat.

My other companion was grief. The triple losses of Mom, a family, and a place to call home gaped before me, too huge to acknowledge. I couldn't make sense of how this utter abandonment had overtaken me. My devastation became my dirty secret. I did exactly what Mom had taught me to do: pretended everything was okay.

I got myself right back into college, graduated with a bachelor's in food science, and was offered a pharmaceutical sales job (and salary) that, on paper, exceeded all of my expectations. Unfortunately, it required me to move to Chicago, which meant leaving my college best friends behind.

Almost exactly two years after Mom died, I packed my car with a few essentials—a lamp; one each of a plate, bowl, fork, knife, and spoon; a pillow; a blanket; and an air mattress—and moved to my new apartment in Oak Park, Illinois, a cute little village outside of Chicago's city limits that reminded me of Grand

Avenue back in Minnesota. Wandering through the rooms, the place reflected my universe back to me: empty. That first night there, I couldn't figure out the thermostat, so I slept in four layers of clothing and my winter coat and cried myself to sleep.

The dread of "What if?" haunted me. I'd just moved to a big, unfamiliar city for a job I wasn't sure I could do, without a single friend and no savings to speak of. What if I hurt myself and couldn't work? How could I support myself if something dire happened? Who could I call to help me? My father and I weren't on speaking terms after I'd asked him to help me financially and he'd refused. My brother had retreated into the solid embrace of his wife's family, and I certainly could never, would never, call Stepdad. I was well and truly alone.

Oak Park lasted about a year, as did the pharmaceutical job. I got a position working in publishing, briefly, before Kraft hired me and off I went to Fort Wayne, Indiana. Two-plus years later, dying to escape small-town rural life, I found another job, this time working for the candy company M&M/Mars. The fact that I was thrilled to be moving to Rockford, Illinois, for the new position, at the time deemed one of the worst places to live in America because the Dodge plant located there had closed, said more about my feelings regarding Indiana than anything else.

I sold drugs, books, cheese, and candy. I didn't last at M&M/Mars for long and took different positions in different companies, always searching for the thing that was going to fulfill me. I looked for more money, a product I believed in, a better location. Like Goldilocks, I searched and searched, but nothing was ever just right.

Each job required me to relocate, which was fine with me. I loved moving. Not the actual transport of furniture and such, but the prospect of finding a home. In each new place, I painted the walls of my apartment bright colors—covering up the this-could-be-anywhere white and living surrounded by seafoam green, lavender, peach, and periwinkle. I bought myself a perfect couch, a green-and-white-striped comfy one, along with the matching oversized chair, which was squooshy and soft and enveloped me. Eleven months in, when the new lease agreement arrived, asking, "Would I stay?", the answer was no. I painted the place white again every time, and I ran away to the next location, hoping.

My college roommates, all of whom were married by now (we were in our late twenties, after all) remained my closest confidantes and were a long-distance phone call or six-hour drive away. I returned to Minneapolis several times a year, and they came to visit once or twice as well, although of course nothing could match the daily intimacy that had grown from living together. I made friends wherever I lived, usually through work or from meeting neighbors, who were often transplants like me. During the holidays, I became the dog/cat/house sitter when they went home to see their families. Christmas tasted sour, and I hated it, the day when the Christian world rejoiced while my mom died during the wee hours when Jesus was born.

Besides friends, there were men. Discovering that I could beguile someone, no matter where I was, turned out to be a beautiful distraction from my sadness—and the pattern lasted for too many years.

My mantra, the refrain of the song in my head during this time, was, "I can always change my mind." The truth of it offered me an odd comfort: knowing I could keep reinventing myself, a brave exhilaration to be so untethered, and a rush of knowing my possibilities were endless.

Underneath all of this busyness and movement, however, lived a still, deep well of sadness. I stood at its edge, again and again, scared to fall, stopping myself only with the distractions of new men, new jobs, and new places. Each time I ran away, I didn't realize that I waded deeper into the pool of grief I was drowning in. Each time, I was left alone, again, with no one to save me from myself.

How this all unfolded began to concern me.

A few months after my thirtieth birthday, my dad died. Although we'd reconciled before he passed, our relationship had never fully recovered. With Dad gone, I felt even more keenly what I was: an orphan.

One evening, I lay on my green-and-white couch, wallowing in my grief, completely uncomforted. Tears fell, rolling down my cheeks faster than I could stop them; snot clogged my nose; and hoarse sobs tore their way out of my throat. I had broken up with another guy. I wanted to sell the town house I had recently bought, and I wanted to quit another job to do something I couldn't even articulate. Tired. I was so tired of all of it. I had reached a breaking point. I couldn't stand myself.

My thoughts careened around my head, smashing into each other, throwing up a fog of confusion as I cried and cried and cried my unstoppable tears. Oliver, the kitten I'd recently adopted, sat regarding me from his post on the armrest of the sofa, his wide green eyes watching me, calming me as the haze cleared. He seemed to be saying, or maybe I wanted him to be telling me, "Please calm down. You can't run away right now. I just arrived and need you to stay here."

Exhausted, I accepted that maybe I just didn't want to be me anymore, didn't want to be here anymore. But what could I do? I couldn't run away from myself. *Could I?* I thought about giving up, about dying, as I lay on the couch on my side, limp as an old, wrung-out dishrag.

Oliver walked carefully across the cushions and onto my chest, where he curled into my armpit, purring. The thrum of Oliver's vibrations spread like a warm blanket, soothing my sadness. *No, I can't do that,* I thought, right before I fell asleep. I had mixed-up dreams about rescuing Oliver from the shelter but he was saving me, giving me a reason to keep going, to live. The next morning when I awoke, I picked up the phone and asked for help.

Six months later, I sat with my therapist, Jennifer. She reminded me of my mom, with her short dark hair, sparkling eyes, and ready smile. She hugged me after every session. I'd spent the session talking about how I wanted to break up with the latest guy who, only two weeks previously, had me swirling in a tizzy of infatuation. Jennifer was nodding, then said, "Aha! I finally get it. Everything, everyone, everywhere, has an expiration date."

"Yes!" I exclaimed, so relieved to have my uneasiness articulated. If I knew what my problem was, then perhaps I could fix it.

Jennifer challenged me. "I have an assignment for you. Are you up for it?"

"Of course!" I said eagerly. If there were such a thing as a teacher's pet in therapy, I claimed the position with Jennifer.

"Okay! Here it is: You can't break up with him. You have to stay. I'd prefer a month, but I don't think you'll be able to do it, so I'll say two weeks. You have to wait to break up with him for two weeks."

"What? Noooo," I moaned, whining. "But I don't like him anymore."

"You've got to get past this." Jennifer emphasized with her hands, chopping the air. "Just stay for two weeks. Then you can break it off if you still want to."

"Fine," I huffed, my desire to please winning out. "See you in two weeks."

I lasted only one week after that, and in our next session, we analyzed. I was finally understanding how remaining when it became real, when I became itchy, maybe even imperfect, was a different kind of agony than aloneness. I became aware of the fear I carried with me into every relationship—that if I allowed myself to be vulnerable, to need someone, it was inevitable that they would either hold it over me (Stepdad) or leave me (Mom). That terror triggered me to take off. It was the first time in my life that I realized my running was much more than a physical activity I loved. It was a metaphor that *was* me. I had been running away ever since my mom had died.

And then I met Doug.

When I told her about him, Jennifer observed, "He sounds different. Is he?" She asked, "What if he's *the one*?"

I didn't know how to respond to Jennifer's question, so I didn't.

Three months later, still with Doug, I found myself, predictably, searching for an excuse to break up with him. I woke up in the middle of the night, lying next to him, tears leaking from my eyes. I could stop this now, cut off the love, but if I stayed . . . ?

I was beside myself because I didn't know how to remain in a relationship. I could not envision a way to stick it out. My compulsion to leave was a mosquito bite, an itch that was never satisfied no matter how voraciously I scratched it. Yet, there in the dark, I realized Doug *was* different than the others. I couldn't manufacture an excuse to abandon him. There wasn't anything wrong—except with me.

I told Jennifer, "I'm scared."

"Hasn't the worst already happened to you?" she asked. "Your mom? Your stepdad? You survived all that. And here you are now."

Here I was now. Could I risk it? Should I? The whispers of desire—to stay—were strange. But I listened. I decided to stay.

CHAPTER 15

DOUG

D oug was thirty-three and I was thirty when we met. A few months prior, I'd had another epiphany in therapy: I wanted to quit the corporate world to go to social work school. Once accepted into a program, I'd moved from the suburbs to Chicago proper—the Lincoln Park neighborhood, to be exact. I was finally having the postcollege experience that seemed to be a rite of passage for twenty- and thirty-somethings from smaller towns across the Midwest. I spent my days running along the lakefront path, meeting up with friends for cocktails, and planning the next phase of my life on the pages of my journal, waiting for grad school to begin.

The week before school started, a girlfriend convinced me to go to a party at Kelly's Tavern on Halsted Street, one of dozens of hole-in-the-wall Irish bars that populate Chicago's neighborhoods. We walked from the summer evening into the dimly lit tavern, and there he stood: a tall, dark-haired, blue-eyed guy leaning by the first table inside the door. Even though he was talking to someone else, we made eye contact as I passed by.

"Who was *that*?" I asked my friend.

"That's Doug," she said. "He's a nice guy."

Apparently, Doug was busy trying to figure out who I was too. The host arranged an introduction, Doug procured some drinks, and our first conversation centered around the new navel ring shining just below the hem of the crop top I wore. A few days prior, I'd pierced my belly button as an outrageous (for me) way to mark this new stage of life. Showing it off was fun, but I didn't realize it would so effortlessly attract my soulmate, not that I knew then it would be Doug. We nestled into two chairs at the bar and began to discover what we had in common.

I learned he worked at Arthur Andersen, the big consulting/tax company; he played beach volleyball, which was how he knew the host; and he'd grown up in Oak Park. We both marveled over the fact that when I'd been living there, he'd lived about a half mile away from me. It turned out the two of us had frequented the same restaurants and bars but never met. For me, this sprinkled some magic over our conversation, a little bit of "meant to be."

Doug asked me, "Do you like to travel?"

"I do," I told him, "but mostly in the States. The most exotic place I've ever gone is Mexico. What about you?"

"I love to travel!" he said. "My job takes me all over the world, so I'm lucky. My mom worked for American Airlines growing up, which was great because my family always took trips."

I mentioned my brief stint in flight school, which Doug told me later made me stand out to him, contributing to his attraction to me.

"The last time you went somewhere, where did you go?" I asked him.

"I just got back from the Outer Banks in South Carolina. My whole family went."

"Really? Tell me about your family. And the trip."

"It was my dad, mom, and younger brother, plus my two sisters, who are both married, and their husbands and kids. I have five nieces and nephews who were all there."

"That sounds like a lot of people!"

"It was, but we rented a big house on the beach, so we were all together."

The happiness on his face as he relayed details of their trip fascinated me. It sounded so idyllic. Did people really have families where multiple generations traveled together willingly? Loved each other enough to spend twenty-four seven with each other on their precious vacation days? I couldn't imagine it.

We kept talking, trading questions and answers, while I admired his cobalt eyes set off by a summer tan. My stomach started to fizz, pleasantly, with feelings of attraction and connection. The tavern was darker now, and the pendant lighting over the bar illuminated a cozy circle only for the two of us. Friends came up to chat, eventually taking their leave or inviting us along for a bite to eat at a place down the street, but we remained.

I watched him as we talked. He held a beer bottle, and when I studied his hand—long fingers, nice nails, beaten up just enough to look manly—I wondered what it would be like to hold that hand. After a while, we noticed we were the only ones from our whole group still at the bar. When the bartender announced last call, Doug offered to walk me home, and I accepted.

As we strolled, Doug stopped me in Oz Park, somewhere in the middle, equidistant from the Dorothy, Toto, and Tin Man statues that gave the green space its name. The darkness of the late August night and the smell of freshly cut grass surrounded us.

"Look at the moon," Doug said, pointing, his other arm nestled around my shoulder in a half hug. The moon was full, a golden orb floating in a sea of midnight blue. *Oh jeez*, I thought, *how completely cheesy.*

And then his hand came down to cradle my cheek, turning my face to his for our first kiss.

Our lips had barely touched when a bright light interrupted us, shining like a spotlight. "The park is closed!" yelled a voice through a bullhorn.

On the street by the edge of the park, we could see a Chicago Police vehicle, white and boxy, along with two policemen.

Doug shouted back, "Really? Don't you have anything better to do?"

"Don't make me throw you in the paddy wagon!" the cop threatened.

I grabbed Doug's hand and said, "Let's go."

I'm still not sure who led who out of the park, but we got out, and I felt safe.

While Doug made me feel safe when I was with him, safe was not the word I used to describe Doug to my friends; in fact, he was probably a little too exciting for me. On our second date, about a week later, we walked home again, but this time on the lakefront path. Doug paused by the chess pavilion, a cement structure with chessboards painted on the benches where folks played checkers or chess while the world ran, walked, biked, or skated by on the ribbon of path flowing past. At this time of night, the pavilion stood empty and the expanse of Lake Michigan stretched to infinity in front of us. We snuggled on a bench, and he leaned in to kiss me. Just as we were settling into each other, a voice called out, "Hey, what's going on over there?"

Two policemen walked down the path toward us, flashlights in their hands bouncing circles of light around the benches. Again.

One of the officers said, "What are you two doing? No one can be in the park after eleven! Go home!"

We both stood up and waved. "Okay, okay. We're leaving."

As we walked away, I looked at Doug and asked, "What's your deal? Do the police follow you everywhere, or just when you're trying to kiss me?"

"I don't know!" Doug replied, laughing. "This has never happened to me before." We kept our hands to ourselves as he walked me home, and then, in the safety of my apartment, he kissed me without interruption.

Our encounters with the police probably influenced me to see Doug as a little more dangerous than he actually was at first, but as our relationship grew, I realized I was dating one of the "good guys"—a genuine, kind, loving man. One afternoon we came out of Twin Anchors, a barbecue restaurant so exceptional the wait time usually exceeds an hour. Because the portions are as big as the wait time is long, Doug carried a large bag of leftovers, which I was looking forward to eating the next day (a fact of which Doug was well aware). A few steps outside the door, a woman who appeared to be very down on her luck sagged against the building, holding the hand of a ragamuffin little girl.

"We're very hungry. Can you spare any change?" she asked.

Doug said, "I'm sorry. I don't have any cash, but I'm happy to give you these, if you'd like them."

"Really?" the lady said. "That place smells so good!" She smiled a piano key–toothed smile and took the bag, hustling the little girl down the street to find a spot for their feast.

As we were walking away, I told Doug, "That was really nice, but I kind of wanted those ribs for tomorrow."

"I know. So did I," he said, "but she—and that little girl— needed them more."

Was Doug turning me into a better person? Perhaps, but I wanted to believe studying social work in grad school affected me too. The combination of intensive learning and Doug—his steadiness, his authenticity, his taste for adventure, and especially his family—demonstrated a different model of how to be in the world. It was quite foreign from my broken familial relationships and set an example that soothed the scared little girl inside of me, who still walked on eggshells and waited for explosions, holding herself tightly, trying to be perfect.

And that was us. In matters of the heart, he kept pushing me to the edge of my comfort zone. He was always willing to lead the way, while I hung back, trying not to get messy, trying not to make any grave errors.

A little over a year after meeting, Doug and I moved in together. We weren't engaged, and I was slightly sensitive about living in sin, especially considering Doug's Catholic mom. To compensate, I invited his family over for a home-cooked dinner. Showcasing my suitability as a girlfriend extraordinaire, I attempted a recipe from the Martha Stewart cookbook his mother had given me for Christmas: rosemary pork chops with red-pepper applesauce.

After planning and shopping, and peeling and braising, the pork chops were leather; the applesauce practically smoked, it was so fiery hot. I warned everyone, "You guys, this is all terrible. Can we please just order a pizza?"

"Oh no!" they all said. "It looks really good."

But after only one bite of the meat, Doug's gracious mom said, "It's delicious, but I'm so full!" She then proceeded to dump her portion onto Doug's brother Greg's plate. Poor Greg's protests were drowned out by the sound of coughing as their mother choked on the lone bite of red-hot apple sauce she tasted.

This meal went down in Armstrong history as the worst meal ever, yet they still wouldn't let me order the pizza. Instead, we laughed, and I wondered at the grinning faces surrounding me, enjoying ourselves even when something went so entirely wrong.

When Doug and I got engaged four months later, I said yes. I knew he was the one for me. We decided to get married fast, because Doug's large extended family had been planning to visit Chicago that summer already.

Planning a wedding so quickly didn't faze me one bit. The thought of a traditional ceremony, in a church and reception hall, where parents walked brides down the aisle and father-daughter/mother-son dances were the norm, triggered sadness for my orphan status. But I was determined to focus on what I was gaining, not all that I had lost.

There was a moment during our wedding day that perfectly encapsulated how far I had come. As I made a toast, I looked around the room at over 150 raised glasses, and waves of love and acceptance washed over me. A million light-years away from my childhood home, where Stepdad raged and I had cowered, I stood there, surrounded by support and soaked in their benevolence. I raised my glass. "To us!" I said, staring into Doug's eyes and clinking glasses.

The Armstrong clan challenged me and my beliefs about family. The summer after we got married, I joined them on one of their epic family reunion vacations. His oldest sister rented a huge beach house in Naples, Florida. Their parents, Doug's other sister, his brother, his brothers-in-law and nieces and nephews—along with the two of us—converged for ten days. I adored vacations involving the sun and sand, so while I was excited to be there, I was decidedly less excited about spending ten days with fourteen people, including five children, most of whom I didn't know very well.

I went into the trip imagining that the Armstrongs traveled as a pack and that everyone expected me to join the group for every meal, every activity, every conversation. Additionally, I pressured myself into believing I should present myself as a cheerful and enthusiastic participant in whatever the family decided to do, regardless of whether I wanted to or not.

So I did. We all cooked breakfast together. We all went to the beach together. We all went out for dinner together. We all played games or watched movies at night together. Everything. Together.

After about four days, I resented all of this togetherness. But did I express any of my less-than-stellar emotions? Of course not. Which is how I ended up one afternoon, seven miles down the beach, literally having run away from all of this Armstrong togetherness when no one was looking.

My thought process, during the two hours I ran, went something like, *This isn't* my *family, because I don't* have *one, and I'm tired of having to pretend that they* are *my family and that I enjoy being around so many people* constantly. *It's all too much!* And on and on, my mind spiraled and spun, until it realized, until *I* realized, how completely ludicrously I was behaving.

Suddenly, my feet skidded to a stop on the beach. I turned around and looked at the line of footprints that had led me to this moment, this place. *God, I'm such an idiot.*

Heaving a huge sigh, I picked up my right foot, then my left foot, building up steam as I followed my tracks, a line of zigzag breadcrumbs, back to the house. Soon, the reality of my stupidity started swirling, gaining speed along with my feet. *Now I'm seven miles away and I feel like a* fool. *I am a fool. What's wrong with me? How will I* explain *where I went and why I left? And why I've been gone for hours? Uggghhhh . . .* The soundtrack of shame played on repeat in rhythm with the drumbeat of my shoes on the sand.

The best thing about running, especially when my mind raced, was that the farther I went, the calmer I became. By the time the house appeared, I had accepted three things: One, it was stupid to run away. Two, I needed to express my emotions to the people around me before my fears caused me to do things I regretted. And three, I had to face them.

I approached the semicircle group on the beach, shame coating the words waiting in my throat. Everyone either lay on the sand, splashed in the surf, read a book, or chatted with one another. They looked totally relaxed and content, lost in the company of themselves and each other.

As I neared, Doug saw me and called out, "Hi, honey!" His voice sounded like he was asking if I was glad to see him. The others turned their heads, the sight of me bringing happy expressions to their faces.

"Did you have a good run?" he asked.

His voice held no anger or worry. No cloud of resentment hovered above his head. *Was it possible that no one was mad at me?* "Umm, yeah," I said in an uncertain tone. "It was good."

Confused by this positive reception, I looked around and said, "Sorry I was gone so long by myself. And that I didn't let you know I was going."

"Don't be sorry!" Doug's mom scolded. Then with a big smile she said, "Everyone loves a good walk on the beach, sweetie. Did you have fun?"

I nodded at her, the corners of my mouth turning upward. Sitting down next to Doug in the sand, he kissed my cheek and said, as if I were being silly, like it was no big deal at all, "I'll always be here, Betsy, waiting for you."

CHAPTER 16

MIYA'S STAY

The morning after Doug and I brought Miya home, I woke up with a pounding headache after a restless night. I dreamt of a hellish labyrinth where I lost Miya and where my maternal doubts and fears chased me as I desperately searched for her. The breathless helplessness of the dream clung to me as I went down to the end of the hall and knocked on Miya's door, not entirely certain she would still be there.

I found her up and alert, hugging her knees and shivering. The air-conditioning in our house blasted in the July heat, and poor Miya was freezing, sitting on the end of her bed, dressed in her traveling clothes from the day before.

"Oh, sweetie," I exclaimed, "come here, let's warm you up!" I went to the dresser to find one of the Gap sweatshirts I'd bought and held it out for her to slip over her head, as I mentally chastised myself for lowering the thermostat the previous night. Barely forty-eight hours in, and I was already failing at this.

For our first day together, Doug and I decided to take Miya to the Lincoln Park Fest, one of the countless street fairs that popped up every summer weekend in various neighborhoods in Chicago. Usually, Doug and I attended in the late afternoon or evening, shopped at the booths, listened to the live music, and enjoyed a few drinks while mingling with friends. The day we brought

Miya, the three of us arrived at 11:00 a.m. sharp, when the festival opened. For the first time in our lives, Doug and I ventured into the kids' area, a place we'd studiously avoided previously.

With our encouragement, Miya took full advantage of the activities. She rode a pony, climbed the climbing wall, made a beaded necklace, and got her face painted. I snapped pictures and smiled at her, glad she appeared to be enjoying herself, but a joyless vigilance buzzed within me. I played the part of a parent, but I wasn't comfortable, and my mind raced with questions. *Was she happy? Was she too hot? Did she need something to drink or eat? What should I do?* Of course, Miya couldn't express herself, and her face remained resolutely stern, giving nothing away as to how she felt.

At one point, Miya tugged on my shirt, clearly wanting something. She kept repeating the word "voz-doosh-are" with increasing volume, attracting the stares of a few other parents. I began to get flustered, but when she stamped her feet and pointed at a balloon, we finally realized what she meant. By then, we were so relieved to comprehend what she wanted, we probably would have bought her the pony too, if that's what her heart desired. By 1:00 p.m., activities exhausted, Doug and I both had a single beer. I don't even like beer, but this one tasted like the first blast of air-conditioning on a sweltering summer day.

Being responsible for Miya felt like walking across a field filled with buried land mines, every moment of every day. Suddenly, everything in our house was a danger. My mind raced with potential tragedies. Miya could open the door and walk out, not even knowing where she was or how to find us. Miya could turn on the oven without even realizing it and set a fire. She might start the blender and stick her hand in it, even though it was unplugged. She might accidentally let Oliver, the cat, who was always trying to escape his cushy indoor life, outside, and he would be lost forever.

She could fall down the stairs and hit her head. She might break something fragile and cut herself. The dogs might knock her over if someone rang the doorbell and they rushed at the door to bark, which they did all the time. She might turn on the bathtub and let it overflow, or scald herself with hot water. The possibilities for harm ran endlessly through my brain.

Three days into our visit, Tatiana came for dinner. Miya was ecstatic to see her friend and to be understood once again. I so wished Miya smiled like that for me, and even though I wasn't exactly jealous of Tatiana, it stung to know that I wasn't a source of comfort for Miya when I very much wanted to be.

We would be sending Miya to day camp the next day, which was part of the deal we struck with the agency, meant to enhance her American experience and surround her with American children. Tatiana explained to Miya where she would be going the next day, and as the knowledge sunk in, Miya's demeanor changed.

Tatiana translated back that Miya, obviously pleading not to go, would like to stay home by herself. She promised she would keep the doors locked and she wouldn't answer the phone or let anyone in. She didn't need to eat. She would wait all day, being a good girl, as long as she didn't have to go to camp. It was clear to all of us that Miya had needed to say these things to someone else, somewhere else, sometime in her life.

The mystery of where Miya's behavior came from was impossible to solve. The agency provided few, if any, details of her background, and we had been coached to avoid explicit questions about our little visitor's life back in Ukraine. Tatiana helped Miya see that camp was required, and thankfully Miya climbed into my car the next morning without incident.

My spirits rose when I introduced Miya to the camp director, who told me that there was another camper who'd been adopted from Russia, and who might be able to talk to Miya in her own language. I handed Miya over, along with her backpack, water bottle, and lunch bag, and sent a prayer up that Miya would enjoy herself.

Five hours later, I returned to pick her up. Miya's hair was still wet from the final activity of the day, swimming, and she sat alone on the cement stairs of the park district building, waiting for me. She looked resigned, as if she were merely tolerating this whole camp thing. When I inquired about Miya's day, the counselor looked kindly at me, saying, "She keeps to herself, and I have to coax her to participate. She seems lonely, but she'll be okay."

The time with Miya continued on like this, and I ached for her. Often, I found myself sobbing, working off my nervous energy about having her here as I went about the day. From nine in the morning until two in the afternoon, Monday through Thursday, I could lower the veil of vigilance that hung over every moment with Miya. I was ashamed of my need for a break. It made me question whether or not I was up to the task of being a mom.

In contrast to the anxiety that caring for Miya brought out in me, Doug was a natural, so much better with her. One evening, we took Miya to the local beach. It was a warm summer evening and the waves rolled in gently, lapping at the sandy shore. Against the lavender sky, Doug and Miya swam together, laughing and splashing in the golden glow of evening. They looked relaxed and happy; they were having fun. I don't know what kept me from diving in and playing, I just simply couldn't make myself. Instead, I watched from the sand and worried about what to make for dinner.

My inability to bond with Miya scared me. I wanted her to like me, love me, even, and I wanted to like and love her. Before meeting her, I'd hoped our hearts could meet halfway, finding each other in the middle of positive mutual regard. As our time together went on, my hopes began to fade, and my anxiety took over.

There were a few things I discovered she liked, though. One was banging on the keys of our grand piano, loudly and discordantly, for as long as I could stand it. I tried not to startle when she hit a particularly disturbing chord combination, but between the volume and dissonance, and my ever-present nervousness, I couldn't take the jarring noises emanating from her hands. After ten minutes, I always told her, "Enough," and closed the keyboard, which also shut down the gleeful look in Miya's eyes.

The other activity she loved was to play with her Barbie dolls. The feminist inside of me was appalled that I spent my money on these persistently sexist toys, yet I also wanted Miya to have the accoutrements of her American peers. I purchased several Barbies, with multiple outfits, and the Barbie Dreamhouse I'd once coveted as a child. Miya took no joy from changing the dolls' outfits. She didn't like rearranging the furniture in the house. But what she loved doing was sitting Barbie on one of the tiny chairs, knocking her off of it, and laughing hilariously at poor Barbie's mishap. I played along, but it disturbed me to watch these small scenes of abuse play out from Miya's imagination. I may have read too much into it, but it didn't seem so funny to me.

Miya was also enamored with our mobile phones and, although she didn't like to be in pictures, she loved to take them. Doug gave her one of his old cell phones, which she adored. She often pretended to be having a conversation, speaking Russian purposefully to her imaginary listener. I longed to understand what she was saying, certain the key to her heart existed in the one-sided dialogue pouring into the speaker.

Miya used the camera to take snapshots all day and brought the phone to Doug each night. While Doug downloaded the pictures into our computer, she leaned into him, choosing the ones she wanted for her memory book. Nyet, nyet; dah, dah. No, no; yes, yes. Doug printed out all her dah photos and helped her tape them into the album. Observing them together made tender tears flood my eyes. Doug was meant to be a dad, no question. If I couldn't figure out how to act like a mother, I'd be robbing Doug of his paternal right, to say nothing of what would be lost to any child lucky enough to become his son or daughter.

And yet, Miya was hard for me to handle. She was prone to meltdowns, probably like any seven-year-old would be. If she didn't want to do something, she exploded. One night I prepared the tub for her bedtime bath, and without any provocation I could see, she began shrieking, "Nyet, nyet!" Trying to calm her only made her worse, and I wondered if I was really cut out for this.

But then there were times when I could turn the situation around or make Miya smile to keep my hope alive. One time I put in a Disney DVD, featuring what I thought were all the various Disney princesses, pictured on the cover in their pastel cartoon splendor. Miya sat on the couch, shaking her head and scowling. She brought the DVD cover over to me, pointing at one of the princesses and babbling in Russian. She stabbed at one of the princesses with her pudgy little finger, pink nail polish glittering from our semi-successful attempt at bonding over a manicure. I realized Miya wanted *this* Disney princess and no other. All the others were nyet! Unfortunately, the Disney princess she loved wasn't on the actual DVD, but I couldn't explain that to Miya.

What I did instead was figure out it was Sleeping Beauty that she wanted, and I went on the hunt. When I presented her with a Sleeping Beauty DVD and the matching doll, her eyes lit up, and she gasped in delight. For the first and only time in twenty-one days, Miya launched herself at me for a big hug. I didn't want to let go; I wanted to savor the feel of her arms grasping my neck.

About halfway through the stay, the agency asked the big question: Will you adopt Miya? And her brother? What will help you decide? I spent almost two hours on the phone with another mom who had adopted the year before. Her daughter was receiving services to help her adjust. Speech therapy, bonding therapy, physical therapy, therapy therapy. It was fine. It was to be expected. It was all normal.

I had no idea if anything about this was normal, but one thing the agency suggested was to take Miya to the pediatrician. I promised to bring Tatiana to translate, which was the only stipulation given, except for not having anything "invasive" done. I couldn't imagine what that would even be, but was told, unbelievably, that a past host family had gone so far as to have their host child examined for signs of sexual abuse. Of course, I promised not to do that.

The doctor was the same one who had spoken to me over the phone after reviewing the paperwork for our potential matches, the "blond cuties." He was renowned for having adopted five Chinese daughters, and for being an expert at assessing internationally adopted children. When I met him, he was wearing a Superman tie, and he had pictures of his golden retriever, T-Bone, decorating his office. He kept up a soothing patter, all translated as agreed upon, as he examined Miya—weighing and measuring her; having her stand on one foot, then the other; asking her to touch her nose and stick out her tongue. The doctor made Miya giggle, especially when she found out she wouldn't have any shots. And he gave her candy. He pronounced Miya perfect. He said that usually these kids have medical problems. He said, "You hit the jackpot with this one!"

I wanted to believe him, but I wasn't sure.

CHAPTER 17

SHOULD WE, OR SHOULDN'T WE?

A s the end of Miya's visit approached, Doug and I discussed what to do. Doug's impression of Miya was steadier than mine, but Doug was largely unburdened by all the emotional baggage I carried. He had never seen this jittery, overwrought side of me and was unsure of how to respond. This was one of the few times in my life when I felt completely incompetent and unprepared. I had never been responsible for a child before, and there was no way to compare it with anything I'd done. At college or work, I had studied and practiced in order to build skill over time. Now I truly didn't know what I was doing, and I was nervous, a taut guitar string that, if plucked, would snap. Thinking of my own mother and her demise, I couldn't help wondering if motherhood, if Miya specifically, was part of a legacy I was meant to fulfill, or something I would come to regret?

Sometimes, Doug attempted to pep me up with "You can do this" messages. I responded to these by tamping down my negativity and reminding myself to take deep breaths. Other times, he told me that I didn't *have* to do this, that we could walk away. Perversely, I received this message with some relief, but remembering his tenderness with Miya, I couldn't bear telling him that I agreed, even on my worst days. I saw just enough to believe strongly that Doug wanted to be a dad, and more, deserved to be a dad.

No talk of adopting Miya was complete without considering her brother, Viktor. When the agency addressed this during the matching process, we understood it was likely we would be required to take an additional trip to Ukraine to meet Viktor before proceeding to adopt both siblings. We also knew that Miya and Viktor were a package deal.

It wasn't until we spent time with Miya and agonized over the adoption decision that the full weight of moving forward, with Viktor as an unknown, bore down. It reminded me of the probability problems I'd studied in math. If I couldn't handle Miya by herself, how would I fare with both of them? Would it be easier if they were together? Would my challenges be simply doubled, or would they turn exponentially more difficult? Was Viktor easygoing or temperamental with adults? What if the siblings constantly fought with each other? My head spun with questions no one could, or would, answer.

As the days counted down, the agency applied pressure upon us to choose: Would we simply say goodbye to Miya, or would we have the Adoption Talk? The Adoption Talk meant telling Miya we wanted to adopt her and make her part of the family. Our Adoption Talk, if we proceeded, would include adopting Viktor too. The Talk also had to navigate the careful lines between hope and promise, between uncertainty and guarantees. Even if we had the Talk, the outcome of the adoption would remain uncertain until the final moments in a courthouse over in Ukraine, when the boom of a judge's gavel would seal all our fates forever.

Searching my heart, I realized even if I couldn't arrive at a wholehearted yes, I still hadn't gotten to a flat-out no, either. That distinction felt important to me. I usually made decisions, even important ones, guided by my gut. My instinct, this time, told me to stay on the path, even if I didn't know where it led.

After endless mulling, Doug and I decided, yes, we would have the Adoption Talk with Miya. Doug and I were both curious to gauge Miya's reaction to the idea of joining our family. We reasoned that perhaps the upset of the trip and unknowns of her future drove some of Miya's challenging behaviors, and if she were aware that she and Viktor would be together, Miya might even respond favorably.

We set up the Talk for the second to last night that Miya stayed with us because the date coincided with a visit from the Ukrainian caregivers. Participation in the Bridge of Hope program required us to host the Ukrainian adults for a couple of days in Chicago, taking them sightseeing, feeding them, and allowing them to observe our interactions with Miya. Since we were the only Chicago family hosting a child, just one caregiver traveled to us, Aleks, and we chose him to translate for the Talk. Tatiana wasn't available. We figured Miya could speak freely with Aleks, since he'd been a caregiver at the orphanage. We hoped that because Miya knew him, she would trust what he told her.

Aleks was tall and handsome, with piercing blue eyes. From the moment we met him, he burst with confidence and bluster, full of larger-than-life stories about his life in Ukraine. Aleks told us about his career as a professional wrestler and then as a pastor at his church. For Aleks, it was a foregone conclusion that we'd be coming to Ukraine, and he offered his "extra" services to us, explaining that he would be our driver, our interpreter, and our guard. How he came to be working at the orphanage was murky, but what was very clear was that Aleks was a hustler.

Instead of sightseeing, Aleks wanted to be driven to one cell phone store after another, and then to Best Buy to purchase more phones and electronics. He asked Doug to take him while I stayed with Miya, which seemed counter to the purpose of his visit. No matter where we went, he constantly excused himself from the meal or conversation to talk on his own cell phone. I wondered if all the computers and phones he purchased were for his family, or for some other business proposition he'd undertaken in his beloved country.

Although Aleks preferred to talk about Aleks, Doug and I were anxious to talk about Miya and to have the Adoption Talk with Miya. Finally, the last night Aleks was with us, the second to last night before Miya went home, Doug and I sat around our dining room table, waiting for Aleks to begin the big conversation.

We told Miya, while Aleks translated, that we loved her, that we wanted to come visit her, to meet Viktor, and to bring both of them back to live with us in America. We said, in order to not promise too much, that there were a lot of rules we had to follow, and papers to fill out, and people we had to please, but we were going to try, very hard, to make this happen. We asked Miya, through Aleks, "What do you think? Would you like that?"

Aleks and Miya had an extended conversation in Russian.

Doug and I moved our heads back and forth while they talked as if we were watching a tennis match. Neither of their faces gave anything away, but I recognized the tone of a salesman in Aleks's voice. Was he trying to convince her? I could barely stand the protracted negotiation.

Finally, Aleks said, "Miya says yes. But"—he paused—"she is worried because her grandma has a birthday in April and she doesn't want to miss her grandma's birthday party. She will see you after April!"

At this, Aleks smiled his very white smile and said, "Congratulations!" He clapped his hands together once, as if to put a period on the discussion and signal its finish.

Doug and I were confused. He asked, "She wants to be adopted? You're sure?"

"Oh, yes," Aleks replied. "As long as she can see her grandma." His face remained neutral, as if Miya's response was the most ordinary thing in the world.

I burned to ask questions about this grandmother and whether she was allowed to be involved, and, if so, then why didn't she take care of Miya? Why was Miya even in the orphanage? And if the grandma wasn't allowed to be involved, then why did Miya think she could see her? Between Aleks's closed expression and the agency's instructions forbidding us host families to ask questions about the children's family situation, I bit my tongue. I didn't want to disturb whatever delicate balance we had achieved. But had we?

Later, after Aleks left for his hotel, Doug and I reviewed the puzzling conversation. We picked apart the facial expressions of both Miya and Aleks and the tone of their voices. Neither of us felt very comfortable about the conclusion Aleks had announced, but we had nothing to point to as evidence. It was weird, we both agreed.

Later, lying in bed and unable to sleep, I realized I never heard Miya say dah to Aleks, but she hadn't said nyet, either. I wondered if Miya felt as conflicted as I did.

One of the Barbies I bought for Miya had a traveling outfit, complete with a miniature rolling suitcase. Miya was obsessed with the suitcase. She often brought me the tiny piece of luggage and spoke to me earnestly in Russian. She acted out the scene of rolling her own case behind her in the house, and saying "*dom oy*," which I had learned during the weeks we were together meant "go home." Miya had begun saying it as soon as she got in the car, or "*MAH-sheen-ah*," each day after camp.

As the time approached for Miya to leave, she asked me, through Tatiana, when she was going to get her own suitcase. All the orphans seemed to know that kids who visited America, who arrived with their plastic bags in their hands, would leave America with their very own suitcases, stuffed with the toys and clothes they had received during their trip. Miya was beside herself with delight at this idea.

The last night before she left, I presented Miya with her very own rolling bag. Covered with pink and purple flowers, it was small enough that she could pull it herself, while still meeting the carry-on requirements so it would go with her all the way back to Ukraine. We carefully packed her clothes, her toys, her pictures— there wasn't room for everything. Difficult choices were made. Miya selected a sweater that Tatiana had given her as well as a winter coat I'd bought for Viktor. All of the Barbie dolls stayed behind.

For the first time in twenty-one days, Miya couldn't wait to go to bed. She wanted morning to come, and quickly, and it did.

Miya was wide awake, waiting and already dressed when I went to her room at 5:00 a.m. Refusing breakfast, she grabbed Doug's hand and impatiently pulled him toward the door, trying to get him to abandon his coffee cup so we could drive to the airport. She danced around our house, saying goodbye to each of the dogs and Oliver, the cat.

Miya rolled her bag out to the car and climbed in willingly. I flashed back to our first trip home from the airport and how hard it had been to console her. I sat in front with Doug this time. We arrived at the airport quickly, well before the morning rush hour. At the check-in gate, Aleks was waiting, trying to negotiate checking extra suitcases. He had two of them opened, filled with his electronic purchases. He sorted it out and looked at his watch, announcing it was time and they had to go.

So suddenly, it seemed.

Aleks put one hand on his carry-on and took Miya's hand with the other. He said, "Say, 'Bye-bye, Doug. Bye-bye, Betsy.'"

Miya didn't say anything. She didn't hug us. She didn't wave. She grabbed Aleks's hand, spun around, and pulled her pink suitcase behind her.

Doug and I stood watching, waving, waiting for the line at security to absorb them, and hoping Miya would turn around.

She never looked back.

CHAPTER 18

TWIN CITIES MARATHON

I didn't know anyone who had ever done a marathon. All of the long-distance runners I knew were middle-aged men who had taken up running after some friend of theirs had a heart attack. In 1988 there were no sports bras or Gatorade, and even people who ran seriously called it "jogging."

The marathon I selected, the Twin Cities Marathon, came five months after my May-day epiphany. I'd decided back on that day that I would spend every ounce of my very being doing what had eluded my mother. When I was gone, not only would I leave nothing undone but I promised myself I would leave something behind—something that would continue, something, I didn't know what, that would become my legacy.

Now here I was, in the best shape of my life, a bundle of potential, poised to burst with the excitement of actually *doing* this thing. It was a brisk October day, cool, sunny, and dry, perfect for running, and I bobbed among the thousands of runners setting off from the Hubert Humphrey Metrodome, leaving the big white marshmallow roof behind to pass through downtown Minneapolis. Before I knew it, I passed the six-mile marker as I went around the sparkling blue waters of the lakes. Lake of the Isles, Lake Calhoun, Lake Harriet, Lake Nokomis—lakes connected by trails. Their loops were embedded in my muscle memory after training on these paths, going around and around and around all summer long.

As the summer had progressed, so had my fitness level. I'd gradually improved from a ten-minute-per-mile pace to an eight-minute-per-mile pace. When I ran past the halfway point, 13.1 miles, I noticed my time was under two hours. I was flying! My legs felt strong and my soul confident as the scenery flashed past me, dazzling with kinetic energy.

Around mile fifteen, the course took me along the west bank of the Minnesota River, exactly where I had run my first years at the University of Minnesota. My roommate and I had named this sinewy rising section of the pavement on River Road the Killer Hill. On any other day, the steep curves of this beast punished me, but this day, I felt unstoppable. The blazing orange and gold leaves that signal the Midwestern fall carried me along as they wafted from the trees. They floated gracefully to their end as my spirit lifted with euphoria. I kept on going.

My two best friends had come out to cheer, after figuring out how to follow and find me multiple times along the way, in spite of the crush of crowds. The people on the sidelines were a constant blur of color, until my friends' familiar faces emerged in focus from the crowd, prompting a swift *thwack* when our hands met in mutual high fives. Then they receded into the background, disappearing until the next time. The one person I searched for, however, would never be there. Memories of my mom, sick and dying the year before, chased me through the roads that delivered me to Saint Paul and the twenty-mile marker.

The pain of my effort finally caught up with me as I rounded the corner for the last stretch: the six miles down Summit Avenue where all of this had begun, back in May. The ease with which I'd been soaring came crashing down and abandoned me. This was the dreaded "wall" that *Runner's World* magazine had warned me about, the state where all my stores of glucose were used up and lactic acid was building up in my muscles. I hobbled and hurt, then psyched myself up to trot, barely, as I passed the twenty-one-, then the twenty-two-mile markers. My pace had slowed dramatically, but I didn't really care about time. This race, I only wanted to finish. *Keep going, keep going,* I chanted in my head. Whenever it hurt too much, I'd think of Mom and the pain of surgery, chemo, and the cancer that ate at her insides. If she withstood that kind of agony, then I could withstand this.

Miles twenty-three and twenty-four passed in a delirious blur. There was a stabbing pain in one of my hips, and my back ached. My feet felt as if they were encased in cement, they were so heavy. I'd run a few steps and then have to slow to a walk. Grinding toward the regal state capitol building where the finish line awaited, my legs were clumsy, but my spirit became lighter with each footfall. When I saw mile marker twenty-five, the knowing began to seep in—I could do this; I *would* do this.

Finally, I arrived at mile twenty-six, just two-tenths of a mile to go. I could see the finish line. I felt my mom watching me, believing in me. She was with me, in my head and the pounding of my heart when I crossed over the marathon finish line. The crowds were roaring, and my throat was closing, tears—happy ones, sad ones—beginning to fall. A medal was placed around my neck. A mylar blanket offered up to hug me. Mom's voice, a whisper only for me, said, "You did it. For me. Now what will you do?"

I had tasted limitlessness. Running. This would be how I lived life to its fullest and guarded myself against the regrets that had haunted my mom at the end. When I ran, I felt exponentially alive. Running made me feel like I could do anything—and I couldn't get enough of that feeling.

CHAPTER 19

GIRLS ON THE RUN

hen I was around thirty-nine years old, a friend slipped me an article cut from the *Chicago Tribune*. "This sounds just like you, a charity that celebrates running and girl power," she told me. "Maybe you'll want to volunteer?"

"She knows what it feels like, and she wants to pass it on," began the story about a woman who had recently started a non-profit dedicated to training young girls, eight to twelve years old, to run a 5K while teaching them lessons about self-esteem, health, and life.

My friend knew me well. I could barely wait to get involved.

Finishing grad school and receiving my master's degree had coincided with my marriage to Doug. I returned home from our honeymoon and began my social services career. As in the corporate world, I bounced around a bit, working a year each in crisis response (*so* stressful), eldercare (everyone died), and as a counselor at a parochial elementary school where the nuns accused me of "bribing" the kids into better behavior with Oreos (guilty as charged). In my defense, I reminded the nuns that in therapy parlance this was called "positive reinforcement."

Right before my thirty-seventh birthday, I became certified in a new field called "life coaching" and opened my own practice. I eventually settled into a niche that, with degrees in food science and counseling, combined with my athletic accomplishments, seemed custom-made for me: helping women achieve their health and wellness goals.

I knew how fluffy my profession sounded, and although a few of my friends jokingly nicknamed me Oprah, I loved motivating people to aspire to and attain their dreams. It wasn't lightweight at all, especially when I began to notice how feeling strong physically set off a chain reaction and empowered my clients to gain strength to change other important areas of their lives, such as relationships and careers. Helping other people, cheering them on to being the best they could be, felt natural and put even more purpose in my life. Echoes of my mom's early death and regrets chimed softly in my thoughts and made me wish I could have helped her too. If there was one message for my clients, it was, "Do it! No regrets!"

Crossing my first-ever marathon finish line had changed something in how I saw myself. I, too, was a girl transformed by running. I'd kept striving to do bigger and better things, and yearning to be *more*. I'd run eleven marathons over fifteen years and begun to branch out into triathlons and ultramarathons— pushing and pushing myself to go farther, to discover my limit. My "No regrets!" motivator had grown into something more— an undefinable desire to make a difference, to leave the world a better place. I remembered how my mom asked me to keep our family together, as if our family was her crowning achievement. There was nothing left of that family. The picture I carried in my head of that family looked like the bombing of Hiroshima: an atomic mushroom cloud of dust. I wanted something different, something sturdier, something larger than family, to outlast me. I wanted my life to mean something, which, by extension, would mean her life meant something too. Could I share the power of running and the limitlessness I'd discovered with others? Yes. I knew what it felt like, and I wanted to pass it on. I loved the idea of establishing a *legacy*. Running, and all it encompassed, would be my legacy.

The organization my friend suggested to me was Girls on the Run, and a new Chicago chapter was being formed. I fired off an email to the address in the paper and became a volunteer coach. At the end of my first season coaching, when the twenty girls I'd trained crossed their first finish line, my heart erupted with joy. These girls, and the lessons we learned together running—discovering that we were all capable of so much more than we believed—inspired me all over again.

Soon after, I discovered the board of directors planned to hire someone to manage the charity, and I wanted the job in a way that twisted my insides with desire and made my palms sweat. I campaigned mightily to become the first (and only) employee, willing to phase out my life-coaching business to do what seemed like a bigger thing, with even more impact. When they said the words, "You're hired!", I felt as if something epic had just happened.

All my grief and yearning had coalesced into a dream job, a mission, and a place where I belonged. I had found a way, finally, to make running my legacy.

CHAPTER 20

WONDERGIRL IS BORN

To say I loved Girls on the Run and the work I was doing was an understatement of gigantic proportion. Girls on the Run wasn't just a job. Girls on the Run became my life.

In the beginning, it operated out of the adorable little house that Doug and I had bought in Roscoe Village, a neighborhood in Chicago, in the first months of our marriage. It was an old two-floor apartment transformed into a single-family home. I had painted every wall, sewn curtains, and created a sunny office with periwinkle walls that boosted my mood as I sat at my computer. Our dark, cobwebby basement stored all the supplies for the programs. Volunteers crowded into our living room on Saturdays, assembling mailers and being trained to deliver the lessons to the kids. Board meetings happened at our dining room table. Eventually, Girls on the Run was able to afford to move into a tiny studio apartment, and then to an actual storefront on a bustling neighborhood street.

After my first year, I got to hire staff to help me, and that was where I found my soon-to-be best friend, Abby. I knew we were kindred spirits when, during the interview, we lapsed from my formal HR-approved questions onto a tangent discussing which kind of Diet Coke we preferred: can, bottle, or fountain. Fountain, we agreed, from McDonald's if at all possible. The day she started, we became a match made in heaven when I picked up the phone to her question, "What's your caffeine situation? I'm at the McDonald's drive-through." Ten minutes later, she sailed through the door, bringing the first of many double Diet Cokes.

It was work, but not work. Early 5:00 a.m. mornings at training runs to talk to runners about volunteering. Harried afternoons when we crisscrossed Chicago and its suburbs, delivering bright T-shirts to schools for the girls to wear as they ran circles around their schoolyards. Evenings spent figuring out the logistics of silent-auction fundraisers so that every girl could run, no matter whether she could pay our fees or not. And the nights, when my mind raced with so many ideas that I often had to get up out of bed to write out to-do lists that seemed as long as a marathon.

When we weren't busy with all that, we were crammed into our less-than-spacious office, answering phones and emails, and singing out loud to the radio, sitting at desks just twenty inches apart. It was about running. It was empowering. It was changing the world, which is how Abby answered the phone sometimes, especially when we knew who was on the other end. "Girls on the Run Chicago—changin' the world!" We were having a blast.

I kept running all along. Marathon after marathon. Triathlons. The Ironman. I crossed things off the top of my "No regrets!" bucket list, and added items to the bottom. My big things were getting bigger.

The year I turned forty, I qualified for the Boston Marathon. For runners, Boston is a mecca, the birthplace of the marathon in America. Because of its hallowed status, not just anyone can run Boston. The organizers require runners to run another marathon within a daunting time standard, and I had managed to slip in two minutes under the qualifying time.

One day, on a sixteen-mile training run for the Boston Marathon, I had a flash of how fun it might be to run the marathon in a tiara. Girls on the Run, over the past two years I'd been working there, had unleashed the irreverent fun girl inside of me, the girl who had been crushed by Stepdad's rage and then left scared and alone after my mom died, then my dad. My work, the running, my husband and friends—the combination had eased my emotional burdens and given my long-buried imagination the freedom to fly. The tiara was an idea that felt as absurd as it felt radical. The tiara represented a taking back of my power—but also a reclaiming of my girl self in a happy, celebratory way. Could I run Boston—the hallowed, crème de la crème of marathons—in a tiara?

And then I did. Although I certainly got looks from some of my fellow runners, my cheeks got sore from smiling at people who called out to me, and my arms hurt from the high fives I'd received. There was a picture taken of me crossing the finish line. The photo showed me in a Girls on the Run shirt, a pink running skirt, and a five-dollar tiara I bought at a party store, arms raised in triumph, absolutely glowing.

The tiara completed my transformation: WonderGirl was born. WonderGirl was an idea that had circled in my head while running, along with the tiara. She was the little me, who was plucky enough to survive—maybe outwit?—Stepdad, while also celebrating the joy and awe of movement. Where I had been silenced, WonderGirl was outspoken; where I had been weak, WonderGirl was strong; where I had been powerless, WonderGirl was powerful. I was ordinary, but WonderGirl? She was a superhero.

Abby and I started wearing tiaras at the office. We were wearing our tiaras when I told her that we were going to create an event especially for the girls of Girls on the Run. It would be a 5K unlike any other, a day of inspiration and girl power, a day where girls from every corner of Chicago would come together to run as a team, a day when every runner would discover the superhero that lived inside of her. It would be larger than life. It would be legendary. It would be the WonderGirl 5K.

CHAPTER 21

WONDERGIRL IN ACTION

WonderGirl came to represent many things—me, my younger self's alter ego, and my legacy, all within the framework of Girls on the Run and the 5K event that we planned for the girls. Birthing WonderGirl was no easy task, but for me, she was a labor of love. I was willing to turn myself inside out and wear myself down to nothing to make her spirit come to life in the hearts and minds of the girls participating in Girls on the Run.

We had about eight hundred girls in the program, and we wanted to get eight hundred adult women to be running buddies to the girls. Sixteen hundred runners! They would all need T-shirts and water bottles and race numbers. And Gatorade and bagels and bananas. And goody bags that would need to be assembled and organized. To set up the race, we needed tents and tables, signage and insurance, ambulances and emergency plans. We needed a course, measured and marked, and hundreds of volunteers in the right place at the right time. We would have to rent trucks to carry all of the equipment, and walkie-talkies to communicate the myriad details.

Sheer logistical savvy was one skill essential to making this event come alive, and I was pretty confident of mine, but the real problem with putting on a race was money. In Chicago, an event of this magnitude costs $25,000–$30,000, which was equal to about a quarter of the total annual budget of Girls on the Run. In the months leading up to the race, I obsessed about finding the money, about securing corporate sponsors who had money to give. Not finding the money, or losing money on the 5K, would put Girls on the Run at risk of closing down. The threat of folding kept me up at night with the thought, *I have to make this work, I have to make this work, I have to make this work*, looping in circles around my brain.

I was on edge—an optimistic, excited edge, but still. The WonderGirl 5K was my baby. I had conceived of it and I worked for it. The more I labored and the closer to race day it got, the larger the scope of WonderGirl's ultimate success or failure grew in size, and the importance of the eventual outcome increased.

After almost a year of planning, the week of the Wonder-Girl 5K arrived. The race was on the first Saturday in June, so on Memorial Day Monday, Abby and I were in the office up to our elbows in all things race-related. She sat at the computer, practicing her Excel magic, mail-merging runners' names, race numbers, and T-shirt sizes onto labels while I systematically went through checklist after checklist, confirming details, and making flow-charts for supplies.

The space looked as if some kind of hybrid tween-runner-su-perhero bomb had gone off. White-and-purple T-shirts were scattered in piles by size; hundreds of pink-and-purple "sporty" plastic tiaras lay in heaps; dozens of Rubbermaid bins were spread out, covers off, waiting to be filled with medical materials, aid-station necessities, and the various and sundry items needed for packet pickup and race-day registration. Once everything was organized, we'd load it into the eighteen-foot U-Haul truck I'd rented for the event.

My house and garage were ground zero because the office lacked the space needed. It took thirty-two trips and several hours to unload all the supplies from my garage. We had built a wall of Gatorade next to a mountain of goody bags covering the concrete where my Ford Explorer was usually parked. The day before the Gatorade was delivered, dozens of volunteers had flooded into my home to assemble almost two thousand drawstring bags filled with fun little surprises for the runners.

On the Thursday and then the Friday before the race, I parked the U-Haul in front of Fleet Feet, a running store in Chicago that partnered with Girls on the Run. Each person received a race number, four safety pins to attach it to their T-shirt, a course map, a goody bag, a bottle of Gatorade, a T-shirt, and a tiara to decorate and wear on race day.

At 9:00 p.m. Friday evening, the last person left Fleet Feet with their goody bag. Abby, some volunteers, and I loaded our remaining supplies back into the U-Haul. I was to drive first to my garage to load all the Gatorade and goody bags left there, then to the Girls on the Run office to pack up final supplies, and finally to Montrose Beach—a wide green space along Chicago's lakefront and the site of the event—to park overnight.

Unfortunately, when it came time to drive, I couldn't find the key to the U-Haul! We searched the store, the sidewalk, and my Explorer, and I became more frantic as the key, on its big triangle orange-and-white tag, remained missing. What if it had fallen into a goody bag that we'd given to a runner? What if it was in my garage? Or somewhere on the lakefront? With all of the shuttling I'd done that day, it could have been lost anywhere. My already-frayed nerves were ready to snap.

I called U-Haul only to be told they didn't keep spare keys for any of their vehicles. They suggested I call a locksmith. One by one, each locksmith I called told me they could break a lock, but they couldn't make a key. Desperate, I widened my search and finally—finally—a guy from Gary, Indiana, told me he could help, but it would take at least an hour to drive to my location. It would cost $500, and he only accepted cash. I didn't say, but definitely thought, that I'd pay just about anything to move the freaking U-Haul.

The locksmith arrived close to 11:30 p.m. I hugged him with relief and hysteria and counted out the twenty-five crisp $20 bills that I'd withdrawn from my personal account at the cash station across the street. I stood, buzzing with anxiety as he worked for the better part of sixty minutes. When he produced a key that fit into the truck's ignition, the tension I'd been holding in my body released, and I almost crumpled to the ground. Instead, I hugged him again and thanked him so profusely I'm certain he thought I was some kind of lunatic, but he waved goodbye to me as I drove the truck away.

I rolled out of bed the next morning at 3:45 a.m. WonderGirl had arrived! The sun still hadn't risen yet when I parked my Explorer behind the U-Haul. Volunteers showed up and descended on both vehicles, all of us eager to get going, to make this thing happen. Within two hours, we had set up tents for registration, packet pickup, medical staff, and various sponsors. A stage and sound system waited for music and announcements, and the start and finish lines were in place with huge WonderGirl 5K banners stretched across the top.

Buses full of girls and coaches began pulling up, spilling hundreds of kids in WonderGirl T-shirts out onto the green grass abutting Montrose Beach. A playlist blasted "Party in the USA." Running buddies were matched up with girls, and groups started chanting, "Girls on the Run is so much fun!" along with other cheers. Coaches affixed pink-and-purple tiaras decorated with girls' names on the girls' heads and pinned race numbers to the front of their T-shirts. The air filled with anticipation and festivity. It was all coming together, just as I'd imagined it.

I stood on the stage looking over an ocean of pink, purple, and white, interspersed with green grass. While the Bally's gym team led the warm-up, I watched hundreds of girls—almost two thousand people total!—bend and stretch in unison, while thousands of hands reached for the perfect blue sky overhead. Those same hands were held over hearts as "The Star-Spangled Banner" rang out. My own heart swelled with emotion, and my eyes brimmed with happy tears. My thoughts were a jumble of gratitude and awe, and I kept reminding myself, *This is it! The WonderGirl—my WonderGirl—is coming to life. Right. Now.*

When the announcement to assemble at the start line came, the sea of runners moved to form an enormous crowd on the pavement, waiting for the gun to go off, ready to begin their 3.1-mile WonderGirl journey. We counted down, "Five, four, three, two, one!" And they were off, running, chasing their dreams, achieving their big 5K goal. I stood at the side of the start line, cheering and clapping my hands until they hurt.

Less than twenty minutes later, runners began to cross the finish line. I watched coaches, running buddies, parents, and girls. They were hand in hand, pumping their arms overhead, smiling, crying, laughing, high-fiving, cheering, and encouraging. Happy faces beamed out from each tiara-covered head as a WonderGirl medal was draped over it. Although we had a few scraped knees and two girls threw up from their effort, overall, the joy in the air was tangible. WonderGirl had cast a spell over all of us, sprinkling us with sunshine and making magic happen.

When the last runner had crossed the finish line, after the last box had been packed up and loaded into the U-Haul, I pulled myself up into the truck. As I drove home, the knowing seeped into me. More than a year earlier, I had crossed the Boston Marathon finish line in a tiara and dreamt up my alter ego. Now, WonderGirl was well and truly alive, not only in me, but in the almost two thousand girls and women who had just completed the 5K. Sitting in the seat of that damn godforsaken U-Haul, I thought, *I did it! I really did it!*

I imagined my mom had been watching, seen how my legacy unfolded, and that she was proud of me too.

CHAPTER 22

UKRAINE SPEAKS

I was torn. The day Miya left, I cried tears of grief. And relief. It was only after the fact that I considered what I had expected and compared it to what really happened. The girl I had hoped for, had imagined might be my little buddy, was gone. I had envisioned looking into the rearview mirror while I was driving with her and seeing giggling brown eyes peering back at me. I had wished for big happy-to-see-me hugs when I picked her up from camp each day. I had wanted sweet goodnight kisses before bed as I inhaled the vanilla-strawberry shampoo scent of her. But the fairy-tale child I'd dreamt up was just that—a fantasy. The reality had been twenty-one days of high alert, of waiting for it to get better, or at least not as awful, which thankfully had happened sometimes. By the end, my adrenaline was spent. Maybe my love and hope were too, because a tiny, mean, childish part of me was glad when she walked away from us without a glance.

I tried to make sense of the experience. I told myself, and desperately wanted to believe, that if Miya were with Doug and me for real, for*ever*, we would both be different. I wouldn't be unsure anymore. She would be more confident with us. The answers to the questions I had were as hard as the questions themselves: How had I failed so miserably? What had I done that made Miya turn away? Was there something wrong with me? I'd always suspected it, and now it was confirmed. In the weeks following Miya's exit, my harsh inner critic excoriated me for not being able to connect with her, and worse, for not even knowing *how*.

People asked me, "Did you just love her? When are you going to Ukraine? What about her brother? Her pictures looked so darling!"

I don't know. I don't know. I don't know. Yes, she was darling. But she didn't like it with us. And I had no idea what her true situation was in Ukraine. She clearly believed she had a grandma who loved her, waiting there. Who was I to tell her that this wasn't the case? Miya wasn't ready, even if the adults in her life were pressuring her that we were the right choice. I willed myself to believe that things would get better with her, but in my gut, I felt myself overriding my better judgment.

In the aftermath of the visit, I spoke with people from the agency, trying to navigate the next steps. This was tricky, because legally we were required to meet Viktor in person to show our intent to adopt him and fill out the introductory paperwork. But the orphanage and government in Ukraine refused to issue us visas to travel there to meet him unless we completed the legal paperwork. This meant paying a fee of thousands of dollars and agreeing to follow through with adopting Miya *and* Viktor, sight unseen.

Doug and I felt uneasy about this plan. One reason we had participated in the Bridge of Hope program was to be allowed to spend a significant chunk of time with the children *before* deciding to adopt. We had been told we would be allowed to visit Viktor, but now we felt we were being given the runaround.

Emails and phone calls flew among Doug and me, our social worker, the agency, the orphanage, and probably the Ukraine government too. Every bit of information we received was second- or thirdhand and needed to be translated. Waiting for responses to our questions was excruciating. Living with even more uncertainty triggered my anxiety, especially after our Adoption Talk with Miya and Aleks. Everything felt up in the air.

Finally, the agency told us there was another family in our same situation, a family who had hosted one child with a sibling too young to travel but who they wanted to meet. The agency was communicating on their behalf and had been told that the Ukrainians might be swayed to allow them visas if they made a "humanitarian trip," and maybe we could make one too. Such a trip would involve bringing gifts and donating to the orphanage in Ukraine. In other words, they wanted money. How much? The Ukrainians delayed answering this question, stringing us all along even more.

Our hopes soared the day we got a phone call telling us to set up a Skype account. The social worker said, "You will be able to actually talk to the orphanage tomorrow! Be able to talk to a person and ask them real-time questions! I think it's going to be Aleks online."

My hopes plummeted at hearing Aleks would be involved. But then she said, "This is very unusual. The orphanage usually doesn't allow parents access until the parents travel."

I asked, "Why do you think there's an exception?"

"It might have something to do with Bridge of Hope, or that you already met one of the kids," she continued. "Be prepared for some very specific requests from them. They have an idea of what they want you to donate."

"What do you mean?" I asked, confused. "Why can't they just tell us?"

"They won't," she said. "The other family was told exactly what to give, but they didn't immediately agree to the orphanage's request. They're still considering it. Unfortunately, for these international adoptions, what one adoptive family does reflects on all of the other families. That works in our favor when things go well, but the opposite is also true."

I wondered why the other family was hesitating. Could it be about the money? International adoption was expensive, and Doug and I knew how fortunate we were to be able to afford it. Maybe we could make up some difference for the other family if we worked together. "Is this the sort of thing where we can pool our resources?" I asked.

"I honestly don't know," she said. "Why don't you write a list of these questions for the call?"

I agreed and hung up.

The next morning, Doug and I called in late to work in order to make the 10:00 a.m. Skype. The previous night, we had compiled a list of our questions: How was Miya? What about Viktor? When might we be allowed to visit them? And of course, how much?

The clock ticked slowly until it showed 9:55 a.m. We sat by Doug's desk and waited at the computer, yellow legal pad in front of us and pens in hand. *Ticktock.* 10:05 a.m. 10:10 a.m. 10:15 a.m.

I emailed our social worker: "Did I get the time wrong? Is the Skype number right? Aren't they supposed to call?"

"Let me check," she wrote back.

More waiting. And waiting. Nothing.

At noon, Doug left for a meeting at work; I was left with the legal pad. I waited, alone.

Finally, around 3:00 p.m., I received a reply: "There was a misunderstanding. The other family decided they won't donate to the orphanage. As you're aware, it's a setback for all of us. We will try to set up another meeting soon."

And then, nothing.

Two days later, I got a phone call at work. "I have some news," said the caseworker.

I closed the door to my office and fumbled in my bag for our crumpled list of questions.

"We have learned more about Miya and Viktor," she said. Instead of sounding triumphant, she seemed reluctant to tell me.

"Yes?" I said eagerly.

"It appears that the orphanage located two more siblings. They're younger. A three-year-old brother and a baby."

"What?" I wanted to believe I had heard her wrong.

"It's pretty common to find more siblings in the orphanages. They get split up because of their ages. Younger ones are sent to different orphanages than older kids."

I was still processing that there were two more kids. I couldn't even fathom it.

She said, "We don't know anything else about the little one, whether the baby is a boy or girl. Would that matter to you?"

"I have no idea. This is a situation I hadn't considered."

"The real issue is"—she paused—"the orphanage wants you and Doug to adopt all four. If you want to visit them, you have to legally agree to take the four of them. They are firm about that."

"What?! They expect us to accept two more? Four kids?" My heart sank.

"That's what they're saying. We're trying to reason with them because we realize it's a lot to ask. Very few adoptive parents are willing to take four children. In our view, it would be better if the four kids were split into two sibling sets."

"I don't know what to say. I'm stunned."

There was silence on the line.

"I understand. There's something else I must share," she said, sighing. "The kids won't be available for adoption for another year, at least. The younger ones need to go through the government process to become available."

"So they want us to adopt all four, and there's not any timetable?" How could the orphanage expect this of us? It was beginning to feel like some sort of trap.

"Yes, and I'm required to inform you that there is always the possibility a family member might step up to care for them. And if no family will, part of the government process requires the orphanage to attempt to find a Ukrainian family before allowing an international adoption. This takes time."

"I need to talk to Doug about this. This changes everything."

After we hung up, I replayed the conversation in my head, getting more furious the more I thought about it. How could they expect us to take two more kids? *Four* kids? And two of them younger! *And* make us wait indefinitely? If we were allowed to adopt them at all?

I felt sick.

Doug was just as angry as I was when we talked about it later. We both felt cheated, as if the Ukrainians had pulled some sort of bait and switch by sending Miya to us. Why had they done that? Had they known about the other kids? Although neither of us wanted to believe they could be so manipulative, to say nothing of involving these innocent children in their scheme, our trust was irrevocably broken.

"I can't see myself with four," I said.

"You don't have to," Doug said. "We're not doing this. It's crazy."

I nodded, silently agreeing.

We sat there for a long time. I thought about Miya and Viktor. About how they were never going to be our kids and we were never going to be their parents. About how, since January, we'd been on this journey, and now it was September. Nine months, just like pregnancy, but then, so abruptly, so suddenly, the children didn't exist for us anymore. It was a miscarriage of my heart.

The idea that I'd never see Miya again brought tears to my eyes. Bits and pieces of our time together floated through my mind. Sleeping Beauty, and balloons on a hot summer day. Barbie being knocked off her chair, over and over. Swimming in the sunset, speaking Russian into an old cell phone, and the way she used to say, "*Dom oy*," on our way home from camp. She had wanted to go home. And now, she would never come back.

CHAPTER 23

DEAD LINE

After the WonderGirl 5K success, the national office of Girls on the Run, aka National, tapped me to work for them on an offshoot of WonderGirl—Team Tiara. Once I'd seen the inspiration that running in a tiara had brought about, I'd formed an adult team of runners who agreed to do the Chicago Marathon (in a tiara!) and fundraise for Girls on the Run–Chicago. Our team raised a significant amount of money, which resulted in National asking me to bring this fundraising platform to every chapter of Girls on the Run across the United States. Even better, they wanted to found a national race series so that every time there was a Girls on the Run 5K race, it would be called the WonderGirl 5K. Another piece of legacy clicked into place, and I was proud.

As part of this job, I went to a meeting at the national office where directors of chapters across the country gathered to talk about best practices. On this morning, the founder had gathered us together to contemplate the question, "What's next?" She meant for the organization, but it was implied that this work we cherished was integral to our individual beings, our way in the world. There was a time when I would have rolled my eyes at these words, like when Mom provided nine-year-old me with my very own copy of *The Power of Positive Thinking*. But now I'd risen to the rank of Believer. I was into it. Every meeting always opened with a visualization, and this was no different.

"Think back to where you were ten years ago."

I had been just thirty-one years old, finally living in the city, still reeling a year after Dad had joined Mom in the afterlife. Saying goodbye to the corporate world in order to go to grad school. I hadn't even met Doug yet!

"Think about who you were then."

Idealistic. Alone. Excited to be following my dream of grad school and hoping to change the world.

The exercise continued. We recalled moments when we'd first heard about the founder and her ideas, the ways we'd connected, the zest that propelled us to this place—this moment. Gratitude cascaded over me as the memories streamed through my mind.

"Let's shift our minds from the past and the present. Project yourself ten years into the future. What do you see?"

I did the addition and thought, *Fifty-one.* And then my mind became white fuzz, and a gauze curtain dropped over the place where the future should have been.

Breathe, I told myself. *Concentrate.* I couldn't.

Get a hold of yourself! I scolded. *Try counting up year by year. See if you can sneak up on your future self.*

Forty-one. Now. I love my life. I love Doug. I love our house. I adore our pets. This job is perfect for me.

Forty-two. Next year. Hopefully I'll have completed the ultramarathon I'm signed up for and be in the best shape of my life. The rest will stay the same.

Forty-three. It will be 2007 and twenty years since Mom died. A lump began forming in my throat.

Forty-four. Twenty years since I did my first marathon, in her honor. I wonder if I can get twenty marathons under my belt, one for each year? Hot tears appeared behind my closed eyes.

Forty-five. Whoa. I'll be forty-five. Is it crazy that children never appear in my life? Maybe. Probably. I just don't see Doug and I with a kid. I wonder if I'll be lonely? I almost chuckled thinking how ridiculous we would be as parents.

Forty-six. I'll be as old as Mom was when she died. She was so young. What if I only have five years to live? The lump returned. The tears reappeared.

I attempted to flash forward ten years, to when I'd be fifty-one, but nothing was there. I couldn't see it. I felt the beginnings of a sob working its way up. I was going to cry. *No, don't,* I told myself. *Fifty-one. Nothing. Don't cry!* My eyes flew open. Assaulted by the glare of sunlight reflecting on the conference room table, I blinked.

Plop. Plop. Two tears fell on the smooth surface. The sun shone on them, turning them into crystal prisms. The founder wrapped up the visualization.

"All right, everyone. Deep breath in. Exhale, and open your eyes. Let's share how our visualizations unfolded. Who wants to go first?"

I didn't go first. Or second. Or any of the places, until I was last. My throat clamped shut so tightly, I knew speaking would release the dam built up inside of me. I couldn't avoid it as the others trained their eyes on me.

"I couldn't see it," I finally choked out. "My future stops at forty-six. There is no fifty-one."

Puzzled faces peered back at me.

"My mom was forty-six when she died."

What hadn't been obvious suddenly crystallized for me. "I think I'm going to die when I'm forty-six. Just like my mom."

I leaned over and rested my forehead on my crossed arms and gave into the emotions. The group gave me hugs, patted my shoulders, and rubbed my back; the motions of concern rained down on me until I pulled myself together.

I wasn't crying for myself but for the sadness of a life cut short—my mom's life. The tragedy was not only that she died young, but she died with regrets, and the family she'd hoped would be her legacy had disintegrated. If I died the same way, would regret visit me too?

There's a saying about how some things, once seen, cannot be unseen. For me, it was the opposite. When I couldn't see my future, my eyes opened to my unconscious prediction, illuminated by the drops of tears glowing on the conference table: my *dead* line.

I worked for Girls on the Run–National, for Team Tiara, for seven months. And then, I broke.

CHAPTER 24

BROKEN

The day I broke was a humid summer Saturday in August. Doug had left for the weekend on his annual boys' bike trip. The trip had become less bike and more fun over the years, something I teased Doug about every time he loaded his bike onto the car rack, only to return home with it unused.

Being on my own, now that I was married, was my absolute favorite kind of weekend—being left solo and to do whatever I desired. And I desired to run, to physically spend myself. Then I would take a nap, wash the sweat and grit off, and polish myself up for a night out. Abby and I were supposed to go to Shaw's Crab House, a fancy seafood restaurant in Chicago, later that day. Abby, who by now had become one of my best friends, had a habit of stating, "I always say yes to fish and martinis." My mouth watered when I thought of us clinking our cosmopolitans together over a plate of steaming crab legs.

The morning Doug took off, I drove the Explorer out to Busse Woods, the site of hundreds, perhaps thousands, of miles I'd run.

If running was my religion, Busse Woods—a forest preserve outside Chicago's city limits—was my cathedral. The green trees closed over the path in the shape of an arch, like church windows, and the sun shone through the stained glass of leaves. I'd worshipped every season there. I knew every bend of the path, the location of the water fountains, where there was cool shade, where the bathrooms were. On occasions when the bathrooms were closed, I knew all the spots where I could sneak off the path to pee.

On my way to Busse, it was my habit to stop at the 7-Eleven for an icy Diet Coke, my morning elixir, to drink along the way. The Indian woman who worked there on Saturdays always smiled shyly at me in my running clothes, and I would compliment her bright pink lipstick.

Back in the car, my bare thighs stuck to the leather seat. I sang at the top of my lungs as I drove, my old eighties mixtapes accompanying me. The sunroof was open, the rays warm on my face. The Kennedy Expressway and exits flew by until I got to Arlington Heights Road. Two turns later, I pulled into the parking lot at the Busse Woods Forest Preserve.

My ritual continued. I took the last sip of Diet Coke, tied my running shoes, turned the waistband of my shorts to hold my little radio, and locked the car.

As I trotted to the path, I felt my right hip twinge.

Pain was my constant companion now, brought on by the combination of my crooked spine and the millions, maybe billions, of footsteps I'd taken. I told myself, *I'm only going fourteen miles today*. The black pavement path shimmered in the heat, and I ran from the sun into the shade of the trees, staying to the right of the yellow line.

Busse Woods was one big loop, divided into two halves by Higgins Road. On each side of the loop were shorter offshoots that runners and bikers used to add distance. I had mapped it in my head, loop-de-looping during the first part to get the miles out of the way, so I'd have a straight shot back to my car on the second half.

As I ticked by the first mile markers, I checked my Timex. I was slower than usual. I chalked this up to the residual effects of a terrible summer of training and racing, from which I never quite recovered: a triathlon, followed by strep throat; a half-marathon, followed by a virus.

I had been doing just enough to get to the start lines, but I couldn't shake the exhaustion that plagued me always, even after the finish line was crossed. The phrase that kept repeating in my mind was *I need a break*. Yet I wasn't willing to give myself respite. In spite of my burnt-out feeling, I had signed up for yet another marathon, my nineteenth. I couldn't stop. Who would I be, and what would I do, if I didn't run?

The pain in my hip increased in intensity, and I tried to block it. I focused on the sun, how it felt tanning my skin; the wind pushing my bangs across my forehead; and the sweat dripping in the crevices of my elbows.

The pain dialed up. I did math problems as I ran: 180 steps per minute times nine-minute miles times the fourteen miles I planned to run today. I calculated my pace, the number of steps I took, and how many miles were left.

As I got to the tenth mile, I turned onto the final path back to the start. Four miles to go.

I could no longer ignore the hurt. Every single time I stepped on my right foot, pain radiated from my right butt cheek in a way that told me this wasn't a muscle ache, but a pain in my very bones.

Whatever thoughts were in my mind were gone, replaced by desperation as I tried, unsuccessfully, to solve the problem of my pain. I walked. It hurt. I ran. It hurt. I limped. It hurt. But I kept going—to the next mile, the next bathroom, the next water fountain. Finally, I was at my car.

And oh-my-God-oh-my-God-oh-my-God, it *hurt*.

I usually changed into dry clothes before driving home, but I skipped that and instead re-calculated my afternoon.

First, I had to get home.

Second, I needed to figure out what to do with the dogs, especially our five-month-old chocolate Lab, Lulu. She was adorable but also a fifty-pound ball of energy who was only halfway through her puppy kindergarten class, and not the best of students. Along with Muddy, our older chocolate Lab who clocked in at 110 pounds, they weren't easy to walk in the best of circumstances. This was clearly not the best of circumstances.

As I drove, I hurt.

I pulled into the garage, fell out of the car, and dragged my right leg behind me. The dogs surrounded me and unbalanced me even more. I couldn't even walk by myself, never mind with the dogs.

Taking the stairs, one agonizing step by the next, I leaned on the banister for support and whimpered. Lulu licked the white crusted-salt granules off my sweaty legs. I stripped away my wet clothes, abandoning them in a mess on the floor.

Questions started to pile up in my head. *What do I wear to the emergency room? What about the dogs? Do I have to skip dinner with Abby? Will Doug come home?*

Reluctantly, I called him. Doug was eight hours away, surrounded by friends after what I imagined was a beer and Bloody Mary–filled morning of golf.

"Honey," I said when I got him on the line, "I just got back from Busse Woods, and I need to go to the ER."

He replied, "What? Oh, honey. What happened?"

I began to cry, and the words rushed out. "It really hurts. I did my long run, and I think I broke something. I can't walk. There's no way to walk Muddy and Lulu. I don't know what to do. I need you to come home."

"Do you really think you broke something? Is it your back?"

"It's my low back, my hip, I don't know. It's wrong. There's definitely something wrong. Will you come? Please?"

The longer the silence continued, the more my heart sank with the knowledge he wouldn't help me.

"Betsy, I can't. I'm eight hours away. We've been playing golf, drinking. I can't drive right now."

"Well, what am I supposed to do?" I implored. *How could he desert me when I needed him? What's the point of being married if it isn't to help each other?*

"There's no way for me to get there in time to help, it would take me till late tonight just to get home. And I'm not sober. Go to the hospital. Then call me."

"You won't come? How am I going to deal with the dogs?"

Doug stood firm. "I really can't come, Betsy. I'm going to stay, and I'll be home tomorrow."

And that was what he did.

In his defense, this fun-loving nature was part of what I loved about him, what had attracted me to him. Wherever Doug went, a good time followed. When we had begun to get serious, our Sundays became epic adventures. After sleeping in (although I would usually sneak out for a run), we would start with brunch, followed by a movie in the winter or a street fest in the summer. Or we might take in a baseball game in the spring, or watch football in the fall. Then we'd meander along a Chicago neighborhood street until we hit a tavern for a few drinks, and keep walking until we were hungry for dinner, or found something else interesting to look at or listen to. Along the way, we called friends, some of whom would join us. By evening, we often had a group around us, talking, laughing, and doing all we could to stave off Monday morning. That's what Doug was doing now. And yet, I was upset, and in my mind, he wasn't supporting me. However irrational, I thought, *It's a good thing we only have dogs, not kids. Jesus. If he can't help me now, will he ever?*

I had to get to the ER, but I couldn't walk. I was alone. I needed some crutches and painkillers.

My happy day had fled, the prospect of a fun evening with Abby slipped away. I called her, and after she answered, my quavering voice gave away my disappointment and pain. When she asked, "Do you want me to come?" the tears came for me.

It never occurred to me that she would help when Doug wouldn't.

Abby asked, "Which hospital are you going to?"

"Northwestern, I guess. That's where my doctor is," I told her.

"I'll drive you."

I couldn't let her do that. Accepting help was anathema to me after a childhood spent learning that anything I received from Stepdad came attached with a price tag of rage and scorn. Even though I'd learned to be vulnerable with Doug, my ability didn't extend much beyond him. I told Abby, "I'll be fine. I promise to call you when I get home from the hospital."

At the hospital, alone, an attendant met me with a shiny metal wheelchair. Relief flooded me when a nurse wheeled me into a green-curtained cubicle. What I was wearing didn't matter, because they'd left me two blue gowns with little purple flowers to put on—one to tie in the back, one to tie in the front.

As I waited for an X-ray, Abby poked her head through the green curtain. I gasped and asked, "What are you doing here?" I was so touched, my throat tightened, and I thought I might cry. "I came to keep you company," she said, as if it was no big deal. She was holding two Big Gulps, and I accepted one with a smile, knowing I wasn't alone anymore. My spirits were further lifted when Doug called to tell me he'd solved the dog problem: a friend had agreed to board them and had already picked them up.

The doctor himself was forgettable, but his words were not. He told me there was a fracture in my sacroiliac joint, where the sacrum and pelvis meet. The angle of my spine, combined with all the running I'd done, had created a pressure point within my body, breaking my pelvis. My pelvis! I'd never even broken a bone before, but now I'd managed to break my *pelvis*? Even as my body throbbed with pain and I wondered about my future as a runner, I felt a small *ping!* of pride at my crazy toughness—that I had just run fourteen miles with a broken pelvis.

The doctor said with my scoliosis, I should never have been running in the first place and that I would never run a marathon again.

My mind replied, *He doesn't know who he is dealing with.*

Abby, in her joking, sarcastic way, said exactly what I was thinking but out loud.

I took the crutches. I took the prescription. Abby took me home.

I visited an orthopedic doctor the next week. She confirmed that scoliosis had contributed to my injury. My stomach sank at her words. Scoliosis had mostly been a nonissue for me. Until now. Her prescription for recovery included more pain medication, no weight bearing for the next two months, and after that, physical therapy to help me strengthen specific muscles so that I could walk again. When I asked her about running, she said, "Let's focus on getting you back on your feet first."

Along with my pelvis, my spirit broke that day. Until then, I'd always been invincible. I'd always been able to go a little further.

Not anymore.

I was forty-three years old. I had run a marathon each year for the last eighteen years, and many of those runs were painful, even before the fateful day when I'd ended up in the emergency room. There had been several summers when I'd finished my long run and gone directly to a massage therapist, every single weekend. It was the only way my body could handle the pain.

Four months after my pelvis broke, I was finally walking, but I longed to break into a jog and accelerate into the weightlessness of running. I missed it. The lightness, the freedom, the floating. The movement, the repetition, the release. I yearned to be the gazelle I'd once been, when I ran with a grace and ease that felt otherworldly.

After recognizing my desperation, my doctor and physical therapist put me on a regimen to return to running. "Only short distances," they told me. "Think about a 5K, not a marathon." The therapist suggested weight training to build up core and body strength, and I was so frightened of reinjuring myself, I hired a trainer.

The specter of surgery hovered. I didn't want to, but I couldn't stop myself from wondering what would have happened if I'd had the operation back when I was seventeen. Who would I have become? I knew I'd be taller, straighter, less torqued, but what else? Would I have been in less pain? Would I still have become the athlete I strived to be? The successful person that I believed running made me? Or would I have built a legacy some other way?

And what about kids? Would I have been a mother by now? My body wasn't the only reason I hadn't had kids, but I had often worried about the effect a pregnancy would have on my crooked spine. The year before I broke, Doug and I had gone to our first adoption information session, the one we left without even filling out the form. If I hadn't felt any maternal stirrings by that point, would I ever? I pushed any thought of children away, tried to heal my back, and yearned to run.

CHAPTER 25

THE CARA ERA

It had been seven weeks since I broke my pelvis, and it was slowly healing. The first time I walked without my crutches, I went to a job interview to become the director of another running organization, the Chicago Area Runners Association (CARA), so I figured I better show up somewhat able-bodied.

The position had opened up around the time I'd hurt myself, and although I loved working at Girls on the Run, a part of me felt that I'd done what I'd been meant to do there, and the time to move on had arrived. A remnant of my younger self, the one always searching for a new place, new job, or new relationship, still existed inside me. Why not accept a new professional challenge? CARA was a lot bigger and more well-known than Girls on the Run—it had six thousand members! The downside? They were all adults, men and women, so I would need to tone down my emphasis on girl power. My ambition, fueled, as always, by the thought of *more*! refused to let the opportunity pass. When they offered me the job, I accepted.

Working at CARA required me to be more serious. These people weren't fifth graders running 5Ks; they were adults who mostly ran marathons. The contrast between Girls on the Run and CARA was noticeable even in their brand colors. The Girls on the Run logo was hot pink and apple green; CARA's was bloodred and midnight black. Although our members covered the spectrum of uber-serious track stars to off-the-couch novices, I considered it my job to get people to lighten up a bit, to remember that running your heart out meant different things to different people.

The people I most connected with were first-time marathoners, and I even had a group that I trained myself. In them, I saw my younger self, the summer after my mom died, struggling to find and surpass my limits, to prove my mettle, to overcome obstacles and achieve my dreams. "You can do it," I told them. And many of them did.

The highlight of my time at CARA was a new event that I conceived called the Ready to Run 20 Miler, or R2R20, as the staff dubbed it. The R2R20 took the final long training run, typically done when training for a marathon, and elevated the experience until it resembled an actual race day. Except instead of covering 26.2 miles, participants covered 20, which is the benchmark running experts use to determine a runner's readiness for the full marathon distance.

The R2R20 at CARA was what WonderGirl had been to me at Girls on the Run—a personal and professional game-changer. In spite of what an ambitious enterprise it was, I decided the R2R20 would be the flag I planted in the ground for the runners of CARA and Chicago. If I was going to do or be *more* at CARA, this was how.

The course ran the entire twenty-mile length of the Chicago Lakefront Trail, starting at Foster Avenue, running north to Howard Street, and then circling back southward until the path ended at the historic South Shore Cultural Center. We planned an extravaganza: separate start and finish areas, timed pace groups, ten aid stations, and buses that would return runners to the starting area after a huge postrace party at the finish line, complete with beer and a band. The logistics of planning and executing an event that (literally) covered so much ground, involved the health and safety of thousands of runners, and required the help of hundreds of volunteers along with the blessing of the mayor of Chicago, who had to sign off on it, were mind-boggling. This is in addition to the pressure I put on myself to bring this baby to life. Something about pushing past the edge of my capabilities fired me up. It made things more meaningful to me, raised the stakes, and became something I could count as another piece of my running legacy, the way I counted the marathon medals I earned.

The night before the event, I found myself in a familiar mindset: excited anticipation and intense worry, self-doubt coupled with waves of nausea, plus a flicker of pride at my audacity for dreaming big. I craved the relief and joy that would come if all went well, but dreaded the unknowns. If something went wrong, I would let down the thousands of people participating, and worse, I'd disappoint myself and likely be fired from my job in disgrace.

As the sun rose over Lake Michigan on a perfect September morning, I stood on a stage counting down to the start. Three thousand runners had registered, a number that thrilled me because it solidly surpassed what most inaugural events drew. The runners were organized into pace groups of fifty people and, from my perch, I sent off one group every minute, so the runners would stretch out along the lakefront path.

An hour after we'd started, the last group left. The staff hurriedly broke down the start area, and I raced in the rental truck—no lost key this time!—down Lake Shore Drive to join the finish-line-party preparations. Looking to my left, out over Lake Michigan, I witnessed what I thought of as *my* runners, a continuous line of silhouettes dark against the brightening sky as they trotted toward the finish line twenty miles away.

I watched them, doing what they had set out to do, knowing this day would forever change the way they perceived themselves, second only to the day of the marathon itself. My heart opened, and a warmth spread throughout my body. These runners would sweat; they would push themselves past the pain and into triumph, the place where dreams were achieved, goals were surpassed, and this huge item on their bucket list was checked off.

In the truck, watching the runners, I slowed and rolled down my window, honking, waving, and cheering. Happiness flooded me. I soaked it in, and I sent them silent prayers: *I wish you well on your journey. Have a safe, good run.*

Just as the WonderGirl 5K had unfurled perfectly, so did the inaugural Ready to Run 20 Miler. Later that day, surveying the exhausted runners lying in the grass by South Shore Cultural Center and listening to music, I was visited by the same magical feeling of accomplishment as I had been on the WonderGirl stage. I'd helped thousands of runners believe they were ready to finish a marathon! I thought about Mom and me, sitting outside the airport, watching planes take off and return, and how I had vowed to fly away. It hurt knowing that I had actually done it and left her behind, but what hurt even more was realizing that my mom never had, and never would. I tasted the bitter of the past with the sweet of the present, happening before me.

Three weeks after the Ready to Run 20 Miler success, October 11, the day of the 2007 Chicago Marathon dawned, and the thermometer showed an unusually high reading. Runners arrived to the CARA tent on the marathon grounds, bursting with a mix of excitement and trepidation. The magic in the heated air was tempered with a dizzy feeling in my stomach. I hoped, so badly, that these people would have a great race, or at least a good one. Per usual, I was invested in everyone's experience, wanting so badly for each runner to finish. Toward this, I beamed every ray of positivity I possessed at the crowd. *Yes you can,* I thought. *Yes you will.* I punched the button on my iPod marathon playlist, kicking off "Let's Get It Started" by the Black Eyed Peas, and steered runners toward the bagels and bananas that CARA provided.

Soon, runners began leaving our tent and making their way to the start, trotting off in singles, pairs, and groups to join the throng of forty thousand waiting for the gun to go off. My team and I hustled to clean up, sweeping the prerace debris into thirty-gallon trash bags. The sun beat down, the humidity already saturating the air. It was so steamy that even when I stood still, sweat dripped from my forehead, with no breeze to evaporate it. The heat, combined with the humidity, made October feel like July. Running a marathon in this kind of weather was exponentially harder, and I was worried.

It had been over a year since my injury, and I'd slowly become strong enough to run again. My doctor wasn't thrilled with my distance-running dreams, but I wasn't ready to let go. I'd signed up for marathon number nineteen.

During the marathon, there would be hours between when runners left the tent and when they returned. I had decided to fill that time with an easy eight-miler. My strategy was to run four miles on the back of the course, watch the winners pass me, then turn and run with the crowd to the finish, with the aim of being back at my CARA post before the masses began to return.

As I stepped off on my run, the black pavement of Roosevelt Road radiated heat up at me. I noticed the wail of a lone ambulance and wondered who needed it as I ran past big groups of volunteers who were setting up the later water stations. With each notch of the sun angling up in the sky, the temperature followed, increasing degree by degree. I ran by a flashing sign displaying the time and temperature, 8:30 a.m. and eighty-seven degrees. *That can't be right,* I told myself.

Barely two miles into my run, I decided the sign wasn't far off. I was boiling hot. My inner alarm bell dialed up several decibels, and I scolded myself, *Stupid, stupid, stupid.* I'd broken a cardinal rule by leaving my money and cell phone behind as I ran into this inferno. I couldn't grab a cab or a cold drink, or communicate with anyone while I was out here.

I paused for a moment to gauge my ability to continue running. The heat had filled my brain with pure red, burning me on the inside with a throb that built to explosive intensity. My black tank top with the CARA logo was glued to my ribs with sweat. The sun baked into my dark clothing while the tar road sizzled on my shoes. Multiple ambulance sirens echoing in the distance made me uneasy. *Why were there so many of them?* I decided to keep going, but slowed down and began to run into any shade I could find, trying to escape the suffocating fire that engulfed me. When I finally got to my turnaround point at mile twenty-two, I panted in the sweltering air, grateful for a chance to rest, and drank the aid-station Gatorade. It tasted like warm lemonade.

The lead vehicles began to pass while I waited. I was impatient to return to the safety of the CARA compound. The elite runners followed. When enough time and people had passed, I got back onto the course, eager to get back to the finish line, even as the heat slowed me down and drained me.

Once out on the course, what I saw was less marathon and more like a scene from an apocalyptic movie. There were runners whose skin was the pink of barbecued meat, not merely sunburnt, but crisped over. Others' faces were bloodless, white, tinged with gray. A guy next to me cramped up and fell, there one minute, down the next. I noticed more people sitting on curbs, slumped over at aid stations, crumpled as if whatever starch they had started with was depleted and they were just piles of bleached clothing unable to hold themselves up. I gritted my teeth, kept going, and finally arrived back at our tent.

I grabbed my phone and saw I had over twenty messages. A sinking feeling took over as I listened to one from the marathon emergency alert center: runner down, unresponsive, transported to hospital. *Unresponsive?!* Two messages later, a friend's voice informed me, "We've had a death. I'll call with official details as soon as I can, but it's bad. Don't share this news with anyone."

Someone *died*? What if it was a CARA runner? My stomach turned, and I almost threw up. *Please, please, no.* Guilt threatened to overwhelm me. Anyone dying during the marathon was unthinkable. I wanted it not to be true.

With each passing minute, ragged runners staggered into the tent. Stories were being cast about—a lack of water at the first aid station, then the second, and then the third. People panicked as they realized there was *no* water and miles to go. The atmosphere, such a contrast to the prerace euphoria, was a rising hysteria about how awful the conditions on the course were. I believed them but tried to remain calm.

By around noon, runners were returning with new tales, rambling vignettes that seemed far-fetched but were repeated and confirmed by person after person. Their words tumbled out in a chaotic jigsaw of big, hot, terrible mess.

"They canceled the race! Can they even do that?"

"The police drove up and made us start walking. 'No running!' they yelled from the squad car."

Others reported that volunteers were using bullhorns to tell runners the race was over and to go home.

"Did anyone see the helicopter?" another runner asked. "It swooped down over us, the radio blaring, 'Stop running. No more running.' I thought we were under a terrorist attack." The woman relaying this began to cry, the terror of it all overwhelming her.

This was turning into a nightmare. After all the races I'd done myself, I had never seen *anything* like the scene unfolding before me.

"Help!" a voice shrieked outside. I burst out of the tent to find a woman lying on the ground, her skin alabaster, eyes rolled back, and her whole body convulsing. Her friend was bent over her, trying to jostle her into awareness. "Help her!" she yelled at me.

I froze for a second, then began issuing orders to people around me, thankful for the first aid–CPR classes I'd completed. "Get ice. Lots of it. Pack it in her armpits, around her neck, her wrist. Wet icy cloths for her head. Elevate her feet!"

I whipped out my phone and dialed 911. *Ring. Ring. Ring. Ring.* I hung up and dialed again. *Ring. Ring. Ring. Ring.* "Fuck!" I yelled, just as an operator answered.

After I explained the scene, she told me she'd send a medic and wheelchair, but it might take a while. I was about to return inside the tent when one of our most veteran marathon coaches came storming through, calling out, "Man down! Man down!" He ran in circles without direction. I knew he'd been in the military, and I wondered if he was having some kind of flashback to a war zone.

I grabbed one of his shoulders and he turned, pulling me by my hand behind him. An athlete from his group had fainted and was lying on the ground, breathing shallowly. I knelt down just as another runner tapped my shoulder, whispering, "I'm a nurse. Let me help. You keep calling 911."

I surveyed our tent. It was a wreck: survivors washed up on the trampled grass, sitting in hushed groups, consoling those who reclined like tattered rags. It wasn't supposed to be like this.

On any other marathon day, we would have been reveling in the marathon aftermath, celebrating. CARA members, runners— my *people*—would have been hugging and high-fiving, giddy with exhaustion and accomplishment, finishers medals hanging around their necks. They should have been euphoric, floating in the certainty of their hard-earned achievement.

It wasn't like that. It was a pile of rubble, a surreal bubble I inhabited with a sweaty phone slipping in my hands, 9-1-1-9-1-1-9-1-1 a nonsense jumble, the inescapable smell of rotting bananas and body odor, and the terror of the word *dead* echoing through my consciousness. In the moment, I didn't have time to think or mourn, I only felt a rising hysterical anxiety that this day had to end. We needed to get everyone out of there before anything else happened.

My staff and I scrambled around the tent, imploring everyone to leave, to be safe, to get home and cool off. They finally did, and we moved through the tent like robots, packing up, going through the mechanics of finishing up this apocalyptic day. After everything had been loaded, I sent my team home, but before I left, I took a last disbelieving look around the tent. Then I turned my back on the field of destroyed dreams and walked away with tears brimming.

The relationship between CARA, a nonprofit, and the Chicago Marathon, a for-profit business, involved a difficult history. Although it preceded my tenure, this history still affected how CARA did business—and their bottom line. In the early stages of the development of the marathon, CARA had been the official training program for the event and accepted sponsorship money to promote the marathon and grow its participation. Once the marathon had grown enough to sell out prior to race day, its support for CARA dwindled. One of the reasons I'd been hired was to reverse this trend and find new sponsors willing to write sizeable checks—the R2R20 had successfully accomplished that goal. But the marathon relationship, tied to CARA's training program, remained of utmost importance to the reputation and revenue of CARA.

The running community of Chicago was small and rife with politics. Some of it was an old boys' network formed by former track stars who once competed against each other and who operated all of the city's running events. Part of it was the city's political machine and the permitting required from the mayor's office to put on events in the city. There was also running-community infighting, which, for me, boiled down to the marathon race director being bent out of shape by my predecessor's firing of a CARA employee with whom the director was close. I suffered the repercussions of that and exhausted myself trying to work the organization back into his good graces, while trying to project confidence to CARA members who weren't aware of the tenuousness of CARA's position with the most important event in the annual race calendar.

The 2007 Chicago Marathon happened, for me, against this backdrop. I had no idea of what went wrong or how it had happened, but I knew CARA members would look to me to demand answers. Worse, I hadn't a clue if anyone at the marathon believed I was important enough to include in any postmortem meetings regarding the event, but according to the sinking feeling in my gut, I suspected not.

The Chicago Marathon was typically held on Columbus Day weekend, which normally gave the city and the runners, and everyone involved in the race community, a free day on Monday after the event. But that year was not a normal year, and I knew I needed to go into the office that Monday, the day following the race. I expected some sort of backlash, but "the hot marathon" turned out to be so much more than I could have expected.

On my drive into the office, I called the marathon race director. I simply asked, "What happened?"

He paused. "We're looking into it."

Silence filled the line. Was that it? All he was going to say? I said, "Some of my runners didn't have water. You don't know anything?"

"From what I can gather, the early runners used up the water," he said, "dumping it on their heads to cool off. Then the volunteers couldn't keep up as more and more runners came. And those back-of-the-pack runners? They shouldn't have been running in this heat."

He was blaming the runners and volunteers? While it was a plausible explanation, it didn't sit right with me. "Not enough water" didn't explain the chaos. Why had people reported so much confusion on the course? Why hadn't there been more medical support at the race? Did he understand how terrified the runners had been? I *really* wanted the truth, but he stonewalled me, seeming determined to shut me out. I kept asking; he kept evading. I finally hung up, feeling very small and very alone.

When I arrived at the door to the CARA office, a FOX news reporter was already there waiting. He shoved a camera in my face, asking me for a statement. I just said, "No comment," and nudged my way past him. Tension cramped my neck and my shoulders, and I could feel the pressure of a headache beginning.

The media called all day long, dozens of outlets, trying to bait me, to get me to blame someone or something. I refused. The events of the day devastated me, but how could the fault for something so complex, involving so many people, be pinned to one person or reason?

The newspeople weren't the only ones searching for a scapegoat. My inbox was swollen with hundreds of angry emails from runners who were totally pissed off, feeling robbed of what they believed was their rightful marathon experience. A significant number of CARA members rose up and demanded "justice." They wanted me to charge into the marathon's offices and insist on a refund for every runner. They begged me to "set up another marathon for next weekend." Their suggestions were not based in reality; they were impossible.

As the leader of the organization, I understood their frustrations, but I couldn't give them back that day and make it right. No one could. Meanwhile, the director of the marathon received death threats over the outcome of the event.

It stunned me that no one recognized Mother Nature—the heat—as the main culprit. It had been so devilishly hot! As the week wore on, news came confirming what the race director had told me about early runners dousing themselves with cups of water, which started an unstoppable domino effect. The emergency medical team at the marathon hadn't been sufficiently staffed to treat the masses of overheated runners. And when people began calling for help, the entire city of Chicago's emergency response teams—the ambulances, hospitals, and 911 operators—had been completely overwhelmed. It was the perfect storm for a complete shit show.

I was catapulted into an alternate universe after that, a world where the members and runners, my people, turned on me. The attacks were vicious and unrelenting and followed me everywhere I went. A group run? Someone made a nasty dig about the marathon. Phone calls? Filled with vitriol at how it turned out. Emails?

Asking for impossible remedies. I started to avoid running on the lakefront path because I'd be recognized and asked about it. I was reminded of how it felt to be in Stepdad's sights when he was on a rampage, triggering my own propensity for taking on blame, even when it wasn't my fault. I couldn't get away from it, and CARA became unrelentingly awful.

I took every single rebuke and insult incredibly personally. By attacking me, attacking my precious marathon, attacking my very intentions, they chipped away at my legacy. I felt destroyed.

My back recovered that year, but I never did.

I stayed at CARA for another sixteen months, for the second Ready to Run 20 Miler and for another Chicago Marathon. I hid my despair and disillusionment, but it was there, lying in wait, ready to pounce on me any time I got an email or phone call from a runner complaining about something. One day, more than a year after the fatal day, I came across a message board blistering with bitterness about the aborted marathon, where my harshest critics condemned me, calling for my resignation.

Yes. Actually, yes, I thought. *They were right. I should quit.*

Deciding to resign didn't feel like giving up. The thought of walking away from these horrible people and choosing not to take their shit anymore empowered me. A long time before, I'd learned to fly away from a bad situation. I knew I could do it again.

So I did.

CHAPTER 26

BACK TO GIRLS ON THE RUN

In what felt like destiny, when I decided to quit CARA, the person who had replaced me at the Chicago chapter of Girls on the Run resigned. When she called to tell me, she said, "Do you want your old job back?"

We laughed. And hung up the phone. Girls on the Run had been such a happy place. WonderGirl remained there. What was I waiting for? My dream job existed. And so I returned. I was forty-five when they rehired me.

The relief I experienced being back in a world full of silly, fun girl power and inspiration, surrounded by pink, purple, and green, soothed me. My nervous system settled down, bit by bit. My belief in myself and my legacy was still shaky, but it grew more solid month by month. The shadow side of the sport I loved, the sport that "made" me, receded, and the light of the girls helped dissipate the gloom. Still, giving everything to my work, and taking the fallout so personally, kept me vigilant.

Two years later, Doug and I attended the Bridge of Hope adoption information session, which coincided with the biggest Girls on the Run race ever: ten thousand runners. Planning a race with attendance in the five figures was daunting.

Unfortunately, it was also a disaster.

The WonderGirl 5K was supposed to be the pinnacle, the peak experience for the girls. It was supposed to be a day when a young girl who doesn't believe she can do it runs 3.1 miles. Paired up with an adult running buddy, who coaxes and cheers her through this grueling event, she must find her inner grit and keep going, overcoming her doubts. And when she finally crosses the finish line, she's beside herself with confidence and inspiration. This event was meant to give the girls *the* moment of their lives. When *She. Believes. She. Can.*

My legacy and me were the template I held in my mind. I desperately wanted the feelings, hopes, and yearning I had experienced at my long-ago marathon finish line to come to life for the kids. The words in the newspaper article I had first read about Girls on the Run were never truer than on a race day: "She knows how it feels, and she wants to pass it on."

However, the morning of this race, the first Saturday in June, was also the first truly warm day of summer—eighty-five degrees. It was as if every sun-starved Chicagoan descended upon the lakefront path, converging with the girls, 150 buses, and five thousand runners who got stuck on the two-lane exit off Lake Shore Drive, delaying the start of the race as the temperature ticked upward.

And in a cruel, ironic twist of all the things that could go wrong, we didn't have enough water, nor enough volunteers to hand out the water we did have to the masses of runners. Last, we lost the water that sat in bottles at the finish line, unguarded, because it got used up by thirsty parents, soccer players, fishermen, bikers, adult runners, and random others wandering the lakefront on this hot day.

In a flash, the heat, the lack of water, the tired runners, and the angry people returned in a tsunami, and I drowned all over again. Only this time, the catastrophe was *my* fault, and it destroyed the only happy place I had left: Girls on the Run.

There wasn't any press this time, but there was social media, and angry emails and texts saying I had almost *killed* the girls who ran. Reading that almost killed *me*. It certainly sounded a death knell for the ruined spirit of my legacy.

That was June 2011. Four weeks later, Doug and I flew to New York, hoping to meet Miya, the little girl who might become our daughter. My not-so-imaginary deadline still glowed somewhere in the back of my mind, lighting up the idea that maybe my real legacy was still on the horizon, waiting for me to fulfill it.

PART TWO

CHAPTER 27

ANDREI AND SVETLANA

fter our failed adoption, Doug and I felt defeated. All the hype, preparation, and my anxiety had amounted to nothing. No child, no visit to Ukraine, nothing. My heart ached each time someone asked about Miya and then broke all over again when I explained the outcome. I didn't realize how many people we'd told, until I needed to circle back around to answer everyone's questions.

I returned to Girls on the Run, reluctantly, after Miya left. While Miya hadn't given me any reprieve from my anxiety, she had provided a distraction from the disastrous 5K. The residue of the terrible hot race still blanketed everything at Girls on the Run, just as the boiling marathon aftermath had ruined my remaining time at CARA. I layered my devastation regarding Miya on top of the calamity at work and spiraled into darkness. I felt hollowed out and emptied of joy, unable to imagine a next step, anywhere.

The agency pressed Doug and I to continue to explore adoption. Our experience was the exception, not the norm, they assured us. I wasn't sure I could manage the process a second time, especially if it went the same way. But the stubborn streak in me, the part of me that persevered through marathons, overrode my caution. They told us about another sibling set and urged us to think about adopting those kids.

Their names were Andrei and Svetlana. He was eleven, and she was eight. They were Russian and had visited the United States for three weeks, like Miya. The host family they'd stayed with on the East Coast had already adopted four kids from Russia, and taking two more was too overwhelming, even though they'd loved Andrei and Svetlana. That's what the agency told us, anyway, but I was grateful when they offered to put us in touch with the host parents to discuss their time with the kids. This was one small step toward mending our broken trust with the agency.

This first family sent Doug and me pictures from Andrei and Svetlana's visit. Unlike in the oddly formal portraits sent from the Russian orphanages, Andrei and Svetlana were smiling. They looked like real children instead of blank-faced dolls. Andrei held up a fish he'd just caught, beaming at the camera with every ounce of his blond, blue-eyed being, a pair of sporty sunglasses perched upon his head. He was shirtless, painfully skinny, but so proud of his catch. Svetlana stared at the camera, holding a Tootsie Pop in her hand. Bright orange nail polish gleamed from her fingernails, and her long light-brown hair was blowing back from her face. Her blue eyes were stunning. She looked like a miniature supermodel coolly evaluating her photographer.

In spite of the lovely pictures, I was beyond leery. I knew what it was to fall in love with the photos, with the idea, instead of the child. I needed more than pictures and words from the agency this time.

I talked to their host mom, Trixie, on the phone, huddled in my office at Girls on the Run. She was earnest in her assessment and so nice, especially after I told her about Miya. Trixie reassured me, saying she'd been through the process four times, and even the best-case scenarios brought challenges. She'd been surprised that having six kids to care for was so much more work than having four! They had to take two cars everywhere so everyone would fit. They chose not to put the kids in camp, because the family wanted to spend time with them. They rode bikes. They swam. They went to the beach. They'd had fun, Trixie told me.

I kept probing for a problem, but there didn't seem to be one. When I asked Trixie about the Adoption Talk, she explained Andrei's and Svetlana's reactions when they realized they were leaving the United States without a forever family. Svetlana burst into tears. Andrei looked away with a trembling lip and heaved a disappointed sigh, struggling not to cry. I couldn't stop myself from comparing this with Miya's response.

"They are really good kids," Trixie said. "They deserve a good family. I will always think about them and forever hold them in my heart."

I thought I knew what she meant, because I wondered about Miya too. What would happen to her? Would she ever be adopted? I wanted the best outcome for her and Viktor, but what would I say to another host family who was considering adopting her? Even though it would be difficult, I decided I'd be truthful. What good would it do to sugarcoat the experience?

Doug set up a time to talk to their host dad, Mike, who repeated the same things. Andrei was a lot of fun to be around. Mike called Svetlana "Sweet Lana." It was difficult to say goodbye, knowing what great kids they were.

I read the summary Trixie provided, which offered in-depth information about the kids and her experience with them. The form reminded me of a SWOT analysis at work, outlining strengths, weaknesses, opportunities, and potential problems. Trixie effused over Andrei and Svetlana. They were wonderful. They seemed healthy. And quite smart. They treated each other well and were kind to her other children. Calm. No problems, although Svetlana cried a few times, and Andrei threw up grape pop in the car.

On the last page, she wrote, "These kids would thrive in a family where they are the only two children. Andrei is all boy and needs a father to look up to. When he gets praise, the look on his face is like watching the sun come out. Svetlana is all girl and will love having a mother all to herself. When you hug her, she never lets go first, and she seems like she doesn't ever want to let you go at all."

How could Doug and I resist *that*?

We decided to try again. We talked to the agency and requested that Andrei and Svetlana visit us for the winter Bridge of Hope program in January. When we said we'd move ahead, the orphanage informed Bridge of Hope that Andrei and Svetlana wouldn't be allowed to make a second visit because they had "used up" their chance to be adopted with Trixie and Mike. The orphanage preferred to send new children who would be more successful at charming their prospective parents into choosing them.

Doug and I thought this was ridiculous and cruel. We campaigned mightily to get the orphanage to relent and to get the agency to try a little harder on our behalf. Around Thanksgiving, we got an answer.

It was yes.

CHAPTER 28

GIVE ME A SIGN

Aaahhh! *I am not ready for this. I am not ready for this. I can't do this. I can't do this. I-can't-do-this-I-can't-I-can't-I-can't!*

I paced around our house, crying. Up and down the stairs. I circled the black granite island in the kitchen. Doug was at work, so Lulu and Roscoe watched me and followed, round and round, thinking I was playing some kind of game. Everywhere I looked, I saw something pressing to do, something important to think about. *Doug's shirt is on the back of that chair. Should I wash it? Wash. I need to do laundry. Clothes. I have to buy clothes for the kids. What do they need? I don't know! Everything! And food. I have to grocery shop. I have to make a list. What will these kids want to eat? How am I supposed to know? I am not ready for this.*

I kept doing laps. My mind kept racing. I kept crying. On and on. *This is crazy*, I decided. *I am becoming unhinged.* Yet I kept going.

The upside of this meltdown was that I got a lot done in between crying jags and anxiety attacks. Twelve days had passed since I took a second leave of absence from Girls on the Run, and Christmas had happened in a blur. Instead of celebrating, I prepared for Andrei and Svetlana.

I bought a bed, pink nightgown, and new Barbies for Svetlana. I moved my office furniture down to the basement to open our extra bedroom for her. I hired movers to rearrange our stuff to make room. After learning that children under eighty pounds were legally required to be strapped into car seats, I bought booster seats. At eleven years old, Andrei weighed only fifty-five pounds—his weight didn't even appear on the growth chart. I bought clothes and toothbrushes and winter coats.

Shopping for Andrei really threw me for a loop. I had no idea what sorts of things eleven-year-old boys liked. Like everyone in the world, I didn't want to go to Toys "R" Us in December, but I did it for Andrei and Svetlana.

My mind spun around the thought that they were coming and I had to get ready for them. On December 28, their arrival was just three days away, and I still had so much to do.

The fragility of my mental state led me to try to find a therapist, but because it was the week between Christmas and New Year's, I couldn't get through to anyone. I thought about calling my primary care doctor for Valium or Xanax, but stopped myself. If the adoption went forward, I couldn't admit to any kind of drug use, legal or not. And certainly not a mental health problem! My doctor would need to fill out a form for the adoption that swore I was drug-free and perfectly capable, mentally and otherwise, of caring for children. Was I capable? I wasn't so sure.

Our friends suggested we were nuts for trying this again. No one could believe it. So we told fewer people. A few of our close friends used words like "brave" and "optimistic." I wasn't feeling either of those things in the moment.

To prepare, Doug and I talked a lot. Most nights over dinner, Doug said, "You were so anxious with Miya. Can you please calm down this time?"

"I don't want to get so weird," I said, "but it's hard for me. I'm so nervous."

"They're just kids. They're not Miya," Doug said. "They want to be adopted. They're available. Remember what Trixie and Mike said?"

"Yes. They told us Andrei and Svetlana are good kids. They want a family." I went on, "They don't have any brothers or sisters . . . that we know about. Oh my God! Oh my God! If that happens again, I think I really will go off the deep end."

"Honey, stop." Doug grabbed my hands and looked right into my eyes. "You're fine. We'll handle this together."

The night before Andrei and Svetlana were due to arrive, I sat in my car outside Jewel grocery store. People rushed around the car, buying food for their New Year's Eve parties. Their boots crunched on the mounds of snow littering the black pavement. Tears cascaded down my face. My body heaved with sobs. The subzero weather, combined with my crying, overheated the inside of the car so the windows were all steamed over. I was glad no one could see me.

Sitting there, I thought, *What if I am insane? Or bad? A bad mom? What if it was all me? Why didn't Miya love me? What did I do? Or not do? What if these kids don't love me, either?*

I realized how scared I was, so scared they wouldn't love me. I realized I really, really, really wanted them to love me just a little.

More tears cascaded from my eyes. I didn't know what to do, but I knew I couldn't go on like this. I didn't want to be a basket case for these kids. I wiped my hand across my face and blew my nose for what felt like the hundredth time.

Staring into my reflection in the rearview mirror, all my makeup was cried off and my eyes were bloodshot red. "Deep breath," I said out loud. "Just take a deep breath. Calm down. Calm."

I closed my eyes and thought, *How did my mom love me? How did I know she loved me? Hugs, kisses, time spent together. She just loved me. My mom loved me. She didn't have to think so much about it. And I loved her back.*

I inhaled another cleansing breath and resolved to do just that—love Andrei and Svetlana. I decided I would love them the best I knew how. I didn't have to be perfect. They didn't have to be perfect. We could find our way to each other.

Then I promised myself, if Andrei and Svetlana loved me back, even a little, if they gave me a sign, any sign, even a small one, I would say yes. They would be my children.

CHAPTER 29

IS THIS THE SIGN?

We found ourselves at the American Airlines baggage claim at O'Hare airport, sitting in the bank of black plastic chairs closest to the Starbucks, facing the silver circular structures that went around and around and around. People arrived and left, picking up their luggage, receiving hugs and handshakes. They put on coats and hats and stamped their feet before going out into the New Year's Eve freeze.

Doug and I waited alongside four other families, plus a coordinator who was there from the agency to make any potentially awkward introductions go more smoothly. As Doug and I had learned, there might be a child who cried, who didn't want to go. I desperately hoped it wouldn't be mine this time. There were nine adults, but only five chairs. We took turns sitting and pacing.

Even when I sat, my feet jiggled and bounced with nerves. I made small talk with the other moms, trying to mask my panic. They all smiled and laughed. They seemed so excited and appeared so sure that this would all work out. Their confidence was daunting. I looked down at my hands, which twisted and clutched the cute stuffed golden puppy that was to be Svetlana's welcome gift. It appeared as if I were strangling the soft toy. I let go and smoothed the blond velour fur. I needed to get a grip. *On myself*, I thought, *not the stuffed animal.*

Doug came over to me and sat. He leaned over to my ear and whispered, "Calm down." He put his warm hand over mine and, together, we squeezed the toy.

The coordinator's cell phone rang. "They're here!" she announced gleefully. "They're walking through the terminal. Five minutes max!"

All the hopeful parents stood up and turned toward the silver-framed, white double doors, as if we were flowers turning toward our sun. Doug planted himself behind me, his hands on my shoulders anchoring me as I leaned against him. His grip was solid, in spite of what felt like my swaying. I don't remember breathing. I don't think I did.

And then I saw them.

Andrei wore a navy-blue winter coat that engulfed him, reaching almost to his knees. His close-cropped hair was pale against his even paler skin, but his eyes were alive, scanning the crowd, searching for us. He looked solemn but not unhappy. He guided two little girls, holding their hands, taking his task as a leader quite seriously. One small girl was too small to be Svetlana. She was not Svetlana. The other . . . was.

Svetlana was decked out in a shiny fuchsia coat, which I noticed as she got closer had ripped pockets. Her hair wrapped around her head in complicated French braids, and she chattered excitedly in Russian to her brother. She was smiling.

All the children wore the same cords around their necks that Miya had, with pictures of their potential parents on one side, their own names and images on the other. Svetlana eagerly gripped the photo of Doug and me with the hand Andrei wasn't holding, trying to recognize us, looking. Two other children and a translator-escort accompanied Andrei and Svetlana, but everyone except them faded into the background like white noise.

The distance between the two groups, one of parents and one of kids, closed quickly. Svetlana saw us and dropped Andrei's hand, running over to me.

"Mama?" she said in her little-girl voice, looking up at me with her blue, blue, blue-sky eyes.

My throat was tight; I could only nod. She launched herself at me in a fierce hug. I wrapped my arms around her tightly and found my voice. "Hi, Svetlana!"

I looked up at Doug, who was receiving a more modest, one-armed "guy hug" from Andrei. They were facing me. Andrei's aqua eyes captured my green ones, and when I smiled at him, he smiled back immediately. His voice was shyly hopeful when he said, "Hello, Mama. Hello, Papa."

Watching us, the coordinator said quietly but with confidence, "I don't think you're going to have any problems this time."

Our little group clustered together, just like each of the "new" families, as we all waited for our turn with the interpreter. Doug stood while Andrei leaned against his leg. Svetlana sat on my lap on one of the baggage-claim chairs. Vladimir, the interpreter, was a young Russian whose family had immigrated to the United States when he was six. He was wiry and serious, dark-skinned and raven haired, but with white teeth that shone out from his beard when he smiled. Because there were four families and only one Vladimir, he had asked his older sister, Katya, to meet the group and help translate. Katya shared Vladimir's dark hair, but she was fair-skinned and softer, a bit more mature.

Both of them were busy with other families, so while we were waiting, I pulled out a mini Etch A Sketch and showed it to Andrei and Svetlana. I drew the four lines for a tic-tac-toe game and handed the pencil over to the kids. Andrei willingly grabbed it and marked the first *X* with a grin. He offered the pencil back to me. Svetlana snuggled on my lap to watch while clutching her new stuffed animal tightly. Right away, I felt the contrast between Miya's stormy demeanor and Andrei and Svetlana's sunny attitudes. We played tic-tac-toe, and the children surprised me by reciting the English alphabet and counting from one to ten. Their willingness to engage, to try to connect, to actually *want* to be here with Doug and me was evident, and it made my heart sing.

Katya wrapped up her conversation with one of the other families and sent them on their way. I watched them go, the little-boy-potential-son walking between and holding the hands of his new "mama" and "papa."

Then Katya came over to us and began speaking in Russian to Andrei and Svetlana. Katya was a mother, and it showed. Her tone was warm and sounded happy, even though I had no idea what she said. Everyone smiled. She said to me, "It's okay?" and I nodded.

She proclaimed, "Let's start! Please give me the book."

Like before with Miya, Doug and I had prepared two albums of photos, one each for Andrei and Svetlana, to show them our house, our pets, our daily lives. During their visit, they would add photos to these pages and eventually, the books would go to Russia with them when they returned. The books would serve as mementos of our hopefully good times together and as advertisements for the orphanages that we would make good parents for these children.

The kids bent over the photo albums, poring over the pictures, absorbing all the details and asking Katya questions, which she translated back to us.

"Is this room all for me?"

"Yes, it is."

Wonderous expressions. "We have *two* dogs?"

"Yes, we do."

Smiles of glee, with raised eyebrows. "Will the cat sleep with me?"

"You don't want that. He will pee on your bed!"

Surprised looks, with giggles and shaking of heads. "Nyet! Nyet!"

Katya turned the pages, explaining, answering questions, and smiling. There was lots of smiling. I felt relief flooding my entire body, like a warm bath.

When we came to the end of the book, Katya asked us, "Any questions?"

"Yes! What do you like to eat?" I inquired.

"Ice cream," said both kids.

"What's your favorite color?"

"Black," said Andrei.

"Pink," Svetlana answered.

"What do you like to do?"

"Ride bikes and swim!"

"Are you scared of the dogs or cat?"

"Oh *no*. Nyet! We're excited!"

Katya turned to Andrei and Svetlana, and asked, "*Есть вопросы?*" Any questions?

"*только один вопрос.*" Only one.

"*Что мы должны называть?*" What should we call you?

Doug and I looked at each other, and then I answered by asking, "What do you want to call us? Mama and Papa?"

Katya translated, "*Что вы хотите позвонить? Мама и папа?*"

Andrei looked at both of us. Holding my gaze, he gave a hopeful smile, and said, in *English*, "Mom and Dad."

My throat closed up, and I couldn't speak. I smiled back and gave him a single affirmative nod of my head.

The four of us closed the books, gathered our things, and went home. Together.

CHAPTER 30

RUSSIAN CHRISTMAS

I
t was the first New Year's Eve that Doug and I had children in our house. In sharp contrast to past years of parties, friends, cocktails, and revelry into the wee hours, this year we stayed home—with two little, non-English-speaking strangers we had met a mere four hours before.

We planned to follow the Russian tradition of decorating a Christmas tree on New Year's Eve. This custom was supposedly born out of the Russian people's desire to celebrate a religious holiday and Communism's dictate that there be no religion. The Russians chose New Year's Eve to prepare for Father Frost, the Russian version of Santa, and to party for Jesus. So we decided to make our first night with Andrei and Svetlana a celebration of Russian Christmas, a week late and minus the vodka.

We had bought a small tree, kind of a Charlie Brown tree, except fake. There would be no refreshing smell of outdoor-pine-tree Christmas in our house, but also no threat of fire or needles to pick up. To Andrei and Svetlana, this pathetic tree was a beauty.

Their faces lit up with delight when I opened the first box of ornaments and it dawned on them that they were going to get to decorate! Svetlana clapped her sturdy hands together in anticipation as she watched me thread a hook onto the ornament string and carefully hang it on the tree. I motioned for them to go ahead, and they fell upon the boxes of ornaments. The sheer number of sparkly wonders they found in the boxes dazzled them. Almost every single ornament elicited what seemed to be one of the English words they somehow knew. "Wow!" Or they would say, "*Class!*", the Russian word for "cool."

This was the first time in twenty-four years I had willingly put up a Christmas tree. Christmas Eve morning was the last time I saw my mom, in a hospital bed, shrunken and yellowed, taking her last breath, dying. When she realized her cancer was terminal, her goal had been to make it to Christmas. She did. And Christmas was never the same after that.

But now Christmas was changing again. It was Russian Christmas.

Andrei and Svetlana worked quickly. It seemed as if they were racing one another to open the next box, get to the last ornament. In no time at all, the sad little tree was bedazzled and happy. Overloaded with tinsel, trimmings, and glittery glory, it shone like a beacon in our living room, reflecting light and shimmering shininess. All those waves of color appeared to make the tree move and, if I listened closely, I could hear the musical tinkle of glass ornaments touching each other. Or maybe that was just our big dogs circling this curiosity and wondering if there was a treat hidden among the branches?

The chatter of these two excited, elated children was like a salve, soothing my spinning mind and calming me—these children who might become my children, children who I might become a mother to. I felt Svetlana's arms circle my waist, pulling me toward her in a tight, almost too tight, hug and saw her face upturned to mine, her lips reaching for me, ready to give me a kiss.

I bent down, and she planted it right on my cheek, pushing hard against my face in her fervor. "Mama!" she said. "I love you!"

My heart melted. Waves of nervousness fell away. I told her, "I love you too, Svetlana."

Doug was watching us. "Good job, *Mama*," he said. "This isn't so bad, is it?"

"Nope! Not so bad at all."

CHAPTER 31

THINGS TO DO WITH YOUR (POTENTIAL) CHILDREN

A ndrei and Svetlana had arrived. We had celebrated Russian Christmas. We had twenty-one days—mornings, afternoons, and nights—to fill. My feverish mind jumped with nervous energy. Because it was wintertime, there was no camp for the children to attend. After what had happened with Miya, Doug and I hadn't planned much—actually, anything at all—with family and friends. If things went from bad to worse, we didn't want an audience this time. The question "What should we do?" rang constantly through my head, and the thought of unplanned, unscheduled time triggered alarm bells in my restless mind. I had promised Doug I'd rein in my obsessive-compulsive need to schedule every second of every day and just relax already, and so I tried.

One of our first nights together, we took the kids to see the zoo lights, a holiday light festival at the Lincoln Park Zoo, located right on the windy shores of Lake Michigan. Each night from late December to early January, when the winter sun went down, the zoo lights came up.

It was an extravaganza for the eyes, with lights in the shape of lions, gorillas, bears, and more. This party took place outdoors, in the dark, usually with temperatures hovering around, or even below, zero. All that visual splendor was necessary to distract me from the fact there was no feeling in my fingers or toes.

Luckily for us, Andrei and Svetlana came from a small Russian town named Birobidzhan, which everyone related to the adoption simply called Biro, that was almost in Siberia. The average temperature there in January was an icy negative twenty-two degrees Fahrenheit. Chicago, in comparison, was positively balmy to the kids.

As soon as we got there, I tried to insist the kids put on their hats and gloves. "Brrrrr!" I mimed, making them laugh.

They told me, "Nyet! Is good!" and picked up snow with their bare hands to throw on each other.

Doug thought that was hilarious and joined in. They were having a blast. I was terrified of losing them in the cold darkness, surrounded by hundreds of other children who were, like ours, all hopped up on the cotton candy and hot chocolate being handed out. If we lost them, their lack of English meant they wouldn't know how to ask for help, especially since they didn't know our last names, much less our address or phone number.

In addition to the sugar, Andrei and Svetlana overdosed on the high-voltage display of eye-popping electricity. Green, blue, red, gold, white, purple, and pink lights. Dizzy, dazzling, dancing lights all around us. If winter in Siberia was drab and gray, we had brought the kids to the inside of a rainbow. Their upturned faces reflected the colors of the lights, and their bright smiles bounced pure wonder back to me. We didn't need English to communicate. My nose tingled along with my fingers and toes. And my heart. It was good to see their joy.

As the first week marched on, figuring out what to feed Andrei and Svetlana was a daily challenge. Their favorite American foods were potato chips, bananas, and sweets—not exactly the stuff that the "ideal mother" inside my head preached about serving. I felt compelled to prepare, from scratch, balanced meals of protein, vegetables, and starches, with cold glasses of skim milk, next to a bowl of unsweetened fruit as a treat. The shopping and prepping and cooking it took to serve this kind of meal, which no one even wanted to taste, let alone eat, seemed like a phenomenal waste of time and energy. Then I'd become irritated when the kids wouldn't eat. Andrei, especially, would take less than a crumb, a bite no one could call a nibble, and decide he hated it, whatever it was.

One Sunday, Doug and I were driving back from Target, where we had bought the kids snow pants and ice skates so they could play in the snow. We were all hungry, and I was exasperated by the kids' limitations around food. As we passed Pete's Pizza, a restaurant on Western Avenue, Doug exclaimed, "Is anyone hungry for pizza?"

"Pizza?" Andrei yelled.

"I love pizza!" Svetlana hollered.

Doug nearly gave us all whiplash, he turned the car into the parking lot so fast.

We ordered two large pizzas, one cheese and one pepperoni. Andrei ate the whole cheese one himself. Svetlana did some major damage to the pepperoni. They sprinkled liberal amounts of red pepper on their slices, much to my alarm. But still. "Thank you, Jesus," I intoned, wondering how it had taken us this long to figure out that our kids liked pizza. I mean, really? How stupid were we?

But we learned. And ate more pizza that next week than ever before. So much, in fact, that Andrei finally said to me one night, pleadingly, "Please, Mama, no more pizza."

Part of our agreement with the agency included allowing Andrei and Svetlana to meet up with their fellow Russians. There was another Chicago-based family who had adopted three children from Biro already, and they offered their home up for the festivities. I was struck by their generosity, since ten families were invited to the party, which included dozens of already-adopted kids and their American-born siblings, plus all the parents.

Andrei and Svetlana were soon absorbed into the groups of Russian-speaking, English-speaking, soccer-playing, jewelry-making kids, leaving us to chat with the other parents. Doug and I took the opportunity to learn about the paperwork, and Biro, and what traveling across the world to bring the children to America would be like.

I was curious about the travel, but more curious about how these other moms did it. How they *wanted* this, so effortlessly and easily. At least that was how it looked to me. The agency had been calling us, asking the big question that loomed over me ominously, constantly: Were we going to adopt these kids? Everyone else here had either already adopted or knew they were. How were they so sure? And why couldn't I be so sure?

The party was supposed to be a coming together, but it left me feeling lonely. The divide between knowing and not knowing, between wanting and not wanting, between being a couple and being a family had never felt so vast.

The shame of my ambivalence weighed on me.

To say that I panicked about what to do with the kids is an understatement. Especially when the rest of the children in Chicago went back to school after winter break was over and I found out, one by one, that many kid-friendly places we planned to visit were closed during the weeks after the holiday. Not having things to do with the kids reinforced my dread and showed how much of a rookie I was at this.

I considered it a major triumph when I was able to book two nights in Key Lime Cove. This was an indoor water park complex and hotel—no one needs to go outside in a swimsuit in January!—in the northernmost suburbs of Chicago, with a floating "river," huge waterslides, several pools, an arcade, restaurants, and sleeping rooms.

To the initiated, it was a place where everyone and everything, from your swimsuit to the carpet in your hotel room, felt slightly damp, if not completely wet, all the time. Kids showed off goggle marks around their eyes and the pruney fingers they got from staying in the water for nine hours at a time. Parents sat poolside after taking the obligatory dip with their kids. The adults were eager to get out soon, because the water wasn't only green from the copious amounts of chlorine.

The real partyer parents seemed to have forgotten completely about their children and sat in the hot tub with drinks, laughing and joking with each other, like spring breakers on vacation in Mexico. I wished I could relax enough to be like them, but I couldn't. No, I was Mama now! I was responsible, mostly. I was petrified, even more, because as we arrived at the pool, it occurred to me that I didn't even know if the kids could swim. If I had a drink, and we had an emergency, it might affect my ability to successfully break out my CPR skills.

The skill I used was my growing expertise at charades. As we approached the pool, I mimed running and said, "Nyet!" I pretended to dive in headfirst and repeated, "Nyet!" I squatted and made a *pssssss* sound and then, shaking my finger to reinforce this, "Nyet! Nyet! Nyet!" Andrei and Svetlana looked at each other, giggling at my pretend peeing.

"Okay, Mama! I swim!" And then they promptly ran—yes, ran—over to the pool and jumped in, narrowly missing a couple of other kids. At least they didn't dive.

So the kids could swim well enough not to drown, and this allowed me to relax enough to get an umbrella drink and to pore over a *People* magazine. As children splashed and parents relaxed around us, Doug leaned back, took a long drink of his beer, and put his newspaper down. Staring at me, he said, "I could get used to this."

I didn't know how to respond. Yet.

CHAPTER 32

THE TALK

The agency was relentless in their follow-up with Doug and me. After the Miya fiasco, they monitored this visit closely, making sure we were okay, that the kids were enjoying themselves, that everything that could possibly happen to turn us into an official family was happening. It was good, but the panic that I had felt in the grocery store parking lot before they arrived bubbled beneath my still-not-so-calm exterior.

With these kids, it was all on me. I had asked for, begged for, a sign, something to tell me that it would be okay, that they would be our children. The visit was going infinitely better than our time with Miya, but was that enough? I still longed to feel what was, for me, elusive. A glaringly obvious maternal instinct that didn't whisper, but shouted, "Yes!" I didn't feel it. All I could think about was how my life would change—how it might suck. Because Doug's corporate job was much more lucrative—and required considerable travel—than my nonprofit one, we both knew that I'd be the one to take on most of the daily parental heavy lifting, especially once the kids arrived for good. I'd have to quit my job at Girls on the Run—the job I'd once believed was my dream job—to bring these kids home, to help them adjust to a new world. How could I, would I, know that *this* was right?

I couldn't, but the more time I spent with Andrei and Svetlana, the more they charmed me.

The two kids were eager to please us. For Svetlana, this usually took the form of physical affection. She kissed me fiercely, hugged me hard, and held my hand, all the while calling me Mama. Andrei wasn't as physically affectionate, but he tried very much to be helpful—making his bed or helping clear the table. I was touched, although a little sad sometimes, to see how plainly and openly they wanted us to like them, love them. I related.

Although we didn't want to fill this visit with structured lessons, occasionally we wrote out the alphabet for them, or showed them how to write their names. So one morning, when Andrei brought me the small notepad that we kept by the phone, along with a pen, I wasn't too surprised.

He painstakingly wrote, "MYMY." Then he pointed at it and said, "Is Mama?"

I shook my head. "Try again."

He crossed it out and wrote, "MIMI."

"Almost," I said. "But not quite."

Andrei, frustrated, crossed it out again and then held the pen out to me and gestured that I should write it. I wrote, "MAMA," and gave it back. He copied me, writing underneath, "MAMA."

He pretended to scribble some more, but instead of writing, he returned the pen to me. "What do you want me to do?" I asked.

He pointed at himself, and after that, with his two pointer fingers, drew the shape of a heart in the air. Finally, he pointed at me.

"Oh," I asked, "I love you?"

His blond head gave a definitive nod, and he made the scribbling motion again, pointing at the paper. So I spelled out "I LOVE YOU" and showed him the paper, which he took back, along with the pen. Andrei bent over, circling the paper protectively with one arm, the way kids do when they don't want you to see what they are doing. I stepped back while he slowly traced his own letters. When he was done, he slid the note across the black granite surface of our kitchen counter. I read out loud, "Mama, I love you!" He had added his own exclamation point!

I took the paper and held it to my heart, smiling at Andrei, while he proudly, but with just a hint of shyness, smiled back. Setting the paper down, I took the pen and wrote, "Andrei, I love you!" and showed him.

His grin got wider. I held out my arms. He walked into them. And then we were hugging. Tightly. My heart stirred then, touched by this boy, a boy who kept surprising me with his sweetness. I hadn't expected this.

I put the note on our refrigerator, fastening it with a magnet from some long-ago beach vacation, putting it where I could, and would, see it. Every day.

Talking with Doug, deciding with Doug, only highlighted our differences. He didn't care about the chaos the children brought; he welcomed it. He didn't obsess about the life we would have to let go of but of the life, the family life, we would be stepping into. I knew how petty I was being, but this was huge, the biggest decision ever.

Still, even I had to admit how awesome these kids were. I had asked for a sign that they loved me, wanted me, wanted us. I had gotten those signs. Finally, after spending three weeks with the kids, Doug and I decided: Yes, we would have the Talk. Without really realizing what I was doing, I made a determination that if the children hesitated or seemed unsure during the Talk, then *that* was going to be my sign.

We called Vladimir, who had escorted the group to Chicago, and asked him if he was willing to interpret the Talk. We worried about how it would go, given that Ukrainian Aleks had not been trustworthy and we couldn't understand the language to know if our words were being correctly translated. Still, we hoped for a better outcome with Vladimir.

We chose the day before the kids had to leave to go back to Russia. Andrei and Svetlana would fly from Chicago to New York, then from New York to Moscow, and then from there to Birobidzhan, all the way back to the orphanage. We had bought each of them a suitcase, the same kind of rolling suitcase that had delighted Miya. I did laundry, ensuring all the clothes going to the orphanage would be clean. We had been putting pictures of the four of us into the photo albums that Andrei and Svetlana would carry back to Russia. Everything was prepared, except for this last bit—the most important conversation.

It was a sunny January morning, cold, but not terribly cold. Vladimir rang our doorbell and, predictably, Lulu and Roscoe barked. When he came in, they circled him, jumping and making a stir. Soon, Svetlana and Andrei were circling Vladimir as well, happily chattering in Russian and grabbing his hands to bring him into the living room.

Along the way, Vladimir translated a little. "You had cake for breakfast?" he asked in English.

I heard Svetlana say, "Dah, dah!"

I said, "Yes. We decorated a cake with frosting that said 'We love Andrei and Svetlana' on it. Life is too short not to eat cake for breakfast sometimes."

This was a tradition my mom had started for my December post-Christmas, pre-New-Year's birthday, to make the day special, surrounded as it was by holidays. I was thrilled to repeat it with Andrei and Svetlana and hoped we would have something to celebrate this day.

Vladimir nodded in a way that signaled it was time. Offering Vladimir a drink and gesturing toward the couch, Doug said, "Come sit down, Vladimir. Let's talk over here."

Vladimir called Andrei and Svetlana over. They sat on either side of him on the long side of our L-shaped leather couch, the color a shade darker than butter. Doug and I sat on the other side of the couch, waiting expectantly. Vladimir's bright white smile shone through his dark beard, and suddenly, I had a feeling that this would be all right.

Doug began, "Andrei and Svetlana, we have loved having you visit us."

He waited while Vladimir translated . . .

"Mama and I love you very much. We hope you love us."

More translating . . .

"There are a lot of rules and lots of paperwork we have to go through, but we want to try to come visit you in Russia."

Translating . . .

"And we are wondering, if we can follow all of the rules and get all of the papers, if you would like to come back with us to America. To live with us. To be our children."

Transla—

Before the words were all the way out of his mouth, both kids flew across the room, one on each of our laps, and hugged us, petted us, held us.

"Dah! Dah!" Yes! Yes!

Andrei gripped Doug with his skinny, narrow arms, his smile wider than I had ever seen. Svetlana almost hurt me with the strength of her little-girl-enthusiastic embrace; her lips pressed and pushed on my cheek, insisting that she loved me. Loved us.

Vladimir clasped his hands together and gave a little shrug of his shoulders, nodding his head. He said matter-of-factly, "I think you guys know this. They are excited. They say yes."

FORTY-ONE DOCUMENTS

A courtroom in Russia was our goal. A room, more than halfway across the world, where Andrei and Svetlana would become our family. Doug and I needed forty-one documents in order to get there, papers from specific people or places, with special signatures and exact notarizations. An international notary, called an "apostille," was required on each and every paper, which necessitated presenting the documents one by one to a clerk in an office located in downtown Chicago. The entire packet, signed, sealed, and translated, was called our "dossier," which brought to my mind thrilling CIA car chases, but in reality resembled mind-numbing bureaucratic paper pushing more than anything.

The process was incredibly convoluted. I considered myself an intelligent person, but deciphering the who, what, where, and when of procuring all forty-one documents made me feel stupid. For example: Form C was based on the information in Document X, which could only be signed by Person Z, who was only available from 6:00 p.m. to 9:00 p.m. Central Standard Time on the third Thursday of the month. When Person Z signed, Notary A had to witness the signature. Notary A only worked until 5:00 p.m. but was willing to stay late if paid three times his normal rate. Also, the stamp of Notary A must not expire for one year from the date of signature, a fact that I only found out when Notary B, who had originally signed Document H, had a stamp that expired in February, just a week after he signed our sacred papers. Did that make sense? It didn't to me, either.

There were also peculiar rules in the maze of information, or misinformation, we had entered. The first was that everything, *everything*, must tie back, exactly, to the home study document. The information in our home study, then, took on the truth of biblical sacraments. Our home study was thorough and listed everything from the amount of our mortgage payment, to the age of Doug's siblings, to the fact that I had scoliosis. However, it had been produced almost a year earlier when we began the adoption process in preparation for Miya's stay. Therefore, we had to revisit it when certain details changed—like when Doug got a raise, or our property taxes went up. Changing the home study reminded me of pushing the first domino over—one little nudge caused a cascade of changes in everything else I had set up so carefully.

The second rule, not quite as arbitrary, was that I was no longer Betsy, and Doug was no longer Doug. For the purposes of adoption, we were, respectively, Elizabeth M. and Douglas E. Any document that spelled out our middle names couldn't be used. The "First Name, Middle Initial, Period, Last Name" versions of our names were on our passports. Passport names were the basis of our home study names, and thus, those would become our adoption names too. And by "adoption names," it meant exactly those names had to be printed and signed, down to the period and space after the middle initial, on forty-one separate documents.

The third and final rule was that everything—*everything*— needed to be sent to our agency contact, Chris, for review. I never met Chris in person and only spoke with him on the phone or sent files via email. Although I knew he was only doing his job and helping us, he was maddeningly detail-oriented. He caught errors, such as one extra number tacked on to the end of a seventeen-digit license number, or the fact that in one version of our address we abbreviated the name of the street we lived on from "Avenue" to "Ave." He discovered the error in my employment-verification letter where the notary wrote a date that didn't match the date at the top of the letter, the dates being just one day off and representing when the letter had been printed and when it had been signed. Chris would say in his nasally, East Coast–accented voice, "I'm so sorry, Betsy, but you have to do this one again. We don't want to take a chance the Russians will find any reason to reject you." He sounded sorry, but when I had to redo something for the fourth or fifth time, and get them re-notarized and then re-notarized internationally, too, he made me want to pull my hair out in frustration.

When compiling all of these documents, I often felt forlorn. I saw my mom's name on my birth certificate and recognized that she had been a mere twenty-three years old when she had me, and then remembered she died just twenty-three years later. This made me feel as if there were a strange symmetry to our lives, that we would each get the same amount of time with each other and without each other. Also, comparing what Doug wrote regarding his family with what I wrote left me, once again, questioning my maternal instincts. Would I know how to raise a child when my own childhood had been ruined in the vortex of Stepdad's rage? The other comparison I agonized over was one I'd been making since before I was even married to Doug—that I had no extended family beyond my brother and his wife. Between the lines of these documents, the terrible aloneness of my status as an orphan lurked, and I worried the Russians would judge me. If I had nobody, what could I offer to Andrei and Svetlana?

Besides the rules and Chris, we had a problem with our social worker, Sandra's, state license. Chris worried that the Russians would reject our home study because Sandra purportedly did not have the proper licensure to fill out paperwork for a Russian adoption. If the Russians refused to accept the one document that was the basis for everything else, then we had no hope of them so much as glancing at anything else. The agency assigned us another social worker and, to my bitter disappointment, we had to begin again.

Four months after Andrei and Svetlana left, and on the day when our upstairs washing machine decided to overflow, we welcomed the new social worker, April, into our home. It was judgment day all over again, except with gaping holes in our ceilings, wet towels everywhere, and the damp smell of mildew setting in. So much for my immaculate housekeeping!

April seemed genuinely apologetic. In fact, she never set foot outside of the living room, preferring to take Sandra's word about everything and to copy verbatim the report Sandra had written. April willingly handed over a copy of her state license too. I never truly understood the difference between the two licenses, but I put it in the stack of papers to take to the notary, and then to the apostille, and then to FedEx to mail to the agency so Chris could examine it for mistakes.

The medical assessment form was another problematic document. This form expired after only three months. Three months in "adoption time" was like three weeks. It flew by. Every few months Doug or I, and a traveling notary, would appear again with the medical assessment document. Our doctors would then swear— after we proved by blood, X-ray, exam, or otherwise—that we didn't have: tuberculosis, active or chronic; diseases of the internal organs; diseases of the musculoskeletal system; diseases of the central or peripheral nervous systems; malignant oncological diseases; history of substance or alcohol abuse; infectious diseases; mental illness; any disease and/or trauma leading to disability; any conditions requiring surgery, past or present; hepatitis B; hepatitis C; HIV; syphilis; and—the best category ever—"other."

When we first started this adoption process, the agency had said a "really motivated person" could get their forty-one-document dossier done in three months. Goal-oriented me was uber-motivated, mostly by the thought of Andrei and Svetlana sitting in a faraway orphanage waiting through the Siberian winter for us to come, but also because of my mixed feelings about returning to Girls on the Run.

I couldn't shake the feeling of despair that flooded me when I ruminated about my work, especially about going back. The voices of the angry parents, mad about the disaster of the 5K, echoed in my head. I'd taken my leave of absence for Miya's visit a few weeks after the race, and when I'd returned, the national office, along with some of the people who worked for me, had joined my critics, faulting me for not being more prepared. I felt piled upon, kicked when I was down, especially after Miya's adoption fell through. To be so defeated at the place where I worked my heart out, where I thought I'd built a legacy, devastated me.

I'd purposely asked for extra time off when planning for Andrei and Svetlana's visit. I needed time away. I felt fragile, and I kept thinking, *If I can just focus on the adoption, on getting these papers, and quickly, then I won't have to go back.*

After two months, the forty-one documents were still incomplete and thus not ready to be translated into Russian and sent overseas as our complete dossier. I comforted myself with knowing that, even if I had finished, the next step was to wait some more anyway. Because once the Russians had the dossier, Doug and I were on hold until they selected a court date. Now I'd have to chase papers and worry about Andrei and Svetlana, while also working at a job that depleted me. I wasn't excited; in fact, I dreaded it, but back to Girls on the Run I went.

CHAPTER 34

SUSPENDED

I sat in my office and looked out the window over Milwaukee Avenue. It had been nine months since the catastrophic race, and I'd just returned from my two-month leave with Andrei and Svetlana. It was a gray, raw day, and the black pavement, the steel-colored sidewalk, and the ash-scattered sky blended together in my view. Cars moved. People walked. It had to be noisy outside, because it always was, but the sounds were muted by my anxious, buzzing thoughts. I thoroughly resented being at work. The time off had provided a taste of sweet respite from the bitter darkness that Girls on the Run had become to me.

I couldn't stop myself from comparing this spring season at Girls on the Run with all the others that had come before. The spring season used to be a big deal, the best time, the time when new schools would have new programs for new girls. Springtime always made my work seem limitless with possibility. More girls became more girls who would run! Usually, Girls on the Run grew and blossomed like the perfect pink tulips that pushed their way up through the gritty dirt of a Chicago winter. Not this year. I felt as if I were hanging outside the window, stretched between two worlds, with my fingers gripping the cement ledge, slipping, trying desperately to hang on, when I longed to let go, drop back, and run away from work. I ached to go back home and finish the adoption papers aligned in careful piles on my desk. If only the documents were done and my phone rang with news of a court date! But the work at Girls on the Run took precedence, as it always had.

Anger vibrated inside of me, next to my jangly nerves and feelings of betrayal. In my head, I composed rants railing at the parents who accused me of trying to harm their kids, the national office berating me for my decisions, and my coworkers who made their dissatisfaction with me crystal clear. How had this job, which had been such a dream, turned into a nightmare? What was I supposed to do now?

I couldn't just quit. I'd already taken so much time off for the kids, first Miya and then Andrei and Svetlana. My absences had stressed the staff considerably, and I still cared about these people, even the ones who were angry with me. Although I was sorely tempted to walk away, something—my pride, or maybe the marathon runner in me—wouldn't allow it. I had never simply dropped out of a race; it was unthinkable to me. Pushing past pain for the sweet reward of triumph was in my DNA, and my cells were encoded to keep fanning whatever tiny flame of hope still existed so that I could somehow make it all right again. Normally, I possessed a depth of this steely reserve, but this time, I was far from any finish line and so, so tired.

The only way I managed to get through the days was by bargaining with myself. I would finish out the spring season. I would hang on for one last fundraising dinner in May, and I would persevere through the monstrosity of one final 5K in June. Perhaps believing this was the last time I would do any of it—and that I could make a success of it—would make it bearable.

CHAPTER 35

THE PRAYER
AFTER DINNER

T wo months later, I sat at my desk, thinking about money. The annual Give for the Girls dinner was scheduled for the following evening, and the pressure was on. The god of money could not be ignored. Like all nonprofits, Girls on the Run needed cash. Just thinking about the dinner, about the important people who I would have to charm, about the speech I would have to make, the funding I would make a plea for, made me want to lay my head down on the fake wood of the Ikea desk I sat at, the one I'd assembled myself back in the beginning of Girls on the Run some ten years ago. Like the desk, my team and I built the dinner one piece at a time. Turning screws, shaking hands, making menus, setting it upright, planning a program, and making sure it was sturdy. We had to build it and get it done.

The night before the dinner, besides fighting the inertia that plagued me, besides wishing I could go home and work on the dossier instead, I agonized over my speech, which was not at all close to done. Actually, it wasn't even started. The pressure to be profound paralyzed me.

If there was one thing I had learned about fundraising, it was that "the ask" needed to come from my heart. I had to *believe,* deep down into my soul, into the very soles of my feet and beyond, of my own authentic conviction. It required infinite faith that I was offering someone, a person with their shiny coins, the chance to do alchemy, to turn money into magic, to make a difference that mattered—to the girls. Belief, conviction, strength, and salvation—what I craved—sounded like a religion. Maybe it was, and mine was lost.

As I procrastinated on my speech and typed random words into my laptop, trying to feel inspired, Jessica rushed into my office. She was the rock of our fundraising staff, and we were both working late. She was glowing, her sparkly brown eyes, glossy hair, and gleaming smile shimmering with excitement. She held a white FedEx envelope.

"We have the video for tomorrow," she announced, "and it is *ah-mazing*!" She handed me the DVD and said, "I am so late. I have to go home." She turned on her heels to leave, but paused to tell me, "Watch it!" before she left.

Jessica had met two women documentary filmmakers while I'd been on leave. She'd asked them, in her twinkly, convincing way, to make a movie about the girls—and they'd agreed. They spent two weeks talking to girls, running with them, following them—all because of Jessica. The filmmakers' last documentary had been nominated for an Emmy, and they planned on winning one this time. The five-minute video, which they'd rushed to complete for the fundraising dinner, would be my first glimpse into what the cameras recorded.

I slid the silver disk out of the envelope and snapped it into my computer. The *click-click* of the DVD catching began, and my screen flared to life. As I watched, the power of the clip took my breath away. I recognized the "I can do anything!" magic that running brought forth from the girls. But as powerful as it was, in equal measure it was devastating to me because I had lost the very spark for running that these girls were sharing. Tears dripped down my face, as the realization hit me: My sparkle, my wonder, the young girl inside of me that yearned to be more than she was—all of that was gone.

This place, these people, these girls used to make me *so* strong, *so* happy, *so* inspired. I no longer felt strong. Or happy. Not anymore. I felt like a big fake, simply going through the motions, pretending, and I couldn't stand it. I hated the way I had to lie to everyone, even myself, about how wonderful this was when I was so dark about it all. I had lost my faith.

I wiped my eyes. *The speech*, I thought. *I just can't.* I didn't even bother to turn my computer off before I packed up and went home. The melancholy followed me all night and into my dreams.

The next morning, I rose early and went for a run. My crooked back was painful most of the time at this point, and even though my doctor warned me against running, that morning I needed to move to unblock what I'd locked inside. The spring morning air cooled my bare legs. The trees were tipped in light apple green, the buds dancing against the frame of the dark branches.

I breathed. I ran. Not like I used to, but I ran. I ran with girls' voices, from the video, ringing in my head.

I heard one girl say, "I believe I can."

I heard another say, "I did it."

I heard the last one say, "I'm proud. So proud."

Fourteen hours later, at the Drake Hotel, two hundred people hushed as the video began to play on big screens in the ornate ballroom. I listened to the tinkling of spoons in coffee cups and quiet chinking of forks upon dessert plates, which soon fell silent. In the film, the girls ran. The girls spoke about what Girls on the Run had taught them about themselves. There were smiles, and sweat, and effort, and the sweet glow of self-assurance, all in these young ladies, who seemed lit from within. The crowd watched, mesmerized. The video ended, and I approached the podium.

On my morning run I'd decided that the words I needed to say would somehow come to me. I resolved that the girl inside of me had words she needed to say, and that the spirit I needed to channel for the moment would arrive. As I had run through the spring morning, with the earth blooming and budding around me, I remembered that other May day, when I'd decided to run my first marathon. I thought of all the times my hopeful, loving, and doomed mother had believed in me, had told me that I could do anything I set my mind to, and how proud she was of me. The belief, the doing, and the pride—this would be the message I shared.

As I stepped up to the microphone, I enlisted the audience's wonder and asked them to participate in a call and response, and to say the girls' words, loudly and proudly.

I divided up the audience. To the left side of the room, I assigned the phrase, "I believe I can." The middle section was given, "I did it." Finally, the right side of the room took on the saying, "I'm proud. So proud."

I told them, "When I point at your section, I want you to be the girls. To say what the girls say about Girls on the Run. To feel the magic. Let's create a chorus of all that is in the hearts of our girls."

And so we did. When I pointed to the left side, the people shouted, "I believe I can." And they were a girl.

I gestured to the middle section, and the crowd raised their voices to claim, "I did it." And they were a girl.

And when I gave the signal, the right side of the room said, "I'm proud. So proud."

The entire room rang out with hope, and belief, and pride. We were the girls' voices. We were the girls' words. It felt like a religious experience. And we embodied, from our eager, impassioned hearts, all of the girls. The girls who ran, who believed, who forgot, who remembered. The girls who did it and who were proud. And after all of that, I asked the audience for their support. Gladly, they gave it. We brought in the money we needed, and this speech, the last I would have to give, was magical. Stepping down from the stage, I wished I could freeze time. I had glimpsed, for a few seconds, what had once been my goodness, my everything: Running, my mom, my legacy. Me, WonderGirl, and Girls on the Run.

My faith wasn't restored so much as replenished. Just enough. I came to see that just like the girls on 5K day, I did what I had come to do. I raised money, lifted spirits, made a plea, said a prayer. Even better, the prayer had been answered. I resolved never to forget this moment when, in the midst of darkness and doubt, I persevered. When I felt my sparkle return and had the audience reflect it back to me, multiplied. When I felt as if the entire universe was telling me *yes*.

CHAPTER 36

RUNNING SOLDIER FIELD

I t was three thirty in the morning when I exited the house. That early, even Lulu and Roscoe lay back down on their doggie beds with a sigh after the initial brief commotion I'd caused by rising so early.

It was race day at Girls on the Run. My heart pounded with anticipation, and I shook with nerves. This *could not* go badly. I could not repeat the hot, waterless 5K fuckup that was last year. I couldn't bear it.

Surveying the still-dark sky, I saw stars and breathed in relief that there wouldn't be any rain. I'd been checking the weather obsessively, and although the forecast predicted warmth, at this point I was glad for just about any contingency, in a sports bra, under a tank top, under a T-shirt, under a hoodie, under a raincoat. Every layer had a bright pink-and-green logo with the words "Superstar Staff" embroidered underneath. This was our uniform, what everyone who worked with me wore, so even if we shed or added layers, everyone knew who we were. I had a pair of sporty capri pants, my race pants, with purposely huge pockets for my cell phone, car keys, truck keys, money, ID, and various papers and instructions, along with the walkie-talkie that would blare communications every which way. On my feet were running shoes. We all wore running shoes on race day, just in case we needed to do what every girl was there to do: run.

I flashed back to last year, when I ran through the crowd in a panic, looking for water; ran to the medical tent to check on overheated girls and their angry parents; ran to the stage to make the obvious announcement that it was dangerously hot and begged everyone to please go, get out, go home. I braced myself and hoped against hope that we wouldn't have anything catastrophic happen today.

I pulled myself up and into the truck, which was parked on Western Avenue near my house. Settling into the seat, I did a final run-through in my head and decided, yes, I had everything I needed with me. I actually loved driving those big twenty-foot trucks. Sitting up high in the cab, using the mirrors to see behind me, feeling the rumble of the engine shake the seat as I stepped on the gas and pulled away from the curb, I felt powerful and in control. It reminded me of driving tractors on the fields of my childhood farm, way back before anything bad happened to the little girl that used to be me. It amazed me, reminiscing, that my parents allowed my seven-year-old self to steer a big machine, solely on the basis of my feet being able to reach the pedals, but I supposed there were fewer lines to stay inside of and plenty of room for error back then.

Before I left, I took one of the Valium out of a bag in my pocket and washed it down with Diet Coke. It would kick in when I got there, when I knew I would start needing it. I had to be calm today, and this was part of the plan. I inhaled deeply, sat up straight, turned the key, and stepped on the gas.

The ride to Soldier Field was swift and silent through the dark night, with only my thoughts and the chugging of the engine to keep me company. I thought and spoke to myself in a loop. *Just one step at a time. Get through today. Please let it be okay. One step at a time. Get through today. Please let it be okay.* I guessed I was praying again.

When I arrived, I got swept into the frenzy of setup, a race against time to get everything ready for the runners as the night skies gave way to dawn. Trucks, tents, and T-shirts, volunteers, crackling radios, weather forecasts, and last-minute adjustments. It was a blur until suddenly, the sun was up, people were in place, the girls were coming, the race was happening.

I left the beautiful green lawn and went up into our Forward Command center, a glass box of a room high up in Soldier Field, where all the decision-makers stayed during the race, listening and responding to reports from the ground. After the disaster of last year, when no one saw the big picture of all that went wrong, we had to do this.

Below, I soaked in the sight of hundreds of yellow-orange school buses filing into the parking lot like a line of marching lady-bugs. From the bus drop-off point, there were lines of excited girls in bright turquoise shirts coming off the buses. The blue shirts jumped and gestured with buzzing energy. These teams jittered toward the Great Lawn of Soldier Field, where two-hundred-plus magenta flags flew, each one flapping and snapping with the name of a school. Watching the parking lot blacktop turn from dark gray to orange and watching the spring lawn transform from still green to a moving sea of turquoise took my breath away.

And yet, there were hiccups. Buses got backed up on Lake Shore Drive; too many people swarmed the race-day registration tent; and, worst of all, the temperature was climbing. I walked to the bathroom and, still quaking, took another pill. The other one had worn off hours ago.

As seen from our bird's-eye view, several thousand runners were lined up and ready to go. Because of the sheer number of people, the groups were divided into corrals. Each corral was assigned a letter, *A–P*, and each group stepped off alphabetically. The operations manager, Mike, began calling out over multiple radios and channels to those on the course.

"Mike to course operations."

"Course operations, go ahead, Mike."

"Is the course set and ready?"

"Course is set and ready. Go."

"Mike to aid station one."

"Aid station one, go ahead, Mike."

"Aid station one, are you set and ready?"

"Aid station one is set and ready. Go."

"Mike to ambulance one."

"Ambulance one, go ahead."

"Are you set and ready to go?"

"Ambulance one, set and ready."

It had the hush of a NASA countdown.

One by one, each place, each turn, each mile marker, voiced their readiness. The last question: "Mike to start line."

"This is start line, go ahead, Mike."

"Start line, are you ready for corral A?"

"Start line and corral A are ready. Can we go?"

Mike looked at me, waiting for my response. I looked out on everything that was Girls on the Run to me. At excited girls and thrilled parents. At the blue dream of the sky and the teal-turquoise lake in the distance. At the volunteers who waved happy, sparkly GO FOR IT signs. At the people on my team, who wore our hearts on the sleeves of our uniforms. It was all out there.

I absorbed the energy of the runners. Big, small; young, old; fast, slow; wide, tiny. The runners were my people. This was my place, in the big wide world—the green grass and the black pavement, filled with runners, ready to do what they came to do. I had been them. I wanted, so badly, to be them again. But right there, right then, I knew there was no going back, only going forward. Hopefully, my worst moments were behind me and my best were waiting up ahead.

I nodded. "Go ahead, corral A. Let's start. It's a go."

Off they went.

The rest just unfolded. An ocean of blue-clad girls, pink-and-green cheerleaders, yellow sunshine that was hot but thankfully not too hot as to get dangerous. There was the jumpy energy of "Can I?" at the start, and the bemedaled swagger of "I did it!" at the finish. There were proud girls and even prouder parents. There were cameras and chants, songs and cheers, and a few tears from scraped knees, or jubilation, or both.

Twelve hours later, it was over.

After all the buses were gone, and all the girls had headed home with their parents, I walked to my truck and laid my head down on the big, round, black steering wheel, hot from the by-now-late-afternoon sun, and let it all out. The tension. The relief. My tears drip-dropped down the steering column, to the emptied-out pockets of my capris, to my dusty running shoes. It was over.

And nothing catastrophic had happened. There was no more to get through. Nothing else, with Girls on the Run, to get past.

What would I do now?

CHAPTER 37

RESIGNED

I wanted to quit, but I wasn't sure I should. I didn't know if I could. The idea of letting go of Girls on the Run scared me. The organization had, for twelve years, filled my life with purpose, with energy, with legacy—or so I thought. But the past years, between my broken pelvis and the pain, between the "hot marathon" and all the anger, followed by the hot 5K race and all the criticism, followed by losing Miya and Viktor, had shattered me. Deep down, I felt running and my body had failed me, although I blamed myself. Whether it was true or not, I believed I was the one who failed.

Two weeks after the final 5K race, I went on a trip by myself to the desert in Arizona. The sandy dust and sage-green cactus framed the tumbleweeds of discontent that blew through my mind.

I wanted to escape our house, the office, Chicago, the dogs, the dossier, and Doug. I wanted to bake myself in the arid heat, sitting in the yellow light by the pool, tasting the salty spice of a Bloody Mary and *not* chasing paperwork. I wanted to stop thinking about 5Ks and fundraising and kids. I wanted to erase the questions "Should I?" and "Shouldn't I?" But of course those questions echoed through my mind, even when I was submerged, kicking through the cool aqua underwater of the pool.

As the sun reflected hotly on the cobblestones around the water, I reflected too. I turned over the idea of my legacy and tried to see what was on the other side. From my mother's death to my first marathon, from the years of soulless sales jobs to grad school, and from Girls on the Run to CARA, and back again. I was forty-eight years old, and running had transformed from a teenage way to keep in shape to a path to handling grief, to a passion, to a dream job, to . . . what? Running had breathed life back into me. Running was my spirit, my heart, my home. Running was my identity. Quitting Girls on the Run felt like I was dying.

What occurred to me was that I kept trying to carry, to be, something bigger than I was. The heaviness, the exhaustion, the effort kept chasing me. Or did I refuse to let it go? Yes. I kept pushing, kept forcing, bending and even *breaking* myself to make it work.

Why couldn't I stop? *Why?*

Because I didn't know what would happen with Andrei and Svetlana. Would I become a mother? I didn't know. I'd lost my place in the world, my confidence. Who was I if I couldn't run, if I wasn't changing the world the way I always had, had always wanted to? When Mom died, I'd vowed to leave my mark, to make my life count. I'd believed running—and by extension, Girls on the Run—was the way.

My mind was the empty sky, mirroring the bottomless blue on the water before me. But in that emptiness, I saw that my dream of Girls on the Run was well and truly gone. Dead. I had nothing to push against anymore, except the blank space where my legacy used to live.

I consoled myself knowing that I had kept the promises I'd made when I went back. I had done the dinner and ran the race. It was over. Crystal clarity showed me, more than anything, that Girls on the Run wasn't mine anymore. It never had been. I understood, there in the heat of the desert day, that it never would be either, no matter how hard I worked or how much I cared. If I grasped at anything, it needed to be the wisdom to walk away from Girls on the Run and the kindness to allow myself a different dream—even if I didn't know what that was yet.

I walked to the edge of the pool and dove. The cool water slapped me. In that moment, I made my choice. I would quit.

CHAPTER 38

COURT DATE

Musical tones emanated from my cell phone as it vibrated next to me. The 301 area code appeared on the screen, signaling that some adoption-related news was about to be delivered. It could be only one of two things: good news, or bad news.

The bad news was a Pandora's box overflowing with grim possibilities. A piece of paperwork needing a simple revision that was never really simple, or a true catastrophe that would shut down the adoption. At this point, either was equally likely.

America and Russia had become involved in a disagreement about Syria, where a civil war had broken out. Russia backed Syria's dictator. The United States hadn't taken a stand yet, but if they did, and it was against Russia, the geopolitical balance could be upset enough to threaten Russia's willingness to allow Americans to adopt Russian children. Even though my heart broke on behalf of everyone involved, it simultaneously hardened when I imagined how the Syrian mess might affect Andrei and Svetlana, separating us forever. Every morning, I scanned the world news section of the *Chicago Tribune* as if it were my daily horoscope.

Bracing myself and hoping for the prospect of good news, a court date, I straightened my posture and popped my finger onto the Accept button.

"Betsy?" the female caseworker inquired. It was not Chris, who was in charge of paperwork. The call was not about paperwork.

"Yes, it's me. Every time I see your number, I don't know whether to be thrilled or not answer," I admitted with a nervous laugh.

"I get it! Well, today . . . I have great news!" she said. "You have a court date! August 13! Time to pack and buy the plane tickets!"

Hearing this, it seemed impossible. We had started this process in January 2011 and it was now July 2012. Nineteen months of waiting, of holding my breath and checking my feelings. Almost six hundred days of wondering, *Would this work? Should I do it?* The anxiety and heartbreak of the experience with Miya and Ukraine, followed by the delight of our time with Andrei and Svetlana—was our wait really over?

I had the sensation, as when I used to run marathons, that I had turned the final corner. At this point in a long race, I was usually tired and close to giving up, but the cheers of the crowd energized me enough to make a final turn, and then the finish line appeared.

This call meant the end of our long wait was in sight. I could accelerate safely now, knowing there would be enough energy remaining to cross over to the other side.

A court date!

Doug and I were really, truly going to Russia.

CHAPTER 39

WHAT'S (NOT) IN YOUR SUITCASE?

Doug and I were finally on our way to Andrei and Svetlana via Paris, then Moscow, then Khabarovsk—a Russian city seven time zones away from Moscow. From Khabarovsk, we would take a three-hour car ride to Birobidzhan, where Andrei and Svetlana waited for us. Birobidzhan—or Biro, as it was known—was so far across Russia that the border of China was a mere three-hour car ride away. The kids were more than half-way around the world. Twenty-six hours of travel, not counting layovers or transfers, separated us. Doug and I wished we could fast-forward the clock so we didn't have to wait to be reunited.

In the fourteen days between the phone call and boarding the plane, I turned into a tornado of organization. There were a million things to get ready—not just our luggage, passports, visas, and medical papers, but our house too. I hired a personal organizer who helped me visualize the best ways to use the space, and then I found movers to come, rearrange, and take away the excess, to make room for . . . our kids? Our family? I quivered with anticipation and nervous energy at the thought.

I packed, with precision, for our journey. Our suitcases and carry-ons were filled with unusual things that normal travelers would never place in their bags. Among the socks and underwear and electrical adaptor plugs was:

- An X-ray of my chest, my crooked spine displayed fully—a huge white S slashed across the blackboard of irradiated background. A typewritten lab report was attached, detailing that as of late July my lungs were clear of tuberculosis. Also mentioned on the report under "Other Diagnoses" was "idiopathic scoliosis."
- Various envelopes, innocuously labeled "Moscow Driver," "Moscow Translator," "Moscow Medicals," "Biro Driver," "Biro Translator"—all containing crisp twenties and starched hundreds. We had been instructed to get "new" money since the various people we would pay preferred fresh American dollars. The bills laid in their white pockets as if they were sleeping soldiers, at attention even in repose, straight and new and ready for action.
- Folders and files containing paper after paper full of undecipherable symbols—Russian—and their corresponding English twins, including our home study, letters from lawyers, official documents, and the reason we were on this flight, a formal invitation to a Russian courtroom.
- One formal suit for each of us, plus a pair of pantyhose and pumps for me. Our visit was "official business," according to our visas, so we had to play the part.
- A brightly wrapped care package and a triple-taped official envelope. The first was from a family waiting for their court date, to be hand-delivered to their future child at the orphanage. Families who had traveled before us had ferried similar care packages for us; now, we returned the favor. The second envelope was from the agency, meant to be hand-delivered to the Russian coordinator in Biro.

- Two small bottles, their orange-brown color and white caps familiar to anyone who has ever filled a prescription. These were prescribed for me: Valium and Norco. I didn't take them every day, but they were insurance for what was likely to be a nerve-wracking experience, and in anticipation of back pain from all the travel. I hoped I wouldn't need them at all.

Doug had splurged on first-class tickets from the States, and I was extremely grateful. As Doug and I snuggled into the navy seats and situated ourselves on the plane, we had a celebratory drink and clinked our glasses together.

"This seems kind of unreal, doesn't it, honey?" I asked. "That we are *finally* going?"

"Yeah, kind of." He paused. "I just want to get there and be done with this. I want to be flying home from the other side."

"Me too. I'm just so relieved to actually be on this plane with all those damn papers. So glad." I expelled a deep breath.

Doug said, "Thanks to you, we're on our way!"

We smiled into each other's eyes.

We believed we were ready.

More than a day of travel later, we checked into our Moscow hotel, the Sheraton Palace. The Moscow airport had been a blur of babble and exhaustion as we searched for the stranger who was to be our driver and translator. We finally found her holding a piece of paper saying ARMSTRONG.

I craved a shower and room service in my pajamas, but restless Doug wanted to explore since we were only in Moscow for a single night. I reluctantly agreed, and we set out down Tverskaya Avenue, which was a main boulevard, with the map the hotel gave us stuck in Doug's pocket. It was a lovely, late-summer day, with temps in the low eighties, a cloudless sky, and a light breeze tickling our faces. The sun hadn't set yet, and I hoped the generous sunshine portended a smooth experience in Moscow for Doug and me.

Doug had traveled extensively for work, and his savvy gave him a confidence I lacked in this foreign place. I was frightened to let him out of my sight.

As we found our way, we discovered the hustle-bustle of Moscow. The street was clogged with cars, so crossing it necessitated walking underground beneath the road and emerging on the opposite side. People jammed the sidewalks: Euro-club-looking people with loud clothes, big sunglasses, and cigarettes, next to slick-looking businessmen in suits who yammered into cell phones, with more cigarettes.

High heels were everywhere. Every woman, except the truly elderly, wore them. Even the women dressed in business suits exuded an overt sexuality communicated by the height of their stilettos, their tight skirts, and the amount of makeup on their faces. All of these fancy people existed right next to the old crone in a kerchief selling crappy trinkets on a card table in Red Square. The one thing they all shared was the grim expression on their faces. There were no smiles, which was so odd to me. One of the refrains of my childhood was my mom saying, "Smile, Betsy! Look happy!" and even though I hated the cognitive dissonance her order created, I'd always found that a big, open smile led to connection. That wasn't so in Moscow, and I tried to keep a blank face as we walked past the imperious structures of Red Square and the Kremlin.

Red Square turned out to be a four-mile round trip from our hotel, but it felt good to stretch our legs. We located a café and managed to snag a table on the outdoor patio to avoid the permeating stench of tobacco. All Russians smoked, it seemed, which I despised and was usually quite vocal about. I knew my opinion on smoking would not be welcome in Russia, so I just rolled my eyes when Doug ribbed me about my potential to cause an international incident.

Looking around the restaurant, I felt frumpy in my mix-and-match travel clothes and sensible Dansko clogs. The place was packed with exactly two types of people: beautiful young Slavic girls who could be supermodels, and groups of much older, squat, ugly men. At every table but ours, the males sat, leaning back, the buttons on their shirts straining and cigarette smoke streaming from their nostrils as they considered their choice of females. The girls simpered around them, showing off fabulous cheekbones and flawless legs in lace short-shorts with tiny crop tops and sky-high heels, hoping to be picked. It was obvious that the girls were on display for money, even in this nice restaurant. The whole thing reeked of misogyny.

I recalled something the pediatrician who had reviewed the kids' medical information had told me—that 90 percent of the kids in orphanages who aren't adopted end up as sex workers. I'd thought he was exaggerating, but I believed him now.

The next morning, we were slated for our Moscow medicals. The Russian government required that adoptive parents be examined and approved by a series of Russian doctors. The purpose wasn't completely clear to me, since by that time the Russians had access to all of our medical information in the dossier anyway. In spite of that, we'd dutifully carried all the lab reports and X-rays, as instructed. I believed, or hoped, that the Moscow doctors would just review them and barely examine us to verify their truth, but I couldn't know what to expect.

Sasha, our translator, was a compact woman in her forties with sensible short hair. Her manner was businesslike and pleasant but not exactly friendly. She spoke English with a very light accent. As soon as she arrived, she ushered us into her car.

Before we set out for the medical center, she confirmed what she saw in our hands. "You have your X-rays and paperwork? Do you have an envelope for the doctors?"

I handed her one of the preprepared envelopes. She didn't look at it or count the money, just put it in her bag.

On our way to the medical center, I asked her what we could expect.

Sasha delivered the information matter-of-factly as she drove, keeping her eyes on the road and tossing answers over her shoulder to me in the back seat. "We will go to medical center where families wait. It is one room, so others may be there too. I take your information to doctors to get signatures. Maybe doctors come down to room to examine you? Maybe they ask a question? Maybe they are satisfied, so they don't. We never know how it will go."

"Are the examinations . . ." I struggled for the right word. "Um . . . thorough?"

She shook her head. "Maybe they listen to your heart. Maybe you take your shirt off."

I observed that Sasha, although willing to answer, didn't offer anything definitive, and she gave no sign of stress, confidently steering her car among the throngs of vehicles and people. I was already used to this Russian response to almost every question: maybe yes, maybe no.

When we pulled up to the medical center, I thought it resembled an apartment building more than the hospitals in the United States. The office was like someone's living or dining room. It was arranged with a huge wooden table in the center, surrounded by at least ten chairs, and several couches pushed up against the walls. No reception desk nor receptionist greeted us. The only nod to the concept of a clinic was a tiny, white-curtained cubicle and a sheet-covered cot off to one side. The atmosphere didn't inspire confidence.

Sasha motioned us to a couch and gestured for us to hand over our paperwork. She mentioned, "No other families are here now. This is good. We are first."

She was mindful we were scheduled to leave Moscow that evening on the sole daily flight to Khabarovsk. If we were delayed, it would be necessary to wait another twenty-four hours in Moscow, which could throw off our entire schedule in Biro and make us miss our court date. We were all cognizant of the clock.

Over the next forty-five minutes, Sasha came and went from the room with our papers. Once, a man in a lab coat entered and walked straight over to Sasha, who sat surrounded by forms. They exchanged a few words in Russian, and he leaned over to sign. My eyes never left him except to blink, but the entire time he was in the room, he never glanced at us.

Only one doctor examined us. He brought Doug over to the cot and asked him, via translation, about headaches, dizziness, or seizures. He tapped Doug's knee to check his reflex. Then Natasha called me for my turn. When he finished, the Russian medical man grimaced at me and said in English, "Good."

I smiled back, and once he autographed the paper, Sasha started to pack up.

"We're done?" I asked.

She nodded and smiled. "Yes. Medicals are over. Congratulations."

"That was easy," I said.

Doug told me later what an absolute joke he thought the medicals were. "They barely looked at us!"

Sasha picked up our X-rays, the black plastic film both stiff and flimsy. "Do you want to keep these? Or these?"

She held out the lab report detailing all of our bloodwork.

I decided to keep the paper reports. On the X-rays, I hesitated. They were a pain to pack, large and unwieldy, and required special care to prevent folding or damaging them.

I questioned, looking around, "Where do we leave them? Here? Don't we need them in Biro?"

"Oh, you won't need them! You can put them here." With a sly expression on her face, she opened a door to a built-in cabinet.

"Whoa!"

The closet was packed, stacked floor to ceiling with X-rays. There must have been hundreds, maybe more, all sitting there, unlocked. They looked dusty.

Doug asked, "Are those *all* from adoptions?"

She nodded. I looked at Doug. He looked at me. I had reservations about leaving the X-rays, with our full names and medical diagnoses imprinted upon them, in a random, unlocked closet, but convenience won.

"Let's leave them," I said.

When our plane departed from Moscow, the X-rays were no longer in our suitcases. Even though they didn't weigh very much, I felt lighter. It was as if Andrei and Svetlana waited somewhere up in the sky, and bit by bit, I floated toward them.

CHAPTER 40

FLYING AND DRIVING IN RUSSIA

When we arrived at the airport for our flight to Khabarovsk, we joined a long line of people that snaked back and forth several times. We were already jet-lagged in Moscow and were about to cross seven more time zones, leaving Moscow at 9:20 p.m. and arriving in Khabarovsk just after noon the following day.

The characters who stood in line provided quite a show. Three men in front of us passed a bottle in a paper bag back and forth, as if they were on a mission to finish before check-in, which they did. Behind us, several men wore the trappings of business: suits and briefcases, cell phones glued to their ears. And then, there were the women. The travel costumes they donned for the flight had one theme: tight. The skirts weren't as short as on the streets of Moscow nor as skin baring, but very snug. I wondered how they could sit comfortably over the long flight and was glad that I had opted for stretch pants and my trusty Dansko clogs.

I wasn't looking forward to our flight. Our friends Jacob and Debbie had shared their Aeroflot adoption experience, and they were not complimentary. According to Debbie, the food served on the flight was both unrecognizable and inedible. They felt crammed into their seats, and Debbie's seat belt didn't latch! Flying nine hours in an unsafe piece of junk, untethered, with a bad back appealed to me not one bit. I begged Doug to check into upgrades but, at $1200 each, he nixed it. I should have known, given the Russian countenance, that smiling and talking about my bad back wasn't going to work any magic on the stern check-in agent.

When it was time to walk down the ramp, the crowd introduced us to the nonexistent Russian boarding process. When a Russian voice called our flight, everyone pushed, en masse, toward the gate. There was no "Group 1 boarding . . ." It was a big cattle rush, where elbows flew and people shoved without a single "excuse me." The polite, Minnesota-nice girl inside of me was appalled.

Once we settled into our seats and the flight attendants began serving meals, I realized Debbie was spot-on about the food. I ate the lone slice of bread with butter and passed on what seemed to be a type of cold fish. There hadn't been any familiar food to purchase in the airport, and my stomach grumbled for the better part of the flight. I vowed to remember to bring my own snacks when we flew home.

Finally, we landed in Khabarovsk.

The size of the Khabarovsk airport announced our arrival into the hinterlands of Russia, compared to Sheremetyevo in Moscow. The contrast reminded me of departing from O'Hare in Chicago and arriving in Des Moines, Iowa.

We easily found our translator, Lina. She was young, with long dirty-blonde hair and a few pimples on her chin. Her outfit of jeans, tennis shoes, and a zip-up sweatshirt would have fit right in at any American college.

Before we left the airport for our long car ride, Lina pointed me to the bathroom. "Do you have toilet paper?" she asked. "They have none."

I nodded, feeling proud that I remembered to carry Kleenex in my purse. *Thank you, agency!* I silently congratulated them as I entered the odorous room. I was pleased for the fifteen seconds it took me to realize why it smelled so bad. The toilet was a hole in the ground with an actual toilet seat sitting over the hole. How odd. And who could even manage to sit on that thing? I resolved to squat and pulled my Kleenex out.

Back out in the tiny terminal, I met back up with Lina and Doug, who had grabbed our bags, and out we walked to the car where we met our driver. He was a short, stout man wearing all black from his suit to his shoes, with the exception of a white shirt. When he leaned against the car, his jacket fell open and the butt of a pistol flashed in my vision. Our driver had a gun?! With jet lag crushing me, I decided I didn't need to care.

Smoke streamed from the driver's nostrils, and my anti-smoking radar went off. I cringed inside, hoping I wouldn't have to endure the entire ride in a thick cloud of smoke. But as I climbed in, I felt a rush of relief. It wasn't smoky, and the driver threw his cigarette butt out the window before he began to drive.

The land around us was hilly and green, interrupted occasionally by hulking metal structures that appeared abandoned, they were so decrepit and rusted. Lina told us they used to be factories when this was Soviet country, but now they were mostly closed.

Occasionally we passed a woman or child standing by the side of the road selling watermelon or cucumbers. I couldn't imagine they got much business out there in the middle of nowhere, and the way their heads turned, following us as we blew past, confirmed that their hope rode in the cars that traveled by.

The houses we saw from the road, when we saw them, were humble. There was no glass in the windows, and curtains fanned outside in the breeze. Some of the buildings were less house and more lean-to, just a roof and some walls attached to a barnlike structure. Many of the buildings had visible cracks in them, with boards nailed haphazardly askew. I wondered how the people who lived there survived the way-below-zero winters I had read about when I researched this place where my children might come from.

My sightseeing was interrupted when the car approached a train track and stopped. Inexplicably, the driver turned off the engine and got out of the car. No train, no sound of a train, no other car disturbed the sudden silence.

"What's happening?" I asked Lina, trying to sound merely curious, not alarmed.

"He needs to smoke," she said.

I watched the driver light up. It had to be close to ninety degrees, and probably hotter for him on the blacktop road, especially because he was wearing a black suit, leaning on a black car, in the blinding sunshine. He smoked his cigarette all the way down, then pitched it away and climbed back in. A wave of tobacco came with him but was soon blown away with the wind that roared through the windows as we drove. The driver did this three times in three hours, always at train tracks.

In time, we drove by bigger and better buildings that emitted the vibe of, if not a city, then at least a town. Gradually more cars and people cropped up. The roads began to cross a few other throughways with traffic. Just as I was trying to figure out what made the landscape distinctly Russian, a gigantic gray concrete sculpture covered with splashes of spray-painted graffiti sprang into view. It was a statue of the hammer and sickle, the symbol of the United Soviet Socialist Republic, sitting on the side of the road surrounded by grass and a few straggly shrubs. The USSR had collapsed more than twenty years ago, in 1991, but this symbol was still standing in 2012. Desecrated, yes, but still there.

"That's one of the orphanages," Lina said, pointing to a three-story white building. "We're in Birobidzhan."

"Is that where Andrei and Svetlana are?"

I stared at the building as it receded, memorizing it. The orphanages in Biro, probably in most of Russia, were numbered instead of named. Andrei and Svetlana were in Number Three. They call them "*detsky dom*"—children's home—followed by a number.

"No, I think that's Number One," Lina said.

I asked, "Will we drive by Three today?"

"No, it is the other way. We are going to Vostok Hotel to check you in."

Although we passed by what appeared to be stores, and restaurants, and businesses, and I wanted to ask Lina about them, she was clearly not interested in being a tour guide. She'd told us earlier she was a student, working part-time as a translator. She was clever enough to learn English but not overly eager to practice with us.

Finally, the car made a sharp turn into our hotel, a cream-colored four-story building with a dark green cap of a roof. Lina and the driver got out to unload the luggage, while Doug and I dug through our envelopes, trying to find the Khab-to-Biro Transfer one, along with the appropriate cash to tip the driver and Lina. We're supposed to give each five to ten dollars per day, and Doug, Mr. Generous, gave them each a twenty.

Lina, preparing to go, asked, "Would you like me to come inside?"

"Yes," Doug said, "please."

The sharp tone of his voice told me he was losing his temper. I didn't blame him, since he'd just tipped her at least double what she expected *and* we needed her to do the one thing required of her—translate.

In the lobby, Doug stepped up to the wooden desk, Lina at his side. I watched the back-and-forth between Lina and the woman behind the desk, who seemed offended we had arrived. Lina said, "She is saying there is no reservation for Douglas Armstrong." The way Lina pronounced Doug's formal name was more like "Dooo-glas."

"Well, Lina," Doug said, "can you please ask her what we need to do to get our room?" He paused between each word as if Lina were slow-witted, but this didn't faze her in the least.

After another volley between the younger and the older woman, while Dooo-glas stood impatiently, desk lady finally uttered something that sounded like dah.

Lina rotated back toward Doug. "She found you a room. The last one available. A suite, which is very nice."

"That's what we were supposed to have anyway!" Doug's voice came out exasperated. We both really needed a nap.

We bumped our luggage into the small elevator, leaving Lina behind. Emerging on the second floor, we passed a hotel worker, a woman, who sat impassively on a chair behind a desk in the hall. She saw the key in Doug's hand and nodded impartially.

The dingy hallway had tan walls and brown carpet. A lone window covered by a drape was at each end, the light losing its fight to shine. A small lounge room off to one side revealed a TV with a rabbit-ear antenna and a short green couch, which both looked like the furniture in my grandmother's house circa 1957. A second worker stared, glaring at our interruption. The Olympics, which had started when we were sleeping in our Moscow hotel, streamed across the TV screen. Bob Costas wasn't commentating here in Russia.

We located the door and rolled in, letting our shoulder bags drop to the floor, and glanced at our surroundings. Doug took a step across the room and swept his arm out as if he were Vanna White on *Wheel of Fortune* showing off a Cadillac. "Welcome to Biro, honey. We made it. We're finally here."

CHAPTER 41

REVEAL AND REUNITE

I woke up the next morning with my back killing me after a night on the too-soft mattress, but today was the day we were finally going to be reunited with Andrei and Svetlana! Even in my exhausted state, my energy surged just thinking about them. I shook Doug awake, eager to begin the day.

Before we could be reunited with the children, we had to meet three people. The first two were our translator and driver. *Please don't let it be Lina and the smoking man with a gun*, was all I could hope.

The third person was a member of the State Guardian's office. In Russia, the State Guardian represented the interests of the children, like Child Protective Services in the United States. They came into Andrei and Svetlana's lives when whatever had landed them in the orphanage occurred and were supposed to have been following Andrei and Svetlana's case, making decisions regarding their care.

Over breakfast in the deserted hotel dining room, where a buffet heavy on fish and poached eggs was laid out, Doug and I talked.

"I'm worried about the State Guardian," I said, picking at the apple-filled blini on my plate, the only item on the menu I could bring myself to eat. My picky appetite wasn't serving me well.

"What are you worried about?" Doug asked me, concern bending his eyebrows.

"I don't know, exactly. Well, I think about Miya, and I just hope they don't have any brothers or sisters we don't know about. And I'm scared to hear about what they have gone through." And how could I not be? It was awful to consider terms like "sexual abuse" or "physical abuse." The memory of every Lifetime TV movie I'd ever watched reeled in my mind, delivering frightening images that the word "orphan" conjured up.

"Yeah, I worry about their family too. What if they show up in court and protest?"

That had been on my mind too. The agency had always added this caveat to every conversation: If anyone in Russia stepped up to care for Andrei and Svetlana, the kids couldn't be adopted by us. "That would be terrible. For everyone."

We had a little time after breakfast to explore the square outside of the hotel. Walking out, it looked as if we'd landed on the edge of a shopping center and a farmer's market. To one side were fruit and vegetable stands set up under a huge canopy, all staffed by people who could be relatives of the folks we drove by on the side of the road yesterday. Farmers. Behind the farmers, a labyrinth of booths stretched as far as my eye could see. The closer ones held bins and tables stacked with shoes, T-shirts, purses, DVDs, and loads of other clothing and household items. It was like a monstrous junk sale in the middle of town.

Doug and I found a farm stand where we could purchase flowers. We were advised that whenever we met someone of import, we must present a gift. Then we made it back to our hotel to wait for our translator and our trip to the State Guardian.

"Douglas and Elizabeth?" inquired a young woman while we stood there, me clutching the flowers. When Doug nodded, she continued politely, "Good morning. I am Natasha, your translator."

If there were a word that meant "gorgeous, striking, abso-fucking-lutely stunning" in the dictionary, Natasha's picture would be right next to it. She was medium height but a slender slip of a thing, with a long waterfall of dark blonde hair that hung straight down her back. Her face looked so perfect, it must have been manufactured somewhere—porcelain skin, wide blue eyes, and high cheekbones. Her clothing was stylish but not past the point of modesty that so many women I saw in the past few days exceeded. Her shoes, though, I noted with an internal sigh, were still high heels.

Natasha checked her watch. "Come. We must go now. The Guardian's office has opened, special for you. It's Sunday."

The State Guardian's office reminded me of the early days at Girls on the Run, when all of the furniture was donated and I had to get creative, piling files and supplies in corners. Doug, Natasha, and I crowded into the cozy space, perched around the desk of Darya, the caseworker. She located her papers in one of the many stacks and began walking us through Andrei and Svetlana's situation, answering the question, "What happened to them?"

In adoption circles, an adoptee's story is their own; it doesn't belong to their adoptive parents. What I can say, in the broadest of strokes, is that what we learned from Darya that day was that Andrei and Svetlana had a family, but the parents who were supposed to champion them were not able to meet their needs.

What we learned broke my heart, but the information was also a relief. My worst fears, Doug's worst fears, weren't realized. In the end, the meeting only strengthened our resolve. These kids had been failed, time and again. They needed a family. Doug and I left the office sure of one thing: We did not want to disappoint them as they'd been disappointed in the past.

The drive from the Guardian's office to the orphanage was less than fifteen minutes, but with my anticipation bubbling, it felt like an hour. When Natasha pulled over to the side of the road, she parked across from a building identical to the orphanage we saw yesterday. The structure consisted of ecru-colored stucco, four square stories, and an entrance under a small portico. Kids played out front on a green lawn, most of them shirtless boys with bare feet. We walked by a swing set where two older boys, maybe sixteen or seventeen, rested on the seats. They were not swinging but smoking cigarettes, their sullen eyes trailing us. I felt accused and guilty. *How many more kids are like this? If we weren't adopting him, would that be Andrei in a few years? Oh my God.*

Natasha escorted us past the boys and inside to a large, high-ceilinged room. She gestured to a couch that was newer than the one in our hotel. "Sit down. I will go find Elena."

Elena was the director of the Detsky Dom Tri, Children's Home Three. As Doug and I waited, we watched a few workmen painting one of the walls a pale blue color. A huge area rug was rolled up and shoved to the side. Silence filled the air, the only sound the tapping of my foot, which reflected my eagerness to lay eyes on and hug the kids. Doug expressed his anticipation by squeezing my hand in rhythm with my dancing foot.

Natasha came into view. "Elena isn't here, but another caregiver will go get Andrei and Svetlana. August is vacation time, so she will be back tomorrow." She followed our eyes to the painting in progress. "They are redecorating here. It's not so bad."

In the quiet, I heard the *tip-tip* of footsteps that picked up speed as they approached. My stomach jumped, my throat tightened, and I turned to see Svetlana emerge from a hallway.

"Mama!" she screamed and launched herself at me. Suddenly she was on my lap, petting my face and pulling it close enough to kiss me, over and over, saying, "I love you!" again and again.

Overwhelming, pure joy lifted my heart. How could I not love this precious little girl clinging to me? "Svetlana!" I breathed into her hair. "I love you too, honey!"

Andrei entered from the other side, and a similar scene played out, man-style, with Doug. There was far less effusive touching, but Andrei wouldn't release his iron grip on Doug's hand. Andrei leaned against Doug like a palm tree in a tropical storm. He wanted full body contact and couldn't stop smiling. "Papa! Papa," Andrei said, pulling on Doug's arm.

Natasha began translating. "He would like to show you where he sleeps. He has something for you." There was much back-and-forth between Natasha and the kids. "Svetlana would like that too. She has something too." How Natasha simultaneously listened to the kids' chatter, understood, and spoke it back to us in English floored me.

The kids dragged us by the hands upstairs and through hallways to show off their home. Natasha was right; the orphanage wasn't so bad. It was clean and organized with a huge staircase rising through the middle, separating the boys' and girls' wings, with groups according to gender and age on each floor. Most of the rooms were devoted to sleeping, with single beds (more like cots, really) lining the walls, ten or twelve to a room. Chore charts hung in the hallways with check marks and blank spaces. Towels draped neatly on hooks across the bathroom, like a series of flags all in a row, with no wind to raise them. *Not bad, but not ideal, either*, I thought as I took in the thin mattresses and beach towels used as blankets on the cots. Mint-green-striped wallpaper wrapped the room, and the ever-present brown carpeting covered the floors. Against one wall a small bookshelf leaned, holding a motley assortment of books and toys. A stuffed animal bled its filling there, overly loved by a lonely child, or just forgotten perhaps.

Andrei and Svetlana presented each of us with a homemade card. Natasha told us how rare that was; usually the kids were the ones who expected gifts in these circumstances. She said, "They must have had to trade something to get the paper and crafts."

I recognized the paper from one of the care packages I had sent to the kids during the long months when I compiled our dossier. My card had an elaborate drawing of a rose and a poem written in Russian inside. "A love poem," Natasha told me, which cracked my heart wide open.

On Doug's card was a picture of him on our porch at home, ready to walk Lulu and Roscoe and holding their leashes. This was from a care package too. As we'd waited for paperwork, I'd bought an assortment of craft supplies on a monthly basis, bundled them up with a note I wrote using Google Translate, and mailed them to the agency to be carried overseas by the adoptive parents who traveled before us. This was proof that the kids had received their packages, and I was relieved to know that they knew we were thinking about them during the time we'd been separated.

Our quartet plopped down on the rough carpet, exchanging gifts, hugging and touching each other with abandon as Natasha translated, until it was time to go.

"Tomorrow is court," we told the kids through Natasha. "We will see you after that to celebrate."

CHAPTER 42

OUR DAY IN COURT

The courthouse where we presented our case was a squat white building contained by a wrought-iron fence holding its green lawn hostage. Trees in full foliage fluttered at us as we walked through the gates, down the sidewalk, and into the building. Natasha accompanied us.

"Are you ready?" she asked.

"He's going first. I'll be second," I said, referring to the presentation each of us must make in court. We'd been prepared by Natasha and the State Guardian on the process as well as specific statements each of us must make.

When I was packing for the trip, what to wear to court plagued me. The agency suggested a dress, but the only dresses I owned were made for galas and fundraisers. Too fancy, I'd deemed. I had settled on a suit, a gray mid-length skirt and fitted jacket, accompanied by a light green blouse. My desire to look humble, nice, and trustworthy had somehow also translated into itchy pantyhose and modest, by Russian standards, pumps. Doug brought a charcoal suit with a blue shirt and tie, which brought out the azure in his eyes.

As we stepped inside the building, Natasha began translating with the guards who appeared to be barely post-adolescent. The gravity of their role, however, was made evident by the guns strapped to the belts of their uniforms. Natasha talked us through a metal detector, followed by the kind of rotating belt you'd see at an airport, but smaller.

Once past security, she led us down an institutional hallway into the courtroom, which was set up in a square, with the judge's bench positioned at the head. The courtroom had dusty green carpeting and shiny, dark wood trim, which gave it an aura of tired opulence, contrary to the odor of cleaning agents lingering in the air alongside the faintest hint of perspiration. On the sides to the right and opposite the judge's walnut-colored platform sat long wooden tables and chairs. There was no gallery here for citizens to view the proceedings. Instead, on the left side of the room sat a jail cell, complete with iron bars and a heavy lock barring the entry of anyone not a prisoner. I imagined the floating ghosts of inmates past, waiting for trial and punishment. Exoneration was difficult to visualize. Thankfully, we weren't required to sit in there, and Natasha took us to one of the tables opposite the judge.

"We sit here." She pointed. "Darya, from the Guardian's Office, and Elena, from the orphanage, will sit there." At this she gestured to the table next to us. "And the prosecutor sits there." She pointed at the table to the right of the judge.

We were alone in the room, and I felt dizzy with trepidation, my hands trembling. I looked up at the bench, bookended by two large windows on either side. The sun streamed through gauzy curtains, and the green leaves of outside trees waved at me. The hint of nature calmed me—that, and the fact that Doug would speak first.

"Where do we go when we present?" I asked, noticing that there was no witness stand.

"You stand at this table. You can have your papers in front of you this way."

Both Doug and I pulled out notebooks and put them squarely in front of us. I'd also brought a copy of our home study, the basis of every document the Russians would be reviewing. Everything tied back to these twenty-three pages, and we had reread them dozens of times in order to keep our story straight.

Sticking to the truth according to the home study wasn't easy, since it had initially been prepared in April of 2011 and our court date was August of 2012. Although major facts such as our address had remained the same, our income had changed, thanks to Doug's bonus; the country of adoption had changed, from Ukraine to Russia; and small details, like my weight for instance, had changed. I took comfort in the fact that other families who'd been through this reported that we wouldn't be interrogated on tiny points like this, and also that the whole experience should take between four to six hours. *No big deal. It's all here, and we'll be done this afternoon,* I told myself.

Just as we settled into our chairs, the courtroom door opened. Two women peeked in, Darya and a woman we didn't know. Natasha jumped up to make introductions. "Doug and Betsy, this is Elena, the director of the Children's Home Three. She will be supporting your case today."

Elena was a short, matronly woman who firmly shook our hands. Through Natasha, she said, "I am so happy to meet you. Andrei and Svetlana told me all about their visit with you. They are very excited that you have come for them, and I am glad they are going to America. They will have so many opportunities there."

Elena's support wasn't a foregone conclusion, so her words meant a lot. They signaled that she loved the kids enough to let them go.

After we greeted Darya, Andrei and Svetlana walked through the courtroom door. I turned to Natasha and asked, "They aren't going to be here for the whole proceeding, are they?"

"No. Andrei will wait in the hall with a caregiver until it is his turn to speak."

Because Andrei was over ten, Russian procedures dictated that he got a say in his future. Andrei had to choose us too. Elena and Natasha had prepared Andrei, and he looked ready in his pinstriped gray suit complete with a matching vest, a white shirt, and a black bow tie. They were all a little too big for him, as were the black dress shoes he clomped into the room wearing. The effect highlighted what a little boy he was, small for his eleven years, and so skinny, his thighs were the size of my forearms. My heart hurt for the journey he had taken to be here. Despite the poor fit and thin fabric, it was clear he was proud of his attire, and Doug and I fussed over him, telling him how handsome he looked.

Cupping Svetlana's head with my hand, I felt a swell of mamabear protectiveness. *Svetlana shouldn't be here, much less need to testify!*

Natasha read my mind, saying, "She wanted to come and say hello, that she can't wait to see you later. She is going now."

While we'd been chatting, the prosecutor had entered the room. He sat at the table across from the jail cell. He appeared benign, a middle-aged, balding man in a nondescript shirt and tie. He didn't acknowledge us with even a glance.

Moments later, the judge swept into the room. Her red hair was pinned up in a neat bun, a flash of fire above her long black robe. We all stood.

As soon as the judge spoke, Natasha began translating quietly to me and Doug. A few procedural questions got covered quickly: who was in the courtroom, who was up for adoption, and who wanted to be new parents. At Natasha's prompting, Doug and I answered yes or no.

Then Darya gave her testimony, followed by Elena. Both recommended that the children be placed with us, and neither the judge nor the prosecutor had any follow-up questions for the women.

Once the proceedings started, I noticed a strange cadence to the courtroom, quiet while everyone waited for translation. Russian to English. Pause. English to Russian. Pause. During the silent breaks I searched faces for signs of emotion, hoping to elicit some positive indication, yet the Russians remained curiously blank. I wondered, *Is this just business to them, or do they even care about the kids?*

A caregiver escorted Andrei into the courtroom. He looked so young, walking in his too-big shoes, his overly large pants dragging. My heart squeezed again. Doug's expression told me that Doug also wished Andrei could avoid testifying, but our boy was ordered to sit next to Elena while he spoke. The prosecutor investigated, while Natasha translated. The questions the prosecutor asked were cruel. He grilled Andrei about leaving his Russian family and friends, underscoring that Andrei would *never* see anybody again if he was adopted. Andrei kept his answers to one syllable—either dah or nyet—and he never wavered one bit.

After the prosecutor gestured that he was finished, Andrei offered us a tight smile as he left the room. I wanted to cheer out loud but settled for a quick wink and nod. Doug murmured approvingly, "A man of few words. I like it."

When Doug's moment arrived, he rose and began to speak, glancing only occasionally at his notes, and pausing so that Natasha could convert and convey his words in Russian. Listening to the English version, a swell of pride flooded my heart. In emotional situations, I got nervy and my voice shook, but Doug communicated our strengths confidently while tempering his remarks with the touch of humility the setting required.

He spoke of our wish for children, our wonder at Andrei and Svetlana, and the "Wow!" moment when they said yes to us.

At the end of his speech, he made the following required, and rehearsed, statement:

"Your Honor, we ask you to register us as the children's parents; to change their last name to Armstrong, and to change Andrei's name to Andrei E_____, and Svetlana's to Svetlana E____. We ask you to change their birthplace to B_____. We do not intend to change their birth dates. Thank you, Your Honor."

We didn't understand the request to keep their birthdays the same, but it was part of the script, and Doug followed it perfectly. The prosecutor had questions for Doug. He inquired about Chicago's crime rate, about our dogs and whether we were willing to get rid of them if they ever hurt the kids, about Russian adoptions that had gone awry. Although it had been several years since an American woman put her adopted child on a plane back to Russia with only a note pinned to his shirt, the Russians hadn't forgotten and wanted to ensure it would never happen again. We had been warned about the last question. Doug responded, "We have heard of these cases and would never, ever, resort to that. We intend to care for the children for the rest of our lives. We also have friends and family, along with social workers and others at the agency, to whom we will turn to if we have any problems."

Doug's answers seemed to satisfy the prosecutor, who motioned to him to sit. The whole business about there being a *prosecutor*, who appeared to be trying to find reasons to refuse our adoption, suddenly gave me pause. If I'd been in a US court, I would never have been without a lawyer. I wondered, *Should I be worried?*

The judge called my name. I knew I was expected to say, "I agree with everything my husband says." Under other circumstances, this wasn't something I'd readily admit, but there I said it plainly and without hesitation or irony. Like Doug, I spoke about my experience with Andrei and Svetlana, our bond, and how excited I was at the prospect of giving them a home, a family, and all the opportunities they deserved. I tried to cover everything on the list in front of me and ended, as required, with a verbatim recital of Doug's request.

The audience of two gave me no feedback as to how they received my plea, which was nerve-wracking. I remembered the first time I stood up in front of a crowd at a fundraiser, staring out at a sea of vacant faces. It was exactly the moment I vowed to always be the person in the audience who smiled back, or at least nodded with encouragement at the speaker. The Russian poker faces bored into me as Natasha finished translating, then gestured for me to sit. Doug gave my hand a quick squeeze.

I felt a sense of triumph. Two or three years ago, I never would have imagined this scenario. Doug. Me. Court. Russia. Kids!

We are entering the homestretch! I thought. All I had to do was answer whatever remaining questions they had, and we were home free.

I wasn't prepared for what came next.

The judge paged through the home study, taking her time as if it were the first time she read it. She stopped on a page and underlined the words with her fingertip. She found something. My heart accelerated.

Q: This report says you have scoliosis?
A: Yes. I do.
Q: How does this affect you?
A: It is a curve in my spine, but generally, it doesn't affect me very much. I am very active—a marathon runner. If I do too much, and there are times when it hurts, I take medication.
Q: Yes, it says here you take Tramadol. What is that?

A: It is a medication prescribed by my doctor to help with pain if my back hurts.

My heart jackhammered in my chest.

Q: I've never heard of Tramadol. What is it for?
A: It is a pain medication. Prescribed by my doctor.

I realized I was repeating myself, but I couldn't help it. The truth, which I couldn't say right there, was that I didn't even take Tramadol anymore. This was one of the "small mistakes" in the home study. Back in April 2011, my doctor had given me the medication when my pain flared. She chose Tramadol specifically because it was purported to be nonaddictive and could be taken long-term. My acute pain subsided, and I stopped taking it. But I never changed the home study.

My mind flashed back to our X-rays, collecting dust in that closet in Moscow. Suddenly, I regretted leaving them behind. I wished I could have whipped them out, *Perry Mason*–style, to show as proof of my condition.

The judge and the prosecutor huddled together at the bench, talking quietly. Elena, Darya, Natasha, and Doug stared at me, wide-eyed and speechless. I whispered to Natasha, "It's like strong aspirin. Is it a problem?"

Before she could answer me, the judge spoke.

Natasha translated, "Elizabeth states that she takes the drug Tramadol for scoliosis. I am unfamiliar with this medical condition and medication and need to call a doctor to testify. The outcome of the adoption cannot be decided without this information. The case is continued and will reconvene tomorrow."

Shit, I thought. *Oh shit.*

Our group froze, stunned, while the judge and prosecutor exited the room. Natasha, Darya, and Elena burst into whispers of Russian as soon as the officials left, but Natasha didn't translate. Her lack of communication underscored the rarity of our situation. Doug and I gaped at each other in shock, completely taken aback at the turn of events. What just happened? Would the adoption still go through? What now?

CHAPTER 43

COURT, DAY TWO

The next morning, we returned to the courthouse.

Same clothes. Same guards. Same people, same building—just a different courtroom.

When we'd left court the prior day, Natasha called her boss, Kseniya. Kseniya masterminded the Russian side of adoptions for the agency. She knew the orphanages, set up the trips, hired the translators and drivers, and kept profiles on the judges. Kseniya tried to console Doug and me by letting us know the judge was new. She didn't want to make any mistakes, they told us. It was just a formality, for show, they insisted.

But sitting in court, it didn't feel like a formality. Both the judge and the prosecutor peppered me with questions about Tramadol and scoliosis. How many times a day did I take the medication? How long had I had scoliosis? Why didn't I have an operation to fix it instead of taking drugs?

Every question they asked seemed to scream, "You are damaged!"

Every answer I gave pleaded, "Not that badly!"

Their cross-examination shrieked, "You are unfit!"

My testimony begged, "I am not. Please, I'm fine."

Finally, the doctor stepped up to the stand. She proceeded to explain that scoliosis was the curvature of the spine. *Hadn't I said that already?* She never prescribed drugs for scoliosis, since drugs couldn't cure scoliosis. *I never said the drug was for scoliosis, or to cure it! The drug was for pain.* Tramadol was a very strong painkiller. *No, it wasn't!* She gave Tramadol to cancer patients. *Poor Russian cancer patients! That was all they got? Where was the morphine?!* It would *never* be her protocol to prescribe Tramadol for scoliosis.

The prosecutor looked smug, certain he was on the verge of catching a criminal. He told the judge he needed to be sure I didn't have a condition that would forbid me from adopting a Russian child. The prosecutor demanded I undergo medical exams—in Birobidzhan.

As Natasha translated these words, I fell into a state of shock because all I could feel was Doug droop next to me. I heard nothing, only saw Elena and Darya shaking their heads.

Tears fell as I considered my journey to this moment: my mom's death, my running, my back, my career, my legacy. I was in that courtroom because of my mother, who had abandoned me by dying, and to become a mother to abandoned children. I was there because I didn't die and I couldn't run. Everything was mixed up and coming apart. Words failed me. I shook my head.

The judge pronounced, "To determine if she is healthy and can adopt, Elizabeth must undergo full medical exams in Birobidzhan. The case is continued."

CHAPTER 44

REVELATION

For twenty-four hours, between the second court date and the medical exam, I felt suspended and trapped. Doug and I had come to Russia on a mission, the entirety of which had been called into question, and there was nothing to do but wait to see what truth would ultimately be revealed.

After day two in court, we stopped visiting Andrei and Svetlana. We couldn't bear the thought of maintaining a facade, of pretending we would be their parents when we couldn't control the outcome.

Right after we left court, Natasha pleaded with us not to give up. To further convince us, she brokered a meeting with her boss, Kseniya, later that day. We met her, clandestinely, in the back seat of Kseniya's un-air-conditioned car. With sweat from the humid August day rolling down her temple, she told us in her broken English, "I don't lose no adoption case. You get your children!" I could barely hear her, the buzzing feeling in my head was so loud.

Over these days, Doug and I would learn about the compassion of our companions on this journey—other Americans at our hotel. One couple was adopting a son. They had already been to court and endured the requisite thirty-day waiting period, and now they were back to bring their boy home for good.

Another couple was hoping to adopt a little girl. This was their first meeting because, due to a failing heart, she had been too sick to travel for a visit to America through the Bridge of Hope program. This couple had paid for her operation before they'd even met her, and now they were here to begin the adoption process. As our legal saga unfolded, these two couples were steadfast in their belief that our story would have a happy ending.

The head of our agency, sixteen hours behind us back home, called at 11:00 p.m. Russian time to tell me they were pulling strings with doctors, to stay strong, although there was truly nothing wrong with me. Doug and I discussed giving up, turning tail, and disappearing. We despaired that the Russians were just toying with us, nearly convinced that "dah" would never be stamped upon our file. Everyone kept telling us everything would be okay, but weren't those just platitudes?

Over these days, I also learned, yet again, how much I could count on Doug. During one of the darkest nights of my life, he hugged me tightly, more securely than he ever had, holding me steady in that foreign bed. Lying there, unable to sleep, I remembered my fear that Doug wouldn't be there for me. Yet here he was.

During these two days, I also learned the thing I needed most to know about myself. What I discovered in the darkness of that black night was that I would do anything for Andrei and Svetlana. I found that my boat of ambivalence had tipped over, and I was swirling in the vortex of Russian bureaucracy, almost being pulled under. I learned I would fight. Hard. I would swim to the shore where, hopefully, a family awaited me: Doug, Andrei, and Svetlana.

The time between our two court dates at last revealed something: I wanted children. I wanted Andrei and Svetlana.

CHAPTER 45

MEDICALS, BIRO-STYLE

Twenty hours after the judge uttered the words "full medical exam," I got dressed for my day of medicals in Biro. The business suit hung, abandoned, in the closet, replaced by a T-shirt and khakis. My mind had busied itself, conjuring up one creepy horror house scenario after another. I envisioned rusty needles, radiation-blasting X-ray machines, and barely licensed, sadistic doctors who enjoyed toying with vulnerable American women. What they might do to me and what they might discover terrified me plenty, but even worse was the idea of being forced to abandon Andrei and Svetlana. All because of the angle of my spine and some pills? It was incomprehensible.

When Natasha arrived to our hotel lobby, she wore a grim expression, her beauty failing her for once, as she explained I would see eight different doctors that day. I knew these doctors weren't going to examine me in the lite sense, as they did in Moscow. These doctors were the enemy. They'd been ordered to be thorough. I mustered up the courage to ask, "Natasha, what exactly will they do? What are they looking for?"

"They will give you a full blood test, testing for diseases of concern. Cancer, anemia, poor diet—"

"Wait a second," I interrupted. "I still have my lab results from the Moscow medicals. Can I bring them? Will they take them?"

For a second, I hoped maybe the vampires wouldn't need any more of my blood and would spare me the stick of any needles of questionable sanitation.

"Yes, of course." She nodded stiffly. "But they will insist on the remaining tests."

"What about X-rays?" I remembered, longed for, those flimsy black-and-white slides gathering dust in the Moscow medical closet. Why had I left the X-rays behind?

"They don't care about the X-ray," Natasha answered. "They will do ultrasound tests. And a urine test for drugs. Marijuana. Alcohol. Street drugs."

I felt momentarily uplifted, since I didn't smoke pot or imbibe anything illegal. My mind counted backward to my last painkiller, my final Valium. I wished I could take one now, but I couldn't, wouldn't. A fresh wave of guilt broke over me because I had taken medication. Prescription medication, yes, but would that make a difference to the Russians?

As I hurried back to the room to unbury the lab results from my suitcase, the words "cancer," "pain," "drug," and "addict" rode a merry-go-round in my head. I remembered a woman I'd met at one of the adoption information sessions Doug and I attended who curved toward us, unbidden, and whispered, "If you have *ever* had cancer, even if it's cured, you can *never* adopt from Russia." Her mouth twisted with outrage, and she didn't need to say more about what she'd been put through. But I didn't have cancer. At least, I didn't think so.

I also reflected on a question I had asked Chris from the agency at some point when we'd been paper gathering and chasing signatures. "Have you ever heard of anyone trying to adopt from Russia who was denied?" I'd wondered.

"Yes," was his surprising answer. "There was a man who admitted in his home study that he had been an alcoholic. Even though he'd been sober for twenty years and his doctor specifically said he was fine, the Russians prohibited him from adopting."

There was a possibility, a probability even, that I could be labeled a drug addict. If I tested positive. Which was possible. Now that I was in the thick of this, I considered the worst-case scenario, what I'd been afraid of all along—that I was somehow defective and unable to be a mother. My breath caught in my throat imagining Andrei and Svetlana sitting on the couch at the orphanage, waiting for us, wondering why we never returned. The thought was unbearable. My hands quivered when I handed the lab papers to Natasha back in the lobby. I clasped them in front of me to steady them and imagined anyone looking at me would have thought I was praying.

Natasha read the lab report. "Good," she said. "They will start with the urine and blood tests. We wait for the results before continuing."

"And then what?" I asked.

"I will take those tests to the hospital. We have a document that each doctor must stamp and sign for the judge. Then I will come back and wait with you for the rest of the doctors."

She didn't elaborate, and I wondered if, behind her cool Russian exterior, she judged me. Did she believe me?

Entering the medical center was like shutting out the sun. It was cool inside but damp, and the humidity followed us in like tendrils of fog. The center could have been out of an old black-and-white movie: spare, sharp, angled. Beige tile floor, gray walls, and three gunmetal chairs pushed together to watch outside the bare windows. Natasha moved straight toward a desk, where an unsmiling battle-ax of a woman guarded the brown door that led to the beyond.

A verbal volley of Russian ensued, and Natasha turned to us, frowning. "Come," she said, and we followed her away from the desk and back toward the entrance, to a box that contained paper brown booties to secure over our shoes.

"Put these on?" I asked.

"Yes. Protocol," Natasha replied.

Who did this protect? Me? Them? I tamped down a nervous giggle that threatened to escape and put on the shoe covers. Doug followed. The booties barely covered Natasha's high heels, but she remained unfazed, now breezing past the desk and opening the door. The old lady, seemingly satisfied now that we were properly attired, didn't even look as we walked by.

Outside the exam room, Doug and I sank into a bench to wait for Natasha, who was checking in with the doctors. "I'm scared," I said and grabbed for his hand. We were alone, except for the spooky sound of unseen murmuring voices and shuffling footsteps.

"At least they're doing the urine and blood first," he said, thinking out loud. "If this goes south, we can just get out of here. There's still time to leave for Paris later today." His remark was a bitter reminder that everything was upside down. The trip to Paris had been planned as a babymoon reward, a four-day stopover on our way back to Chicago, since we had to endure the thirty-day waiting period between court approval and coming back to bring the children home for good. We had hoped to celebrate in Paris, after the Russian court approved the adoption. *If* they approved the adoption. "Goddamn it. The kids . . ." His voice trailed off.

I knew what he was thinking. What if this didn't happen? Would we leave without explaining anything to the children? And if we could tell them, what would we say? I was unfit? Their court system failed them? My thoughts were interrupted when Doug said, "I'm going outside to make a few calls to the airline and see what our options are."

"No! Don't go until Natasha comes back." I didn't want to be alone there, in that echoey, odd place with my sad imaginings. We sat in a deserted hallway lined with closed doors in both directions.

Just then, Natasha cracked the door and peeked her head out. "Come in, Betsy. They are going to do the blood test."

Natasha ushered me to a stool at a small gray Formica counter. A lab-coated woman appeared. She was silent, a robot who snatched my hand and roughly wiped my index finger with an alcohol swab.

In my short-sleeved Gap T-shirt, gooseflesh rose on my bare arms, and I wished I could reclaim my hand. I was scared of the needle. I didn't want to risk offending anyone, but Biro was remote and under-resourced, and the hygiene there questionable. But before I could formulate a question, the nurse pushed a device against my finger, and "Oh!" It stung. Expressionless, the nurse siphoned blood from my fingertip onto a series of glass slides.

Natasha handed me a glass beaker. "For your urinalysis. You have to go, right?"

Nodding, I said, "Where is the bathroom?" I followed the direction of Natasha's finger and returned quickly, only to sit again and wait on the bench.

One hour in, Natasha decided to make a few calls and instructed me to sit tight with Doug, who glanced in both directions to ensure privacy and whispered, "How are you?"

"I've never been more nervous in my life," I said. Doug was well aware of the little orange-brown bottles I'd been dipping into. His conversation with the airlines informed him we could still fly out tonight. If we wanted to. Or had to. There were flights every day, but changing the tickets cost $2500. "Thanks, Russian judge and prosecutor." I rolled my eyes.

We waited some more. A few others had joined us. Strangers paraded by, entering and exiting the various doors. An old lady limped by, her prosthetic leg squeaking with each step; a young woman grasped the hand of a crying toddler, her belly almost bursting with another pregnancy; and a shrunken, elderly man muttered to himself. It was a bizarre swirl of foreign sights, sounds, and people roiling around me—a kaleidoscope of weird.

Ramping up my anxiety was the complete lack of privacy. Everyone wandered in and out of rooms seemingly at will and without knocking. Sometimes they were welcomed in; sometimes they were rebuffed and sent back to the benches. I wondered when it would be my turn to walk through a door, simultaneously hoping and dreading what would unfold when I did.

Natasha returned with an air of hustle-bustle. "Your blood is good," she said. "No anemia. No evidence of poor diet. You also don't have TB or any venereal disease. Now I'll go see about your urinalysis."

Doug and I stayed on the bench. Three and a half hours had passed since we arrived and, with a three-hour car ride to the Khabarovsk airport, it looked as if we would likely miss our flight. Emerging from a door, Natasha came out shaking her head. *Oh no . . . shit.* I was entirely sure I failed when she said, "They don't have the results, but come with me. The neurologist is ready for you. We can get his stamp while they finish."

The neurologist was a blur. Echoes of the only doctor in Moscow who truly examined me reverberated through my mind, and then it was over, the doctor taking a stamp out of his coat pocket, affixing the seal and signing over it. The words "Tramadol" and "scoliosis" didn't even come up.

Back on our bench, Natasha had no time to sit before a nurse summoned her. They huddled, forming a wall with their backs, but I observed the nurse pointing as she read to Natasha from a piece of paper. Natasha gave a single definitive nod to the nurse, took the paper, and turned toward us.

"Your urinalysis is good," she proclaimed. I couldn't stop my body from drooping with utter relief. Natasha went on, "All the doctors are at lunch. I'll drop you two at a restaurant so you can eat. Do you like Chinese?"

Chinese food sounded so banal, so normal. It belonged in my real life back in Chicago. Something we'd order on a Monday night when I didn't want to cook instead of a meal I'd consume on the most frightening day of my life. I hadn't eaten since before court, the day before. My stomach was pulled so taunt with nerves that I couldn't imagine forcing a bite down. Even with the drug test over, no appetite remained with all the doctors still looming over me. I looked at Doug, who was nodding, and communicated with a shrug my willingness to go along.

The lunch was a buffet with various bowls of unidentifiable meat in similar brown gravies along with a huge pot of white rice. I sipped water while Doug poked at the mystery stew on his plate. Our conversation was limited to "Thank God the drug test was negative" and "What happens next?" After paying the bill, Doug decided to change our plane tickets. We would pay an extra $2500 to stay, to be put under more microscopes, to stand before our accusers, to know that we left *nothing* undone in our quest to lead Andrei and Svetlana home.

Back at the medical center, Natasha guided me into the first examination room. Doug accompanied us and the three of us stood, penitent with our heads bowed, crowded around a doctor. He sat, his round belly protruding from his white lab coat to rest like an overstuffed marshmallow on the cocoa of his chocolate-brown pants. The doctor was bothered by us, huffing and shaking his head. Through Natasha, I was given a stern lecture about scoliosis and Tramadol, a scolding that assured me the pills would never cure my crookedness. I kept my head down, absorbing the blows of his words until he finally decided to bestow his blessed stamp and signature upon our paper. He never asked about my back. He never even looked at my back. A fleeting and absurd thought occurred to me. *Maybe they thought I'd made it all up.*

The three of us went on to the next office, a psychiatrist. He was a small, ferret-like man who snapped at Natasha until she turned to Doug and explained, "He is telling you to go. He wants to speak with Elizabeth alone."

Doug's eyes telegraphed his reluctance to leave me as he departed. Once he exited, I absorbed the chamber where I stood. The doctor sat at a plain small desk. Next to the desk was an ordinary waiting room–type chair, to which Natasha was directed. I looked past the doctor to see a proper queen-size bed covered with a raggedy striped quilt that didn't look clean. A large bed like that in a psychiatrist's office struck me as creepy and wrong. I turned, looking for someplace I was willing to sit, and I saw the Chair.

It was a Frankenstein chair, really, with leather belts and metal buckles hanging from the arms and circling the front legs, ready to bite into my limbs. Lamps, wires, and other devices fanned out from the tall straight back in a halo of medieval torture instruments reminiscent of a grim peacock's tail. I shuddered, but still it was preferable to the bed.

I balanced on the edge, crossing my legs and arms while leaning forward so none of the clamps or electrodes could secretly capture me. I remained in this perched position for nearly twenty minutes while the Russian doctor educated me on the dangers of Tramadol.

Natasha dutifully translated his diatribe while I perched and nodded my head. "Tramadol is a very serious drug!" he said. "Your US doctor must be an idiot," she detailed, and I wondered which of the words he'd uttered meant idiot. "I could cure your scoliosis, if you let me. Russian medicine is very superior in this area."

I didn't want to show the fear that had seeped into my very being. If this man really *could* read minds, I was in trouble.

Luckily, he released me to join Doug back on the benches, which were beginning to feel like home base. Doug looked relieved to see me. "What happened in there?"

"I'll tell you later. All that matters is we got the stamp."

Doug, who needed to work the phone with the airline, went outside for better reception, leaving Natasha and me to talk. "You are not going to like the next doctors, Betsy," she confided.

"What do you mean?"

"You have to see an oncologist, but before that, you will need two ultrasounds."

"Ultrasounds? Of what?"

"Your thyroid. And breasts."

"Oh." My mind screeched to a halt. A *breast* exam? It was finally seeping in that this whole experience had nothing to do with scoliosis. It was about cancer and screening me to weed us out as potential candidates to adopt Russian children. I flashed upon an image of my mom, tears filling my eyes. I couldn't have cancer. Not now. I just couldn't.

"The ultrasound isn't so bad. The machine touches you, but the nurse won't." Natasha's voice brought me back. "And I'll do what I can to make sure it is a woman who performs the ultrasound."

I didn't know of anyone who eagerly awaited their next mammogram, even in America. But in Russia? And if she couldn't get a woman? That opened a Pandora's box in my mind that contained my worst fears—ovarian cancer, colon cancer, any cancer inside of me in places I didn't want probed by nefarious strangers. "Natasha, they aren't going to make me go see a gynecologist, are they?"

"No!" Her retort was so fast it was reassuring. "Ultrasound and then oncologist."

"What is the oncologist going to do?"

"He will read the results. And . . ." She sighed. "You must do this. It's part of the exam. I'm sorry."

I could tell she was. Then another horrible thought occurred to me. "You will come with me, right? I don't want to be left alone."

"I will not leave you," Natasha promised. "It is my job to translate, and they must allow me there. You will *not* be alone," she emphasized.

"Thank you." She'd been steadfast, and I was grateful for her commitment not only to our case, but to me personally.

While we waited, Natasha shared with me how many adoptions she'd facilitated (too many to count), what the Russians really thought of the Americans coming to Russia to adopt (most were not in favor), what Natasha really thought of Putin (I won't tell), and how many languages she spoke (eight!). We even laughed when she tried to teach me some Russian. My attempts to shape my mouth in the proper position—and my failure—made her giggle. I'd never seen her unable to contain herself, but we were both probably a bit punch-drunk seven hours into our day at the medical center.

When it was finally time for my exam, a nurse led Natasha and I through a series of doors into the largest room I had seen in this place. It was startlingly white. White walls, white ceiling, white-sheet-covered exam tables (four of them), and white clunky machines. The lights glared brightly and reflected off the small sink in a corner of the room. The overwhelming lack of color made it feel as if we'd fallen into a vat of bleach, yet something ominous lurked within the sterile surroundings.

The room was empty, except for Natasha, the technician, and me. I was thankful, as I'd figured out that the four exam tables offered zero privacy if there were other occupants. Through Natasha, I was instructed to discard my shirt and bra, then to lie topless on the table. Flat and facing up, I was exposed, no paper drape or sheet or blanket to cover me. Natasha stood across the room by the door. The technician—thankfully a woman!—wheeled the unwieldy ultrasound machine over and parked it by my head. I shut my eyes.

The nurse squirted gel all over my chest, all over my boobs. It seeped into my armpits, dripping onto the table below me. As the test went on, I was more conscious of my nakedness than I'd ever been. I was also scared. I tried to read the technician's impassive face as she traced circles all around my right breast, then my left, then my right again, then my left again. What was she doing? Had she found something?

I seized upon a memory of when my mom discovered a tiny lump in her breast. We had endured a week of waiting for the surgeon to remove it and test it before learning it was benign. What if I had the same thing? A tear escaped from one eye and ran down the side of my face into my ear. Why was this taking so long?

As these dark thoughts invaded my brain, Natasha translated that the nurse was done and moving to my thyroid. The technician produced a pillow and shoved it under my shoulders, tipping my head back to display my neck. This also arched my back, uncomfortably elevating my gooey breasts up and into the air. A glob of chilly gel landed on my throat. My breath hitched ever so slightly, a combination of the assault on my throat and the trace of tears trying to escape.

The end finally came when Natasha called out, "It's done. You can wipe off by the sink."

I sat up, and the mass of sludge slid down my torso. I lurched, naked, toward the sink, gunk falling onto my stomach and dropping on the floor. I hung my top half over the tiny sink and cleaned up the best I could. Although I felt slimy, the straps of my bra and soft cotton of my T-shirt were like a warm embrace.

Back to the bench I went, this time alone. Natasha hung back, and Doug must have been outside pacing. There was just one more doctor, an oncologist, to go.

Natasha approached. "Come, the doctor can see you now. He is just about to leave, so we have to get you in fast."

We marched down the hall to a large, cold blue room with windows on two sides. The sun and green trees were visible just outside, so different from the interior of this place that they appeared fake. Directly across from the door, a nurse costumed in a starched white dress and white cap, with heavy white shoes, stared impassively, a relic of an earlier time. The doctor stood by her side, his outline darkened by the light outdoors behind him. Natasha selected a chair next to the nurse, facing away from me and toward a wall.

Natasha instructed me to again remove my top and bra. My stomach twisted. Hadn't I just endured this—and now they wanted me to do it again? I was uneasy both because of the circumstances and the thought, *What if something was wrong with me?*

I saw an exam table tucked into one of the room's corners and approached it reluctantly to peel my clothes off. Although there was a privacy screen, it was off in a corner and clear no one intended to pull it out for me. Again, there was nothing offered to cover myself. I hoisted myself up onto the table off to the side, but was called back to the center of the room.

There I stood in the middle of the ice-blue space, exposed, naked from the waist up, as the doctor approached, stopping right in front of me. The invasion of my personal space felt intentional and intimidating. It required conscious effort to hold my ground, not to turn away or step back. I had to get through this, I reminded myself, so I chose to look him straight in the face as his gaze slid down and up my body. I took in his white-gray hair and steel-colored eyes, his blue lab coat and stethoscope. The doctor said something in Russian, and Natasha translated, "I'm going to feel your breasts now."

First, he reached over to grab both of my hands and placed them on my hips. It was a shocking sensation, and I felt for all the world like a caricature of an angry housewife, only naked on top.

The doctor began. Unlike every breast exam I'd ever had administered in my life, I remained in the standing position, the doctor groping my breasts as he stood in front of me, looking directly into my eyes. I pretended to see through him, imagining I was somewhere, anywhere else but there. The buzzing in my brain that I experienced when Stepdad was on a rampage began, new trauma overlapping the old.

The doctor moved to stand behind me. An eternity seemed to pass as he reached through my propped-up arms, pawed some more, and at one point even pressed himself against the back of me. I stared at the nurse, who observed the spectacle without moving a muscle. She watched, immobile and indifferent, adding to my humiliation. I wanted to cry out to her, for her to come to my defense, but even Natasha, who I'd seemed to befriend that day, couldn't help. She remained facing the wall, resolutely looking away from me as the doctor did what he did.

At last, the doctor was finished. From my collarbones to my rib cage, he had left nothing untouched. He briefly paused, then began massaging my shoulders. I stiffened before he wrapped his hands around my neck as if to strangle me, checking my thyroid. I gazed out the window and willed this exam to be over. He didn't *need* to do this. He *wanted* to do this.

Finally, *finally*, his hands fell, and I heard his shoes walk over to the desk. I didn't want to look at him, tilting my head up toward the ceiling so that the tears welling up in my eyes stayed put. The *scritch-scratch* of the pen and *whump* of the stamp were the accompaniment to my dressing. Natasha and I were mute as we walked out.

When we returned to the bench, Doug was there, thankfully. I felt removed from my body, still in shock, and barely able to speak. Natasha reassured him, "We got all the stamps, Doug. Betsy was very brave."

As I realized we were walking out of the building, I heard the pounding of my heart and felt the rush of my blood coursing through my body, carrying wave after wave of sheer relief. I wanted to weep. I wanted to forget. I wanted Doug to hug me. I wanted Natasha to never speak of this, ever. My day in the medical center was over. I passed.

Later, I was livid about what happened, furious to be put through an ordeal that the doctor clearly relished. Angry that the nurse looked on so unfeelingly, that no one stopped it. That none of us could.

I shed tears privately, glad that Doug hadn't witnessed my humiliation. And although I relayed to him what had happened, it seemed he was relieved that nothing worse had transpired. Through it all, one crystal clear point shone through: I wanted to be a mom. I was sure about the kids. I would do anything for Andrei and Svetlana, and I wanted to take them home.

CHAPTER 46

COURT, DAY THREE

The next day was déjà vu. Same courthouse. Same prosecutor. Darya and Elena. Natasha, Doug, and me. We were back in the second courtroom, the one without a jail cell in it. The prosecutor kept his head down as we waited for the judge. Only Natasha would look at Doug and me, but her nerves showed, her hands alternately fluttering about or twisting her wedding band.

I stared—glared, actually—at the prosecutor's bent head. I was furious inside but unable to show it. While I may have passed their medical tests, I didn't want any more challenges or to give them a chance to think up new ways to inspect me. I needed the prosecutor and judge to believe that Doug and I had been humbled enough.

The judge entered from a door behind the bench and claimed her seat as we all reversed the motion and stood. She dove right in, signaled for us to sit, and asked Natasha to give her the precious paper, showing all the stamps and signatures my body earned us yesterday. Natasha's action and deference toward the judge made me long for a lawyer of our own. It never occurred to me, to anyone, that it might be necessary, that the Russian prosecutor would work so hard to prevent our adoption. Then again, I would never enter an American courtroom without an attorney. Yet another chorus of *What were we thinking?* chanted in my brain.

The judge called the prosecutor up to examine the paper. He lingered over it, checking each signature, each stamp, his finger following the symbols like places on a map. At last, he looked at the judge and shrugged. He wouldn't admit out loud that he'd been wrong.

The air in the room suspended and stretched, the judge's decision floating unseen while I held my breath. It was silent, no translation necessary, though Natasha translated as the judge spoke. "The request to register Douglas and Elizabeth Armstrong as the children's parents; to change their last name to Armstrong, and to change Andrei's name to Andrei E____, and Svetlana's to Svetlana E____; to change their birthplace to B_____; and to keep their birth dates the same is granted."

Natasha's beautiful face broke into a wide smile, and she held out her arms to embrace me. I hugged her before Doug. Darya and Elena were also joyous, bursting from their table to shake our hands and clap our backs. It was more emotion than I had seen displayed during the entire trip.

Our merry group quieted at the approach of the prosecutor, who held out his hand to Doug. I knew Doug didn't want to shake the man's hand, but he did. I did too, though he made me sick. This was all his fault. I wouldn't give him the satisfaction of a smile. He exited quickly.

The judge abashedly appeared in front of us and also reached out. She stared intently at me, searching my eyes. Natasha translated, "Congratulations. I had to be sure, and I hope you understand."

I did not understand, not at all, but I nodded. Later, I told myself she was only doing her job, but in that moment, I couldn't summon any forgiveness.

I turned away from her, returning to my safe circle of happiness, these people who had been with me, on my side: Doug, Natasha, Elena, and Darya. Especially Doug, who would carry me back to see Andrei and Svetlana, finally, one last time before we left.

CHAPTER 47

THIRTY-SIX HOURS
IN PARIS

D oug and I gladly packed our bags. We had a last meal of pizza and salad at Café Felicity, and for once I felt as happy as the restaurant's name. I didn't consider how much disdain our waitress projected, because I didn't care. I recognized my buoyant emotions as the carefree aftermath of a race well run. We did it! Dossier, Moscow, court, kids. This finish line was incredibly sweet. Maybe even more so because the trials I went through, both judicial and medical, had solidified in me an inner knowing: I really wanted kids! This feeling that had eluded me forever was now inside of me.

The realization made it more difficult to say goodbye to Andrei and Svetlana. We had to leave them in Biro for the Russian-imposed thirty-day waiting period. In one month, we would return, and they would be ours, our family, forever after.

Doug managed to salvage thirty-six hours of our Paris trip, and we went for it. The beauty of flying toward home was that the clock rewound. By the time we got to France, we gained almost half a day.

The last time I was in Paris with Doug, the city and I didn't impress each other. The people were rude. Everyone smoked. It was dreary November, with cold rain misting constantly, and jet lag plagued me the entire trip.

But this time was different. The French people's classic reserve was downright friendly compared to the Russians. I was surprised to discover no-smoking sections in cafés. Despite the one-hundred-degree heat wave that swept across Europe, we managed a delectable croissant breakfast and a peaceful boat ride down the Seine, and even observed some kind of French spy movie being filmed next to the river. We also strolled past the Arc de Triomphe and through the Centre Pompidou Museum, where I lingered over the art, followed by steak *pommes frites* and a heavenly bed.

Then we were waiting to board our first-class flight from Paris to Chicago. After Aeroflot, first class felt scrumptious, like a buffet of decadent desserts after weeks of starvation. At the last minute, I decided to add to my shoe collection, beckoned by a pair of blue patent leather ballet flats in the airport shop. It was a tradition of mine to buy a pair of shoes, or two, when I traveled, as a happy and useful reminder of my visit. I owned so many pairs of shoes that Doug believed I had a problem, but I didn't see it that way. Some people collected baseball cards or stamps; I collected shoes. And I loved them and the stories I told about them. The blue shoes were another tale to tell.

Once we boarded our flight in Paris, I turned to Doug and said, "Do you realize that the next time we fly this way, we will be taking up four seats in coach?"

"Yep. No first class next time, or ever, probably. Let's make this count." He passed me a glass of wine from the flight attendant. We clinked, swished, and swallowed. And clinked again.

Then I took out my journal and started making lists. We were going to have two kids in a month! I had a lot to do.

CHAPTER 48

NESTING

"Is this what they call nesting?" I wondered aloud. Surveying our basement, it appeared as if I'd been transported to an episode of the reality show *Hoarders*. Falling-apart boxes, papers spilling in all directions, snake nests of electronic wires, and teetering stacks of pictures surrounded me. But the kids were to arrive within the month, and I was on a mission to make the house ready for them.

Once we'd arrived back in Chicago, the thirty days stretched out in front of us. Although I'd prepared for Miya's visit as well as Andrei and Svetlana's first stay with us, those were trial runs. This, by contrast, was for forever. The clarity I'd gained during my medical ordeal—that Andrei and Svetlana were the children meant to be mine—had flipped a switch inside me, transforming me into some kind of flapping mama bird who had already laid her eggs and then suddenly realized she needed someplace to put them so they could hatch. I was building my nest.

I had quit my job, giving notice a few weeks before receiving the call about our court date. When I turned in my resignation, I cried and wondered if I would ever find another place where my whole heart had been so full of purpose, where I'd feel called to the work as if it were my legacy. Running, marathoning, Girls on the Run, the WonderGirl, and the Ready to Run 20 Miler were all linked in a chain of memories that led all the way back to my mom. Leaving them behind broke the connection. I was relieved to have none of the anguish, none of the tension, but what if I never found any of the joy or the sparkle?

Diving into closets and drawers, between sorting and discarding, I discovered artifacts here and there that moved me. In what was about to become my *former* office, the room where Svetlana would sleep, several boxes were stacked in the back of a closet I hadn't explored in years. I opened them and released history. Dozens of my journals were packed away underneath the twin-size peach quilt my mom had made for me, the first one she ever sewed. When I pulled it out and held it to my nose, the absence of her scent brought tears. I traced the intricate pattern she'd stitched by hand and remembered the months where she sat at night, pushing her needle in and out thousands, maybe millions, of times as the blanket slowly came together. I realized I was building a similar sort of comfort for my own daughter, there in a room where my own mother had never been but was somehow still present within.

Also, I found a small oval pillow in the box, with tatted lace around the edges. It was cream-colored with an outline drawing of a little girl joyfully throwing leaves up into the air and the words "You are my everything." Mom had given me the pillow as a Valentine's Day gift when I was still in grade school. It was on my bed throughout my youth, and I remembered the feel of the cool muslin against my cheek. I set it aside, saving it for Svetlana to cuddle in her new home.

In the bottom of the box lay a family picture, the only formal portrait our family had ever taken. Stepdad's bulky frame sat next to my mom, who leaned into him, smiling. His sons and their wives stood behind him, while my brother, Paul, and his wife lined up in back of our mother. I stood next to Mom, the only one in the photo without a partner, which at the time had hurt me, underlining the fact of my aloneness and abandonment. I considered throwing the picture in the trash, but I couldn't bring myself to do it. Instead, I placed it face down back inside the box, covering it up with all the things that represented fonder memories.

The last items to go in the box were the dozens of race-finisher medals I'd earned. Sometimes I wondered if I'd ever be ready to truly release the weight of these objects, or if the legacy I'd believed they contained was actually a burden I'd carried in the years following Mom's death. Running had been my salvation before it was my downfall. Quitting Girls on the Run and packing these memories away symbolized letting it all go. I hoped preparing for Andrei and Svetlana would ease my load and lead me to the next chapter of my legacy.

As the calendar ticked down, my anxiety over our coming children amped up. I lost sleep and woke up in the middle of the nights to jot more items down on my multipage to-do lists, then rose in the wee hours to do whatever was necessary to cross them off. I was determined to roll through (perhaps over) our house, closets, kitchen, and bedrooms—our files, pictures, junk, and treasures. I cleared out the adult trappings of our house and furnished it with kids' stuff. Our childless life diminished, replaced by all the accoutrements of a family. By the end of the thirty-day waiting period, I had emptied my heart of all that ambivalence and felt it swell and overflow with love.

CHAPTER 49

SEVEN STEPS AND SEVEN WORDS

Three days before we were to return to Russia, I made a date for dinner with my friend Abby.

That night, a light rain misted in the air and scattered across our back patio, congregating on the seven steps that led from the deck down to our garage. The steps were wooden, stained dark with age and annual coats of polyurethane. They were steps I had run down, walked up, and stepped upon, without thinking, countless times. The light from the streetlight reflected on the water sprinkled across their glistening surface.

In spite of the rain, I wore my brand-new Paris shoes—the bright blue patent leather ballet flats. The cheerful cobalt color sang to me as an antidote for the gloomy day. My feet hummed with happiness as I hurried. I was late.

I gripped my phone in my left hand and heard the *swoosh* signaling that the text I just sent saying "10 mins!" flew across the air to Abby's phone. I swung my purse over my shoulder with my right hand just as my left foot touched the first step.

And whoa! I slipped. My body shot horizontally as both feet flew up from underneath me like something out of a cartoon. *Bam!* The convex curve in my back slammed onto the sharp wooden edge of the second stair. I bounced and—*bam!* I came down next on my right elbow, smashing it on another step. *Bam.* Bounce. Another step. *Bam.* Bounce. Another stair. My back. My butt. My body boom, boom, boomed.

Down.

The.

Stairs.

And I lay at the bottom, breathless. The wind knocked out of me. Legs splayed on the rainy cement, head resting on the seventh step.

The shock of the fall, the suddenness of finding myself so thoroughly down, gave me a moment of numbness before pain began to blossom. I lay there, scared to move. Slowly, I took stock. My feet could move. My head turned but—oh! The agony! Obviously, something was very wrong with my back. My goddamn back. A memory flashed of an earlier time, years before. Broken. Calling Abby. Calling Doug. Hurt. Hospital. Bad. Broken.

My phone, somehow, remained in my hand. I dialed Abby first. "I'm not going to make it tonight," I gasped when she picked up. My throat constricted as I tried not to cry. "I fell. Down the back stairs."

Abby asked, "Do you need me? To take you to the hospital?"

Abby and I have joked over the years, at Doug's expense and to his great chagrin, about how she rescued me when he would not. She wasn't laughing now, and neither was I.

"Doug's out watching the Bears game, but I'm sure he will take me," I said. "I just didn't want you to sit at the restaurant waiting for me. Oh jeez. Ouch." I attempted to sit up. "Okay, I've got to hang up now."

"Call me later . . . if you need anything."

I took a moment to be grateful all over again for our friendship before a wave of pain swept the good feeling away.

I pulled my body upright and back up the stairs, one at a time, swearing the whole way. "Shit. Shit. Shit. Damn. *Fuck!*" I screamed, not caring if the neighbors heard me. There were droplets of rain shining on the patent of my not-so-happy-now blue shoes. As soon as I reached the seven-stair summit, I dialed Doug.

The sound of his voice triggered my tears. I barely got the details out, but Doug understood. He came to my rescue.

A few hours later, I rested on a hospital bed in a gray cubicle. The nurse provided me two shots of some magic medicine that relaxed me just enough not to jump with pain if I took more than a shallow breath. Even with the drugs, arranging my body into a comfortable position was nearly impossible. Under my gown, a horizontal purple-blue line slashed the middle of my back—the imprint from the edge of the stairs; deep mauve bruises bloomed on my left butt cheek; and my right elbow swelled misshapenly, appearing as if I dipped it in red-brown paint, bloody-colored from the jarring impact. Stunningly, nothing was broken. It only felt that way.

In three days, I had to be able to sit upright, for twenty-three hours, on a plane to Russia. Doug and I would have to retrace our path to Andrei and Svetlana and carry them home. I would have to bear whatever burden would be placed upon me, and act as if there was not a thing wrong. Especially not with my back. I would need to stand tall. I was terrified of what the Russians might do if I was not in tip-top condition. Would they test me all over again? This time, I would fail.

The doctor's name was Virginia, a small detail that stuck in my drug-addled mind. The other thing I would recall later was the first sentence out of her mouth after examining my X-ray. "Your scoliosis is *really* bad, isn't it?"

Yes. I nodded. Yes, it was. And now it was worse. Inside, I silently prayed, *And I hope the Russians never find out.*

CHAPTER 50

RETURN TO RUSSIA

Doug and I boarded a plane bound for Helsinki on Friday night. No first class this time, but, thanks to Dr. Virginia, I had powerful painkillers and slept most of the twelve-hour journey. I woke up to stumble into the spare, modern, gleaming Finnish airport in the early dawn hours. We had a few-hour layover and, before long, our Aeroflot flight left for the two-hour trip to Moscow.

The first trip, we had stayed in Moscow for the useless medical exams. This time we had no judicial reason to spend time there on our flight to Biro but were required to return through Moscow for visas for the children, so we rented an airport hotel room for a few hours in order to sleep in a real bed and take a shower before the daunting flight to Khabarovsk.

Our only objective was to get in, get the kids, and get out. After all that had happened on our first trip . . . well, it couldn't go wrong again, could it?

As we deboarded the plane and reunited with our luggage, we also found Lina, our translator from the initial drive into Biro. She was as young and sleepy as ever, her tousled hair giving away that she had most likely napped all the way there. I let Doug handle the luggage, taking the smaller carry-ons, psyching myself up to pretend that my back was fine.

We had a different driver this time, with a larger car that was clean and well-kept. I didn't know if this driver carried a gun like our first one, but he did smoke, the same way as the other driver, stopping the car at railroad tracks to get out and light up.

The car was silent; no one wanted to talk. The driver drove. Lina slept. Doug and I dozed, too, though my attempts to sleep were interrupted by stabs of pain in my back when the car bumped over a rough spot on the road. The three-hour car journey passed quickly, and I barely noticed the huge hammer-and-sickle statue when we passed this time. I had taken to counting down the legs of each trip: Chicago to Europe, Europe to Moscow, Moscow to Khabarovsk, Khabarovsk to Biro, and then all of it backward. I realized, in the car, that there was only one time remaining that I would make this particular trip, on the road from Birobidzhan to Khabarovsk—just once more, on the way home with the kids.

We arrived at the hotel, its tired splendor unchanged from a month ago. Riding up the elevator, we encountered the Russian hall monitor, still sitting, immobile, at her post. We found our room and realized we had moved up in the world. Just one floor up from our last visit, the room was vast and quite well furnished. The door opened upon a living room, complete with couch, armchair, coffee tables, and a television. To the left was a full-out dining room with a small kitchenette beyond a grand table and six ornate chairs, topped with a tinkling crystal chandelier. Against one of the walls, a china cabinet held red glass plates and bowls, along with other colored dishes: delicate blue drinking cups, tiny aperitif snifters, a full sterling silver tea service. The dining room held the opulence of once-upon-a-time dignitaries being wined and dined there, throwing back vodka after they'd agreed which country to invade next.

We settled in. I wanted nothing more than sleep. The next morning, we would see Andrei and Svetlana. Tomorrow, *four* of us would fill this big hotel room.

Jet lag awakened Doug early, so he went searching the farmer's market and kiosks outside in the hotel square to find some break-fast for himself. I joined him in the lobby to wait for our translator and driver. We weren't sure if we would be lucky enough to be rejoined by Natasha, but I fervently hoped.

Natasha and I never spoke about the ordeal of the medicals, but a sisterhood of sorts had been born that day. It was the bond of survivors. We both knew what had happened, and we both understood that what I had endured had been necessary for the judge to finally say yes. We both believed the children would be in a better place when it was over. We both tried to forget, but we— or at least I—would always remember the small ways we car-ried each other through that day. Bumping against bureaucracy, tears and assurances, nakedness and averted eyes, and ultimately triumph.

As we waited, I fussed with the packages I carried, trying to avoid the jagged surges of pain that ripped through my back. For this trip, in addition to preparing the envelopes with crisp twenty- and one-hundred-dollar bills, I brought gifts. Presents were required for Elena, the orphanage director, and for each of the twenty orphanage caregivers who spent time with Andrei and Svetlana. Kseniya, the coordinator for all adoptions in Biro, also received a token of appreciation. Finally, we had been asked to put together small goody bags for the other kids in Andrei's and Svetlana's groups—the thirty-some orphans they would be leav-ing behind. I had packed half of one suitcase with things meant to be given away.

The other half of that suitcase held two backpacks. One was full of clothes for Andrei; the other was empty, but I planned on shifting the clothes I'd brought for Svetlana, which were sprinkled throughout other bags, into the second backpack. The packing and distribution of our bags was a constant source of frustration and pride for me. Annoying because no one could tell me what, if anything, Andrei and Svetlana would need. The only information provided was when we picked them up, they'd each need an entire set of clothes: underwear, shoes, socks, pants, shirts. All of their possessions and clothing in the orphanage were community property and couldn't be removed. We also had to bring whatever clothing they needed for the twelve-day journey through Biro to Moscow, necessary for all the paperwork we'd have to get through in Moscow before we could take them home with us to the United States. There had been a few items, like shoes, that confounded me. How would I get the right fit? My solution had been to buy flip-flops in two to three sizes, figuring that we would donate any that were too small and keep the large ones for the kids to grow into. Thank goodness for the summer clearance sales at Target!

Of course, I immediately dropped all the packages when Natasha walked through the hotel doors. "It's so good to see you! I'm so happy you will be helping us again!" I said as I hugged her, wincing when she squeezed my back.

Natasha bubbled over with questions for us. "How have you two been? Are you ready to go see Andrei and Svetlana? I've heard that they are very excited to see you!" She smiled and seemed genuinely happy to be reunited with us.

"We're great." Doug and I had decided that my accident wasn't to be mentioned. "And yes, we're very excited to see them too!"

We walked outside to Natasha's car, anticipation quivering inside of our hearts.

The September weather had turned in Biro. The last time we pulled up to the orphanage, there had been a sweeping green lawn and children chasing each other across the grass, while the sullen older boys dominated the swing set, smoking as they barely moved in the heat.

Now it was quiet outside, and the temperature had dropped enough to make me think the flip-flops I'd brought for the kids were a mistake. It was jacket weather. The kids were in school instead of playing. There was no one to witness our small parade to the entrance and through the now-familiar glass doors. The renovations that had been underway in the main room were complete, the walls painted a powdery blue, new curtains hung, and the spotless rug unfurled. We sat down on the sofa while Natasha went to find Elena.

I heard them before I saw them. Footsteps pounded in the hallway, and the sound of voices called, "Mama! Papa!"

It was pure glee when they came at us. Brown hair braided, wearing a black skirt and white tights, and giving a huge hug in which she wouldn't let go, murmuring, "Mama, Mama, Mama": Svetlana. Her embrace pinched my back, but when I felt her small, sturdy shoulders through the gray sweater she wore, I loved her.

Next to her, with a blond crew cut, gray dress pants, white button-down shirt, and skinny arms gripping Doug as if he were a lifesaver: Andrei. Doug ruffled his hair, saying, "Hello! Hello! Andrei, how are you?" Doug's smile beamed, enveloping his boy.

Natasha approached with Elena. "I see you've found each other," she said. Her grin went all the way to her eyes. "The kids are skipping school. They think they shouldn't have to continue since they will be leaving."

"Oh-ho!" Doug was merrily skeptical. "Already skipping class? Can they do that?" But he was jovial. We were finally united. I didn't even let my back pain ruin this moment.

"It looks like they are being tricky," Natasha confided, "but they can't leave here yet. We have paperwork to complete in the mornings, but you can take them out for lunch each day and for a while in the afternoon. The kids will sleep at the orphanage until

Wednesday. We also have to arrange for a goodbye party, if you would like."

The goodbye party had become a tradition in Biro, started by our friends, Jacob and Debbie, who had adopted two sisters from Children's Home Three four years earlier. It had become customary for adoptive parents to bring their child's orphan friends out to the only bowling alley in Biro for games, pizza, and cake before the kids bid a final goodbye to their America-bound comrades.

"Of course we'll do the party! We brought gift bags, and we're planning on it," I said. Doug and I recognized this was something of a status symbol for Andrei and Svetlana in the Russian culture of gift giving, and we didn't want to deny them the opportunity to play host and hostess.

The kids followed the conversation eagerly, even though they couldn't understand our English. It was clear they realized their fate regarding homework was being decided. I'm certain they didn't imagine their party was being discussed, or there would have been campaigning on their part. Whatever they absorbed, they were giddy with smiles. Their embraces were tighter and squeezed my aching back more than ever.

Natasha told us the kids had one question. "What are our new names?" Their eagerness was poignant. Although I had considered what we were asking of these kids when bringing them to a new life, and counting on their resilience to welcome it, the gravity of their devotion floored me. They were ready to give up their names, to abandon the identity they'd had their entire lives.

In retrospect, we were all leaving behind the selves we knew. The kids were becoming Armstrongs, turning back into children with parents. I was at sea in a different way. My career-focused identity, what I had believed was my legacy, WonderGirl Betsy, was being left in the dust. "Mom"—the name I hadn't uttered aloud in twenty-three years and that I never imagined anyone would call me—was now going to be *me*. This very moment in Biro, looking into the blue eyes of these children—*my* children— it finally sunk in. I was daunted. I was excited. I was fearful. I was jubilant. I really should have considered all of this earlier.

We told the kids that we loved their names. Andrei meant "brave"; Svetlana meant "light." They were both courageous and filled with sunshine. They deserved and embodied their Russian names. We explained how we had chosen their middle names. Russians had a different kind of middle name, called a patronymic, which traced their lineage and was often the same name but adjusted for feminine and masculine—think William and Wilhelmina. We had decided to keep the first letter *E* of their Russian patronymic name but had selected American family names that began with that letter, Edwin for Doug's father and Elizabeth for me.

The comical part of this exchange arrived when I explained their new last name. "Arm." I pointed to my arm. "Strong." I flexed my bicep. Svetlana's unspoken response was an expression of puzzlement. She looked more than a little horrified. I supposed if someone had tried to assign me the name "flexible ankle" or "broad shoulder" when I was her age, I would have reacted the same way. But Andrei E. Armstrong and Svetlana E. Armstrong were their names, and, aside from the Armstrong part, the kids seemed quite excited.

Our days in Biro unfolded quickly. Natasha brought us papers to sign in the mornings, or I'd rest my back, and then we went to the orphanage. We visited Café Felicity or another restaurant, Cupid, for lunch with the kids. Cupid was extravagant by Biro standards, situated overlooking the Birobidzhan river and offering an upscale menu that included a delicious roast chicken.

After lunch on most days, I began teaching the kids the English alphabet, using a puzzle I had brought along. The back pages of my journal became filled with doodling and uncertain writing in all caps: "ANDREI SVETLANA ARMSTRONG."

We also had a party to plan. Andrei and Svetlana were invested in making their goodbye soiree the best one ever. They were ecstatic when I showed them the stuff I'd brought from the American party store—all kinds of loot that would go into goody bags for their friends. One afternoon we assembled all the treats, carefully counting out pencils and candy and trinkets into each one. In prep for the party, the lone bowling alley, which doubled as a disco at night, was reserved and the pizza, cake, and ice cream ordered. The party was scheduled during lunch, the day before we left Biro.

One afternoon, we happened upon a wedding party celebrating on the boardwalk by the river. Natasha told us about a wedding tradition, taken from the French: When couples get married, the bride and groom place a padlock on one of the bridges over the Seine and then throw the key into the river. This tradition melds the families together while making the union impossible to break, as the key is lost to the currents. Doug and I had seen Parisian bridges crammed to overflowing with locks, some with ribbons or flowers entwined, proclaiming lifelong adoration and eternal togetherness.

In Biro, outside of the Cupid restaurant, there was a huge cast-iron filigree heart sculpture. The day we saw the wedding, we watched as the bride and groom "locked" themselves together symbolically and proceeded to laughingly toss the keys over their shoulders into the lazy waters of the Birobidzhan river. Natasha explained to Andrei and Svetlana what was happening, and their faces lit up. Their happy babbling was translated to us. "Let's get a lock and throw away the key. We are a family now."

And that was how, the morning before the goodbye party, we found ourselves, all four of us plus Natasha, locking a sturdy padlock onto the filigreed curves of Cupid's heart. Each of us took turns touching the metal, which warmed in the morning sun, and then we all stood by the banks of the river and counted, "One . . . two . . . three . . . go!" and threw the keys as far as we could. *Splish-splash!* It was the sound of a promise being made.

We left the river, the cast-iron heart, and our lost-to-us keys behind and prepared to go to the orphanage's goodbye party. I was leery of the party for two reasons. One was simply my back, knowing I wasn't physically able to bowl with the kids. The second was wondering how it would be. How would Andrei and Svetlana feel when the time came to really, forever, leave the orphanage and all they had known? What was it like to walk toward a better life and abandon your friends to a less fortunate destiny? The party was expected of us, but I was conflicted.

Adding to my uneasiness, Andrei had been subdued the morning of the party. Natasha finally got him to explain that one of his best friends was being left out of the party because there wasn't room on the bus for him. With a quick phone call, a plan was hatched to have Kolya, Andrei's friend, driven by one of the caretakers. Crisis averted and Andrei beaming once again, we loaded the goody bags into Natasha's car and set off.

The highlights of the party were Andrei playing debonair host and Svetlana running about snapping pictures with our cell phones, while kids crowded eagerly around the pizza and cake. Doug and I stayed on the sidelines, giving Andrei and Svetlana as much time with their friends as we could. But there was one little girl who planted herself next to me for the duration of the party. She sat and smiled, her brown hair short and her caramel eyes shining, following my conversation, even as she couldn't understand. She seemed to be pleading, "Take me too." Her name was Nastya. I went so far as to ask Elena about her and was told she wasn't available for adoption, even though she hoped to find another family. I remembered Debbie's efforts to get more of these children adopted and completely understood.

After a few hours, the orphanage bus pulled up to the bowling alley. It was time for the venue to switch to a discotheque and time for the children to return to real life. Time for Andrei and Svetlana to come with us. It was time.

Pictures flashed. Bunches of kids smiled and laughed. Pictures snapped. Friends hung on each other's shoulders. They took a final group shot in front of the bowling alley and then of the bus as it pulled away. Pictures of Andrei and Svetlana as they waved. There was no picture of the moment when the kids both turned to hug Doug and me, the second moment we became family.

CHAPTER 51

MOSCOW, WITH CHILDREN

In the early morning hours, the day after the party, we made the final trip from Biro to Khabarovsk. As the kilometers clicked by, I was reminded of all the times I'd run a race and counted backward toward the finish line. It was likely I would never pass this way again, never have to compete in this contest. That was fine with me. I was glad to retire from this sort of competition.

It was relatively easy to fly with Andrei and Svetlana. They had made the trip to and from America twice already. They knew how far it was and how long it would take. What troopers! We said goodbye to Natasha for the last time at the Khabarovsk airport. She hugged the kids. She hugged me and Doug. I was still trying to hide my back-pain-induced grimaces whenever anyone touched me. "Good luck," were her parting words.

From Khabarovsk, we traveled to Moscow for the governmental business of obtaining visas and other paperwork. Although I held out hope that my pile of papers would diminish, it kept growing, each file being more important than the last. Russian birth certificates, adoption certificates, passports, medical exams. Everything Doug and I had needed, the kids needed as well—in Russian and English. Because these documents were precious and irreplaceable, they were packed in carry-ons and followed us everywhere we went. We took no chances.

Landing in Moscow, we met Yuri, a new driver and translator. He was a bear of a man, black hair, furry hands, lumbering, but all business. Conversation wasn't his strength, and he frightened the kids into silence, although I didn't know why. Trying to make small talk with him one day, I asked, "How many adoptions have you helped with, Yuri?"

Brusquely, he said, "Moscow has stopped adoptions. No more Americans get kids."

I remembered Nastya back in Biro. There must have been hundreds of thousands of kids like her—yearning for a family, for a better life, with no way out.

We tried our best to enjoy Moscow while we waited for the bureaucratic wheels to crank. Our hotel, Peter the First, which Doug had splurged for, was quite cushy. It had a huge underground pool, hot tubs, and saunas, and Doug and I laughed at seeing our little orphans adapt to the luxury of hotel robes and slippers. Svetlana, with her long hair towel-turbaned upon her head, robe dragging like a train, and feet slipping out of too-big slippers, paraded to and fro with the air of an entitled princess. Post-swim, Andrei draped his skinny frame along a chaise lounge and buried himself in the heavy-ply towels.

There were two times at Peter the First where my desire for what a happy family looked like coincided with our family activities. In the first scenario, Doug was seated on a plush armchair in the sitting room of our hotel. Svetlana and I shared the small love seat, and Andrei amused himself spinning circles in the desk chair. Although the TV was on, everyone suddenly became aware of a noise. A noise that meant noxious fumes. A noise that transcended language. The noise of a really loud, really stinky fart. And we heard it not just once, but twice, three times . . . from perky one-syllable toots to four-syllable poop-in-your-pants farts.

They went on and on. The kids looked at me, and I shook my head. "Nyet! No!"

I pointed at Andrei, and he tried mightily to deny through his laughter. Svetlana pointed at Doug and screamed, "Papa!" in a most accusatory tone.

We almost cried at the comical sounds coming from somewhere in the room. Finally, Doug couldn't contain himself. He burst out laughing, pulling his phone from its hiding place behind him, shouting, "It's a fart app!"

The children fell all over themselves to play with this electronic wonder. The music of farts accompanied many of our excursions. Yuri never laughed. But we did.

Our final evening in Moscow, we procured tickets to the world-famous Moscow Circus. We'd been informed it was a once-in-a-lifetime chance to watch the performers, who were precursors to the famous Cirque du Soleil shows already ubiquitous in Las Vegas. The animal portions of the show made Doug and me queasy. I didn't like the whips used on elephants or how eager the tigers seemed to be to earn their meat. They snarled at the trainers, bony ribs showcasing the hunger that kept them obedient. I was relieved when the downtrodden beasts were ushered behind the scenes. And it was my impotent fury at their treatment that made the next part so over-the-top hilarious.

Doug and I couldn't translate the patter of the master of ceremonies, but we understood the good-guy-bad-guy routine of the master and one of the clowns. The clown was misbehaving, and so it was his turn to get into the middle ring with . . . a kangaroo. Dressed as a bride. The clown pretended to dance with her. The bridal kangaroo proceeded, in no uncertain terms, to kangaroo kick the clown-groom's ass. Poor clown-groom bobbed and weaved, but the kangaroo launched herself and punted with her powerful hind legs and tail, knocking the clown back. This happened over and over. We laughed so hard, tears were running down our faces by the time the clown finally turned to run and the kangaroo chased him offstage.

It seemed appropriate. A power struggle. A kangaroo court. The downtrodden underdog triumphing. A story so bad you had to laugh, or you would cry. It was funny and weird. It was our story too.

The next morning was our last day in Moscow. We had an appointment at the American embassy before going directly to the airport for home. The purpose of this meeting was to finalize the paperwork so that Andrei and Svetlana would become US citizens when our plane landed in the United States.

Yuri brought us to the embassy, pointing where to sit before going back to wait in the car. We were directed to a small square room with chairs lining the sides. Every seat was occupied by a set of American parents and at least one Russian child, the vast majority of them toddlers, if not babies. Svetlana sat on my lap, and Andrei stood by Doug. Both Andrei and Svetlana smiled at the little ones, and I imagined these two as babies, feeling suddenly heavy with the toll all these years of waiting might have taken upon them. Were they jealous of the babies? Happy for them? What would have been if someone else had found our kids sooner?

There were excited exchanges with the parents around us, their surprise registering when they realized we were adopting these older kids. It was the first time someone said, "Wow! How old are they?"

When the embassy official came out, I expected some kind of pomp and circumstance, but she was a small and young woman who lacked gravitas. Speaking perfect, unaccented English, she announced, "Congratulations! You are almost done. Please raise your hands, and repeat after me."

Doug and I lifted our hands and spoke the words, patriotic and promising. "Yes," we pledged. "Forever," we swore. All the families together repeated words familiar to our ears and foreign to our children. Then, family by family, papers were stamped. Envelopes were handed over. Instructions were given. One by one, families, now complete, left the room and the embassy to walk out into the world. It was bureaucratic. And sterile. It was patriotic. And emotional. It was an instant in my life, but it was everything.

CHAPTER 52

FLYING HOME

was not sad to be leaving Mother Russia, although she did make me a mother, finally. As the plane ascended, I said a flurry of goodbyes, my head tilted toward the window, watching the earth recede. *Goodbye, Moscow. Goodbye, Biro. Goodbye, Russia. Goodbye, judge and prosecutor. Goodbye, Natasha and Elena. Goodbye to all of this.* I felt like a refugee, running away from a bad place and knowing I'd be safe once I crossed the border. I was thrilled to be going. Home. With my family.

When the plane touched down in Heathrow, Doug and I flew into motion. The layover was tight, and when we got to our gate, we learned we needed to backtrack to another terminal, find a different gate, and go through security again. The stakes rose dramatically because, should we miss our flight, the four of us would be forced to sleep on the hard airport floor since the children, in between their Russian and American citizenship, were forbidden to set foot upon British soil. With my back, I couldn't consider a night sleeping in an airport.

I had no shame telling anyone who would listen that we'd just adopted these kids and they didn't speak English, that we had to catch our flight to the United States. My lack of stiff upper lip— and abundance of tears—worked, and we were given wide berth to jump the bus line and run first off the bus into the terminal.

Doug led us, my back screaming as Andrei and Svetlana, unaware of why we hurried, followed. The kids dragged their suitcases up escalators, taking stairs two at a time to keep up.

We arrived at the second security station, where the line stretched ahead like a long, coiled snake. Sweat dripped down my back, which was cramping from tension and activity. It appeared we weren't going to make it, until I started pleading again and again. "We just came from Russia and adopted these children. We're going to miss our fight. Can we please get in front of you?"

Time after time, people stepped aside. At one point, a British Airways pilot overheard me and interrupted, "Excuse me? Are you trying to get them to the United States?"

At my nod, he said, "Come with me," and it was like Moses parting the waters. We were brought to the front and rushed through.

"Good luck, mates! I hope you make it!" was his cheery goodbye.

And we did. We got on the plane—with our kids.

Once we were settled, Doug and I clinked our water bottles together, as had become our custom, though this time without champagne flutes or the luxury of first class. Whew! We made it. The kids. Our kids. We smiled and clinked. It was the clink of two plastic cups touching, or the ping of hearts shifting into place, or the snap of puzzle pieces that finally fit.

Eight hours later, the wheels of the plane touched the tarmac, and in that instant our children became American citizens. Our bedraggled foursome dragged each other off of the plane at O'Hare airport in Chicago. The melody of English was music to my ears. I knew where I was. I knew what to do. Luggage. Customs. Taxi. Home.

Mom. Dad. Kids. Family. I was not forty-six anymore. I was not even forty-seven anymore. I was forty-eight years, nine months, and three days old. It took a long time for me to arrive. I was a daughter for twenty-three years before I lost my mom. I became a runner for twenty-three more years, but then I lost my sport and with it, my legacy. My losses, combined, felt tragic to me. Yet I was on the edge of something unexpected and new, a legacy I never could have imagined before my forty-seventh birthday.

There have been at least these two times in my life when I've had to balance on the brink of what was and what will be. When I've had to turn myself toward the future and walk into it unsure and unknowing. When I have had to teach myself hope and believe my dreams will be answered, even as they were dashed before. Finally, I made the mother of all decisions: I became Mom. And what I thought was going to be the end turned out to be the beginning.

Watching our kids on the playground after school, four moms surrounded me. It was October 2012, and I was a new addition, with Andrei and Svetlana recently enrolled in fifth and third grades.

The other women were friendly but curious.

"So, where did you move from?" one asked.

"We've lived in this neighborhood for about ten years, but we didn't have kids before now." I explained that we'd just adopted the kids from Russia.

A few foreheads wrinkled, heads cocked sideways, and puzzled expressions appeared on their faces. I could almost see them doing the math in their heads.

"You just adopted them? And they're ten and twelve?"

I nodded.

One of the moms gushed, "Oh my God, that's so amazing! You must be a saint to take on kids like them!"

"No, I'm really not," I said, trying not to show my annoyance. *Kids like them.* "They're great kids."

Another mom chimed in, "Isn't infertility the worst? We had to do three rounds before our twins were born." A few heads nodded in solidarity.

I attempted a sympathetic smile, but held my ground. "I never did infertility treatments. It just . . . wasn't something I was willing to do."

One of them couldn't stop herself. "Why not?" she asked. "Didn't you want babies? Or at least younger kids?"

"Not really." I tried to make light of her question. "I've still never changed a diaper," I laughed. "At this point, I'm on a streak that I can't break! And these kids, they're perfect for me."

That conversation on the playground and countless others I've had since have reiterated an assumption that people have a hard time overcoming—that we chose third best.

Not first choice, a baby of our own.

Not second choice, an adopted baby.

But third choice—adopted older children.

The questions hurt, loaded as they were with the thoughts behind them.

In the early days of our life together as a family of four, I was a mess. Conversations like the one with the group of moms did not help. No matter how prepared I had believed I was, how could I, how could anyone, ever be ready for the moments, big and small, precious and awful, that pile on top of each other when raising kids to adulthood?

Our first ninety days included thirty appointments. Between catching the kids up on their vaccines, taking them to a Russian-speaking educational psychologist to determine their grade levels, submitting their cavity-ridden baby teeth to multiple dental interventions (which involved Svetlana refusing to allow the dentist to administer Novocain while drilling cavities), and discovering that they were both legally blind (poor Andrei even had to wear an eye patch daily for four hours, for six months, to train his eyes back into perceiving depth), our early days were often fraught as we all learned how to be a family, together.

From the start, mornings challenged me. Doug took the kids for their first eye appointment, not knowing how bad their vision was. When the crew arrived home, the kids were wearing contact lenses. Contacts! Then he left for a business trip, abandoning me to the role of (inept) contact lens inserter.

The following morning, trying to get them ready for school, I managed to get Svetlana's and one of Andrei's contacts in, but the second proved impossible. On the umpteenth try, my fingernail accidentally stabbed Andrei's eye, and he became so upset he bolted from the bathroom, ran downstairs, and out the door. We lived adjacent to Western Avenue, a busy, four-lane street in Chicago, and the morning rush was well underway. I panicked.

"Stay!" I told Svetlana, putting my hand out like a stop sign in her face. I had to go after him and hope she wouldn't bolt too.

Out the front door, I saw him running up the street. I caught him just as he approached Western. When I finally got close enough, I grabbed for him. I was out of breath and beside myself, and I inadvertently scratched his neck. The poor kid was furious at me. He didn't want to go home. Instead, he allowed me to walk him to school (following from a distance), where he turned before he went in and said, "I no go home with you, Mama!"

One of my biggest fears was that the kids, who didn't speak fluent English and were still strangers to the area, would run away and not know their way home. That morning, it almost happened, and my hands were still shaking as I walked Svetlana to school, worrying about Andrei and whether he would come with me at the end of the school day.

By the time I picked the kids up, I had enlisted Vladimir, the translator, to be on call in case Andrei balked. I even called Vladimir and handed the phone to Andrei, who exchanged Russian words with Vladimir and returned the phone to me. Vladimir told me Andrei was fine; Andrei had already forgiven me for our morning struggle. I was learning an important lesson about being a mom. You can have little skirmishes, and the love doesn't go away. It doesn't break the bond.

Svetlana had her moments too. On the morning of her first playdate with her new friend, Shawn, she became angry when I refused to straighten the mess in her room. During the ensuing meltdown, Svetlana screamed and cried and finally shook both hands, with her middle fingers, aka double "birds," flying in my face! When I relayed the incident to Shawn's mom, we decided to cancel the playdate. Later this would be funny, emblematic of Svetlana's sassiness, but the incident remains emblematic of our early struggles.

As time went on, we experienced fewer upsets and more good times. That first Christmas, the kids' eyes shone bright. When they held their overflowing stockings, their wide smiles and pure joy left my eyes brimming with happy tears. Christmas had become a symbol of what I'd lost. I missed my mom so much that it felt like a piece of me was missing. Now, my heart swelled with love for these kids. Their gift to me was that twenty-four years after my mom died, Christmas became a celebration again.

My stomach clenches uncomfortably when I wonder what kind of mother I would have been if two things hadn't happened. One was the Russian doctor's assault. At least eight years passed before I would even use the term "assault" to describe what had happened, but the fact endures: The doctor's bare hands touched intimate parts of my body when I did not, could not, give authentic consent. I was a victim then, but I have reclaimed my power by calling myself a survivor, and I consider myself a different kind of WonderGirl now.

The second event was my fall down the back porch stairs. For months afterward, I was startled by pain from the deep purple bruises that remained emblazoned across my back, and even twelve years later, as I finish this book, I have yet to recover fully. I cannot run, and I live with daily chronic pain. I'm sad for myself, for the gaping hole in my heart where my lost identity as a runner lives, but I'm even more sad that my children will never see me finish a marathon, complete a triathlon, or look at me as the unstoppable athlete I once was. I hate that they've known me only as a person in constant physical pain.

Under the shadow of these twin traumas, my anxiety grew from molehill to mountain. I buzzed around Andrei, Svetlana, and Doug, flapping my hands like an ineffectual dodo bird, not realizing that flight was never an option since dodo birds can't fly. I always imagined I'd be the kind of mom who had a lightness about her, who would act silly, and laugh easily. I wanted to be a mom who was unafraid and who modeled bravery for her children. Instead, I was fearful and wary. I felt coiled with tension, ready to spring, like my entire being might explode into a million pieces at the slightest provocation. Thankfully, I've been expending the effort to unwind and ease the tension, but it is hard, slow work. I console myself, knowing that my kids are sure of my love for them. No matter what kind of mother I've been, or am, I love them. I would still do anything for them.

Only recently, I've pondered re-learning to fly a plane. I may not be able to run, but I still desire to fly. Not away, and not forever. I just want to rise and circle the skies, perhaps find my mom somewhere up in the big blue yonder, then know that when I land, my family—my family—will be waiting for me.

Three months after Andrei and Svetlana joined our family, we learned that Russian dictator Vladimir Putin had made good on his threat to ban Americans from adopting Russian orphans. Several hundred families, including one of the couples that Doug and I met in Biro (the family that paid for their child's heart surgery), were prevented from adopting children they had already been matched with and met. My heart breaks for these kids—those we saw languishing in Russian orphanages, waiting and being denied their forever families. Andrei and Svetlana were outraged by Putin's decision, and now, with Russia's war in Ukraine, their anger grows. Andrei knows he would have been drafted. When I think about how likely it would have been that he would have died on a Ukrainian battlefield, my knees buckle under the weight of my emotion. The horrible losses keep mounting.

Today, Andrei stands a lanky six feet tall and works as an electrician. He is stoic and straight-faced, yet the first one to throw out the wittiest of one-liners that crack everyone up. He is twenty-three, the same age I was when I lost my mother, and looking at him, I see my young, vulnerable, sad self. I'm so glad I'm still here for him.

Svetlana is twenty-one, creative, empathic, and the kindest person I've ever known. So kind, in fact, that she used to buy coffee every day for the same homeless man outside Starbucks. Once, when she got his order wrong, she corrected her mistake by purchasing him a second coffee. I'm proud to be her mother.

Now, this many years later, I think about those folks who asked me unanswerable questions: Why never try for my "own"? Why not babies? Why Russia? Why not when I was younger?

Only with hindsight do I know that the decision I made was right for us—the right time, the right place, the right kids. I was, unexpectedly, alive at forty-seven. Because of whom Doug is, I finally believed I could sustain a relationship instead of bolting.

When I imagined children who might be mine, they appeared to me like little people with whom I might share something. Kids who were having a sadder-than-it-should-have-been childhood; kids whose mother made a bad choice that had resulted in their being catapulted into an alternate reality they never asked for but were forced to bear anyway. Kids who had lost their mom, their family, their everything. These were things I could understand and kids I could relate to.

I found Andrei and Svetlana, my first-choice children.

Yet not long after we adopted them, Andrei and Svetlana asked me, "Mama, why did you choose us? Didn't you want a baby?"

Their question made me gasp, "Oh." And my hand flew to my heart. "Oh, no."

"I was here, waiting for you, and I didn't even know it!" I cried. "For years. You, Andrei. You, Svetlana. All along, I was here and waiting for you."

Which brings to mind my mom's last words to me, "I'll never leave you," and I know it's true for me and my children, too. Because of Doug, the kids, and our forever family, I have learned, at last, to stop running, to hold my ground, and, finally, to stay.

ACKNOWLEDGMENTS

I had no idea what I was doing when I decided to write a book. There are so many people to thank! I'll start with StoryStudio in Chicago, where I met the people who first made me believe this was possible. Jack Helbig, thank you for reading my first draft and telling me it didn't totally suck. Annette Gendler, I appreciate the hours I spent with you and all the Advanced Memoir Writers.

Nadine Kenney-Johnstone, where do I begin? You read that horrible mish-mash I called a manuscript and coached me into something that was beginning to resemble a book. My gratitude for you knows no bounds. For all the ladies (& Stan) in Writers Workout and the other classes, thank you for writing with me and listening to my words.

Brooke Warner, you are a superstar! I'm in awe of your talent and business. Finding a home for my book at SheWrites Press was a dream come true. Thank you for the final draft.

I owe the biggest debt of gratitude (and hugs) to all of the folks who wrote with me at one time or another, over the past twelve years: Jen, Rita, Laurie, and Margaret; Ben, Della, Georgia, Hannah, Kim, Peter (RIP), and Vanessa; and The Lit Ladies: Michelle, Peg, Rachel, and Robyn.

Kim Dower, whatever publicity I got for this book is because of you! Thank you for being a master at your craft.

Michelle Redo, you're an audio engineering and producing genius! I'm still pinching myself that you answered, "Yes," when

I asked if we could record this book together. And, in Maine, to boot! Thanks for the lobster roll, along with everything else.

To my fellow motherless daughters, especially the G25s: remember, even if we were raised by wolves, we blazed a trail through the motherless wilderness to find each other, and, we're dragonflies now. We can fly!

To my VVBBFF: Abby, thanks for the Diet Coke, for picking me up when I was down, and for everything else. MLWSWOY and LYM. You know what I mean.

To the Andersons: Dad, you don't need to worry about me, I'm finally okay. Paul and Lynn, I'm proud to call you family. It wasn't easy, any of it, but here we are, all grown-up and out of there.

To all of the Armstrongs: Claire, Ed (RIP), Kathy, Diane, Greg, and the kids, and the kids' kids, thank you for showing me how a family that loves—and likes!—each other works. Just by being you, you've healed me in ways I never could have predicted.

Mom, I hope my love for you shines through on every page. Can you believe this? Everything turned out so much better for me than we ever could have imagined.

Last, to my family—my family! Doug, Andrei, & Svetlana, there would be no story without you. Honeybear, you're the love of my life; Andrei and Svetlana, you are the children of my heart. Thank you for allowing me to tell our story. I'm so incredibly proud to call you my family and I hope you know that I'd do any-thing—anything—for you.

Diana Gran

Betsy Armstrong grew up on a farm in Minnesota, but Chicago captured her country-mouse heart thirty-plus years ago, so she stayed. Betsy is a writer, mom, athlete, and philanthropist who wants to change the world. She had careers in sales, counseling, and the non-profit space. Still, her true passion was running, which led her to become the Executive Director of Girls on the Run-Chicago and the Chicago Area Runners Association. Her writing has been published in the Brevity Blog, The Pinch Journal, and WOW-Women on Writing, and she has been recognized in essay contests in Writer's Digest and WOW-Women on Writing. She and her husband, kids, and pets divide their time between the mountains of Nevada and the lakes of the Midwest.

Looking for your next great read?

We can help!

Visit www.shewritespress.com/next-read
or scan the QR code below for a list
of our recommended titles.

She Writes Press is an award-winning
independent publishing company founded to
serve women writers everywhere.